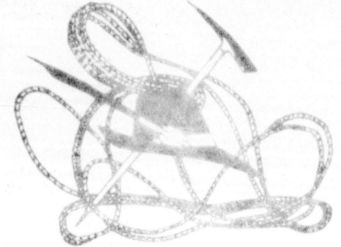

On the Edge of Europe

Also by Audrey Salkeld

Lightweight Expeditions to the Great Ranges
  (co-edited with Dr Charles Clarke)
Climbing (editor)
The Mystery of Mallory and Irvine (with Tom Holzel)
One Step in the Clouds (co-edited with Rosie Smith)
People in High Places
Climbing Everest, the Bibliography (with John Boyle)

On the Edge of Europe

Mountaineering in the Caucasus

Audrey Salkeld and José Luis Bermúdez

The Mountaineers
SEATTLE

ISBN 0-89886-388-0

First published in Great Britain by
Hodder and Stoughton,
a division of Hodder Headline PLC
47 Bedford Square, London WC1B 3DP.

Published in the United States of America by
The Mountaineers, 1011 S.W. Klickitat Way, Seattle WA 98134
Published simultaneously in Canada by Douglas & McIntyre Ltd,
1615 Venables St, Vancouver B.C. V5L 2H1

Photoset by Rowland Phototypesetting Ltd,
Bury St Edmunds, Suffolk

Printed in Great Britain by
St Edmundsbury Press Ltd, Bury St Edmunds, Suffolk

*Dedicated to the Alpine Club
and those nineteenth-century pioneers who pointed the way*

Contents

Acknowledgements

This book drew its inspiration directly from a symposium on the Caucasus, organised by the Alpine Club in November 1991. At a time when access to the Caucasus mountains for outside mountaineers becomes easier than for decades, it seemed appropriate to remember the range's pioneers and, in particular, to celebrate the long love affair British climbers have enjoyed with this unique area.

We are deeply grateful to all the contributors who have allowed their work to be reproduced in this volume, to the families and estates of those no longer living, and to the *Alpine* and *Scottish Mountaineering Club Journals*.

Many friends have been generous with advice and assistance: George Band acted as our Moscow courier, Bob Lawford guided us through the Alpine Club's picture archives, Eugene Gippenreiter and Vladimir Shataev supplied Russian information. In their separate ways Richard Fox, Sheila Harrison, Robin Hodgkin, Lord Hunt, Jill Neate, Michael Taylor, Ken Wilson, have all earned our gratitude.

Especially, we would like to thank Dr Charles Clarke for his unstinting cooperation and encouragement throughout the project, and Maggie Body, our wise and tolerant editor at Hodder & Stoughton.

Audrey Salkeld and José Luis Bermúdez
Summer, 1993

A Note on Nomenclature and Spelling

Due to the inevitable difficulties created by transliterating from the Cyrillic alphabet, there is no standardised spelling for most of the mountains in the Caucasus. Different conventions are adopted in different countries, and most of these change over time. The situation is further complicated because many of the mountains have changed their names over the years, some several times. Confronted with an enormous range of alternative spellings and reidentified mountains we have tried to stick to the following principles.

Spellings have been standardised whenever they occur in editorial contexts (e.g. chapter introductions or ascents list). Most of these standardised spellings are in line with those adopted in the translation of Friedrich Bender's *Classic Climbs in the Caucasus*.

In cases where anthologised authors have employed variant spellings which are nonetheless easily recognisable (e.g. Koschtantau for Koshtan-Tau, or Tchegem for Chegem), these have been retained.

When anthologised authors have written entire articles about mountains which have subsequently been reidentified (as in Dent's account of the ascent of Gestola which he thought was an ascent of Tetnuld) we have changed the text to bring it into line with current usage. Where this is done, however, attention is drawn to the fact in the chapter introduction.

In cases where authors have misidentified mountains which are not central to their articles we have drawn attention to the error on its first appearance, but then left it in the text.

In so doing we have no aspirations towards clarifying the vexed issue of Caucasian nomenclature. But we hope that at least we have not added to the confusion that already exists.

BETWEEN THE BLACK SEA AND THE CASPIAN

0   50   100   200 km

R. KUBAN

• Armavir   RUSSIA

• Cherkessk

CHERKESSKAYA   • Pyatigorsk

Teberda •   Karatschajewsk   R. BAKSAN

ELBRUS ▲   R. TERER   R. TEREK

R. SOUNDTA   • Grozny

SHKHARA ▲   CHECHNIA

Alagir   Ordzhonikidze

ABKHAZIA   KASBEK ▲   Burnaya •

OSSETIAN MILITARY HIGHWAY   DAGHESTAN

BLACK   IMERETIA   Kutaisi

• Poti   R. RIONI

SEA   GEORGIA   KAKHETIA

• Gori   R. ALAZANI

Tbilisi •

R. KURA

CASPIAN

SEA

TURKEY   • Erivan   AZERBAIJAN

ARMENIA

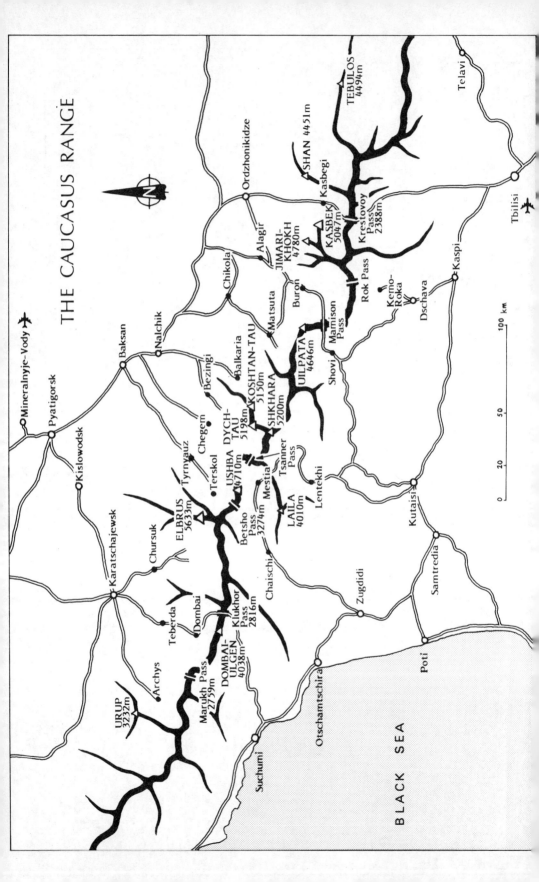

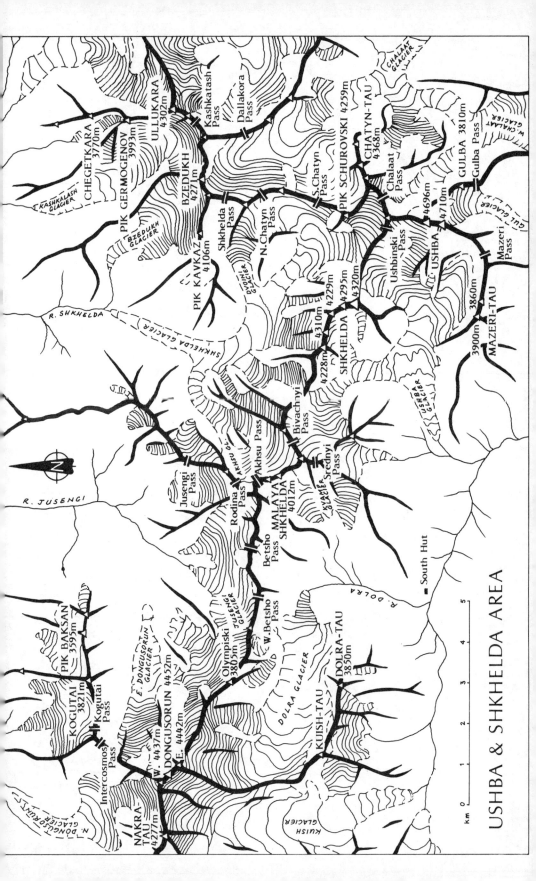

USHBA & SHKHELDA AREA

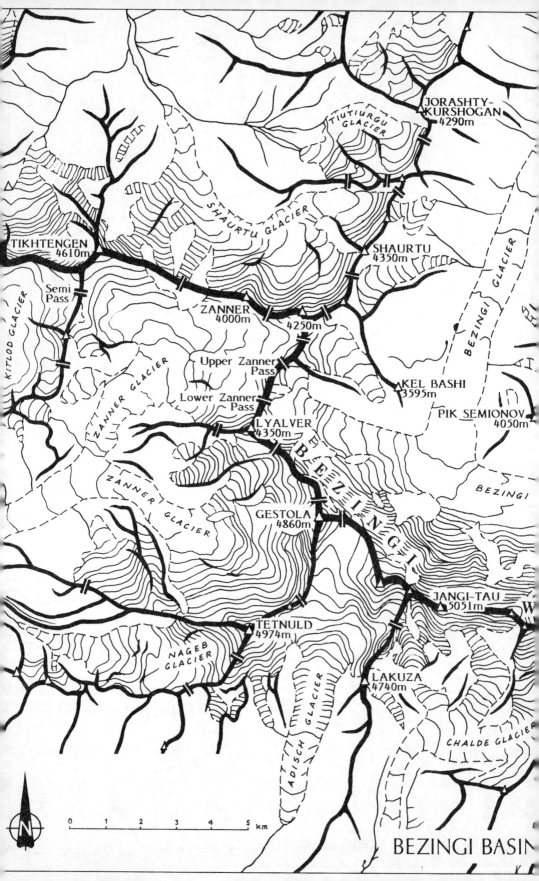

BEZINGI BASIN

BEZINGI

UKIU GLACIER

ULLU-AUZ-
BASHI
4670m

PIK
OCTOBER

ULLU-AUZ GLACIER

TIUTIUN GLACIER

MISHIRGI GLACIER

MISSES-TAU
4320m

KOSHTAN-TAU
5150m

TIUTIUN-
BASHI
4530m

DYCH-TAU
5198m

PIK PUSHKIN
5100m

Sella Pass

KHRUMKOL
4680m

KHRUMKOL
GLACIER

KARA-TAU
3941m

4460m BASHKA-AUZ

PIK SELLA
4370m

BASHKA-
AUZ GLACIER

AMANKAJA
3674m

Dychsu
Pass

ACIER

DYCHSU GLACIER

DYCHSU   GLACIER

SHKHARA
5200m

L L

SHKHARA WEST
5057m

USHGULI
4310m

NUAMKUAM
GLACIER

SHKHARA SOUTH
4350m

SHKHARA
GLACIER

NUAMKUAM
4182m

AILAMA
4525m

AILAMASU
GLACIER

INGURI
GLACIER

TSURUNGAL
4222m

AND KOSHTAN-TAU

Photographic Credits

The authors would like to thank Mrs Clark for permission to reproduce the photograph of the 1868 party from the Ronald Clark Collection; the Alpine Club for the portrait of Donkin, for Donkin's photographs of Ushba and of the camp near the Gulba Glacier, and for the pictures of Fischer and Streich; Richard Fox for the portrait of Harry Fox; Lord Hunt for Dych-Tau South-West Face, the picture of himself with Khergiani and Kachiani, Ushba from the Ushba Plateau, Pik Schurovski from the Shkhelda Glacier (photo: Vilem Heckel); Robin Hodgkin and Dulcibel Jenkins for the North Face of Tetnuld and the British team of 1937; and Mick Fowler for the picture of himself on Ushba (taken by Victor Saunders). All other pictures are from the Salkeld Collection.

1
The New Playground

To think of there being peaks higher than Mont Blanc within ten days from London, and that we should not even know what to call them! Is it not a disgrace to the Alpine Club that the words 'nameless peak' should have been left all these years in the middle of one of the grandest mountain groups in the world?

W. F. Donkin, 1887

In the middle years of the nineteenth century, as new railways thrust into Europe to bring Basel and Geneva within easy reach, British gentlemen-travellers suddenly discovered the joys of climbing Alps. And since this was the heyday of the London Club, they wasted no time in banding together to form an élite brotherhood. The Alpine Club, first of all alpine clubs, came into being in the last days of 1857, firmly establishing mountaineering as a 'sport' – and the Alps as the chosen 'playground' of Europe.

During the dozen or so years that make up what is conveniently called the Golden Age of Alpinism, British climbers bagged no less than thirty of the thirty-nine great peaks of the Alps, culminating in 1865 with Whymper's ascent of the Matterhorn. But that climb cost the lives of four men and severely dented the sense of infallibility that had hitherto been the hallmark of Victorian mountain enterprise. Until then, Alpine accidents were considered very much the result of the bad mountaineering practice of foreign climbers or inept tourists. This disaster was altogether too close to home and resulted in an appalled *Times* leader demanding that the Club manage its affairs better. What right had its members to throw away the gift of life? With the growing feeling that in any case the Alps were almost played out and fast becoming vulgarised by the trappings of tourism, disenchantment seeped into British mountaineering. Many Clubmen resigned. Those who still had a taste for virgin summits, and the leisure and means to indulge their appetite, began casting around for fresh fields to conquer. One young Oxford University student, with thirteen Alpine summers behind him, looked east towards Europe's loftiest mountains. In 1866, the year of his graduation, the aptly-named Douglas William Freshfield planned the first serious mountaineering exploration in the Caucasus range.

For more than six hundred miles, stretching north-west to south-east, linking the Black Sea with the Caspian, and with no less than twelve summits surpassing the height of Mont Blanc, this tangle of peaks separates Europe from Asia. Local legend tells how, after God had created the world, he decided it was too flat. Snow-capped mountains and green hills were needed to give it spice; so he filled a large sack and set off to scatter some over the earth. But the Devil, jealous that man should enjoy such wonders, sped after him and, as God flew between the two great inland seas, slit the sack with a knife. All the precious mountains tumbled out in a heap to form a wild barrier from coast to coast. This is the reason, its people say, why the Caucasus is the most beautiful land in the whole world.

The main chain is a near continuous spine, with few (and high) steep passes. At the eastern end the ranges fork into what is known as the Caspian Flail. Even today there are few road-crossings of the system, the most important breaches being the Klukhor Pass, crossing the Abkhazia chain; the Mamison Pass, linking the Rioni and Ardon river valleys, south and north, and bearing the old Ossetian Highway; and the Daryal gorge, connecting with the Krestovoy Pass and Terek valley, which gives passage to the Georgian Highway linking Tblisi with Ordzhonikidze. Climatically, there is great variation west to east, warm and humid on the Black Sea coast with subtropical vegetation, becoming increasingly arid through Daghestan to the Caspian, where the snow cap disappears. Climbers recognise three distinct sections: the Western Caucasus from the Black Sea to the Klukhor Pass, its highest peak being Dombai-Ulgen (4040m); the Eastern Caucasus between the Georgian Highway and the Caspian dominated by Shan (4451m); and by far the most important alpinistically, the Central Caucasus, between the two, made up of the Svanetian, Digorian and Ossetian chains, and containing all the major peaks.

To the ancient Greeks, the Caucasus mountains represented the boundary of all that was known. They were lands of myth and legend. It was to 'Mount Caucasus', probably Kazbek, that Prometheus was banished after stealing fire from the gods, there to languish, shackled to a rock with an eagle preying upon his liver, until Hercules at last delivered him. On the mountains' southern slopes lay Colchis, where Jason's Argonauts sought the Golden Fleece, and where too dwelled those formidable virgins, the Amazons. The charmed highlands were home to the durable Hyperboreans – and even today tales abound of vigorous centenarians living frugally and happily in sunny Georgian valleys.

The Mountains of Kaf of the *Arabian Nights* are traditionally identified with the Caucasus; the fabulous giant roc (which could truss elephants in its talons) had its eyrie on Shalbuz Dag at the eastern end of the range. The Old Testament tells of Gog of Magog, a monstrous ruler dominating the far, dark side of the range; while local folklore claims this wilderness as the last refuge of a yeti-like wild man, the *almesty*. As recently as autumn 1992 a scientific investigation reported taking cast of mysterious footprints, and rigged caves and other possible hideouts with self-triggering infra-red cameras to ambush the elusive hominid.

Venetian travellers and, later, Elizabethan merchants were among the first to bring to Western Europe tales of this fabulous region. Two centuries ago, the Empress Catherine of Russia despatched a scholar, one George Ellis, to gather information about the warlike tribes which offered such stubborn resistance to Russian dreams of conquest: his memoir of the Caucasian states with their exotic mix of peoples was published in London in 1788. In literature, Georgia can be said to be the poetic homeland of Russia. Pushkin travelled there; the tragic soldier-poet Lermontov drew inspiration from the 'golden peaks' of the Caucasus where he was exiled for eight years before meeting his death in Pyatigorsk in 1841, victim of a senseless duel. With more than a dash of romantic imagination, the Caucasus, too, coloured the writings of Dumas and Tolstoy. Even so, it has been said that in Western Europe in the mid-nineteenth century less was known of these mountains than had been of the Alps in the Middle Ages. An expedition such as that envisaged by young Freshfield was a serious undertaking indeed.

Politically, the Russians had been firmly established on both sides of the Caucasus from the beginning of the century, though holding only a narrow line of communication through the mountains themselves (the Daryal gorge link). The country's southern frontier was constantly shifting and the hills to the west and east, Circassia and Daghestan, were the refuge of proudly independent tribespeople. These would not be absorbed into Russia until after the Crimea War, and then uneasily, enjoying brief periods of independence in times of Russian turmoil. Mingrelians, Gourri, Svanetians (Balkarians and Ingooshi/Chegen-Inguzes), 'Mountain Jews', Circassians, Ossetes, Tchetchens, Tartars, Armenians lived on in their remote villages, quick to feud with their neighbours, much as they had for centuries. The three principal languages were Ossetian, Turko-Tartar and Svanetian, though as many as forty dialects and variations had been identified. The break up of the Soviet Union in modern times has renewed old conflicts, as separatists seek once more to splinter the mountain republics.

Freshfield had been attracted to the Caucasus through his love of classic literature and poetry. He knew little beyond the existence of its two highest peaks, Elbrus and Kazbek, extinct volcanoes in the central section of the range. Most maps denoted the mountains merely as a series of furry symbols resembling nothing so much as a nest of caterpillars, while an authoritative encyclopaedia unequivocally announced that all Caucasian mountains were either flat or cup-shaped, and that the existence of glaciers was uncertain. Freshfield did well, early in his plans, to team up with Adolphus Warburton Moore, a fine climber, slightly older than himself, who was employed by the East India Company. The two pored over Russian survey documents in the India Office, and a map prepared in Germany from the latest intelligence smuggled out of Russia. It showed the existence of a group of rugged and extremely interesting-looking mountains – anything but 'flat' – lying between the two known giants, and including Dych-Tau and Koshtan-Tau. A high-level route was worked out from Kazbek to Elbrus, which – Freshfield afterwards wrote with some pride – 'we subsequently carried out in all its details'. The sources of the rivers, he added, proved to have been plotted accurately enough (except in the case of the Skenis Skali), but of individual peaks and passes there had been little detail. Nothing then available in English literature had been of the slightest practical use to a mountaineer.

Freshfield travelled via Constantinople to approach the Caucasus from the south. He caught his first glimpse of the mountains from Batum on the Black Sea coast and remarked: 'It is curious that no one that I know of has written of the splendid distant panorama of the chain seen from the shore on a fine morning. To the left the sharp crests of the mountains west of the Klukhor Pass rise above the waves, in the centre is the unique dome of Elbruz, and to the east the peaks of the central group. Snows without name . . .'

The slender, gleaming pyramid of what we now know as Tetnuld particularly captured his attention. At Kutais, Freshfield's party was shown a postal map and learned for the first time of the many high-level passes that crossed the main chain. In Tiflis (Tblisi), where Moore joined them, they met Russian and German surveyors, who had taken part in the early exploration, and from them obtained official charts and documents to help them on their way. Even so, there was still scant knowledge of land above the snow line.

Freshfield was an avid chronicler, lyrically recording this first journey in his book, *Travels in the Central Caucasus and Bashan*. The mountains more than lived up to his youthful expectations. They had a vigour, an extravagance, he would afterwards say, and the hollows between were filled by such enormous firths of ice: there could be no doubt any more of the nature and glaciation of the area. Thereafter not a book or bulletin, not a scrap of Caucasian information escaped him. He noted all activity, every little anecdote, each clarification of nomenclature. It became a life's mission, and in 1896 his findings were distilled into the monumental two-volume *The Exploration of the Caucasus*, lavishly illustrated with photographs by the master artist of the camera, Vittorio Sella. By this time Freshfield had been three times to the region, traversing the main chain eleven times by eight different routes. He had crossed in and out of Svanetia by no less than seven variations.

Contemporary reviewers hailed his opus as 'rather a library than a book', adding that it was unquestionably the best illustrated in the whole literature of mountaineering. Its particular value today is as a Rosetta stone, post-dating, as it does, the confusing claims, counter-claims, and sheer speculation that attended early mountain and glacier discoveries. From one travel account to the next, one official Russian survey to the next, names would dance about on the map, making it hard to reconcile the information gleaned. After 1888, for instance, the old Tetnuld became Gestola and Koshtan-Tau Shkhara. Guluku was briefly Koshtan-Tau before settling as Dych-Tau, leaving the old Dych-Tau to be reidentified finally as Koshtan-Tau!

Further changes came in the wake of the Russian Revolution, as the more blatantly Communistic names will doubtless be supplanted in today's post-Soviet era. Still, Freshfield's scholarship ensured clarification of the major peaks.

Another of the pioneers, Clinton Dent, described the High Caucasus as without doubt 'the grandest chain of ice mountains that Europe can claim'. And he was not exaggerating. They surpass the Alps in height and scale, offering a challenge to the climber midway between those mountains and the Himalaya. The main Caucasian chain comprises steep-sided parallel ridges and spurs with literally hundreds of dramatic tops. Snow lies permanently above a level between 2500 and 3000 metres (8200 and 9850ft). The highest mountain is Elbrus at 5633 metres (18,383ft), though this, with its rounded twin cones, is atypical. Elsewhere the peaks offer serrated crests to the sky; they are hung with glaciers and icefields. The Central Caucasus, lying between the upper basins of the Kuban and Terek rivers, encompasses (at either end) Elbrus and Kazbek (5047m) – though both lying to the north of the main chain. In its ten square miles can be found as many as twenty distinct summits over 4270 metres (14,000ft). The early climbers, seeking to describe this wonderland to the uninitiated, felt obliged to borrow Alpine imagery. Shkhara, its five-crested ridge conspicuous from the southern plains, was the Monte Rosa of the Caucasus, the Bezingi glacier its Gorner Glacier; Kazbek from the Daryal Pass offered the Jungfrau view, or the Matterhorn seen from Riffel Alp, though Ushba, too, was frequently claimed as the Matterhorn of the Caucasus. Jangi-Tau conjured images of an enlarged Breithorn, Cheget-Tau was the Biancograt, Tikhtengen the Shreckhorn, and the 'sky-cleaving pyramids of Koshtan-Tau and Dych-Tau' made even the Schreckhorn and Finsteraarhorn seem small.

In the decade between 1886 and 1896 most of the major summits were climbed and, with the exception of Merzbacher's ascent of Gimarai Khokh (4778m) and Sella's of Ullu-Auz-Bashi (4670m), all by Alpine Club parties. The pattern was similar to the Golden Age in the Alps. By the turn of the century, as with Alpine development, British parties relinquished dominance to other nationalities, and eventually, rightly, to Russian mountaineers. Even so, Britons retained their special relationship with the range and sporadically in the years of this century have made highly productive visits.

Clinton Dent once remarked how so much of the information gathered by successive travellers in the Caucasus was hidden away in journals, and some only to be found in private diaries and notebooks. Nearly a hundred years on, you could make similar comment. Despite recently available guidebooks, the bulk of Caucasian literature is still widely scattered or difficult to obtain. Freshfield's compendium has long disappeared from all but the most exclusive antiquarian shops, where a presentation copy today fetches well over a thousand pounds. It seems appropriate, therefore, and especially with the prospect of easier travel in the Caucasus for non-East European mountaineers, to remind ourselves of the history and literature of the range.

It will be some years before we learn the full story of Russian activity during the years when the mountains were closed to outsiders, but we are especially indebted to Eugene Gippenreiter and Vladimir Shataev for supplying a wealth of route information that has been incorporated into this narrative and into the History on page 219.

2
Snows Without Name

Douglas William Freshfield's background was in many ways typical of the members of the Alpine Club during the first years of its existence. Educated at Eton and Oxford, he inherited a considerable private fortune, allowing him to devote his life to climbing and exploring in the great mountain ranges of the world. What was uncharacteristic about him, however, was the wealth of mountain experience he acquired at a relatively early age. When he climbed Mont Blanc for the first time in 1862 he was only seventeen years old and still at school. During the next five years he spent each summer in the Alps and made a significant number of first ascents and first crossings of mountain passes, including the first ascents of Presanella (3556m) in the Lombard Alps and the Tour Ronde (3792m) in the Mont Blanc massif.

When Freshfield decided to make the first serious exploration of the Caucasus in 1868 he was just twenty-three years old. His companions were not much older. Charles Comyns Tucker was twenty-four. A friend from Oxford, he had accompanied Freshfield in the Alps during the seasons of 1866 and 1867, a time which Freshfield describes rather laconically: 'In the summers of sixty-six and sixty-seven I climbed with my college friend Comyns Tucker in most of the districts between the Graians and the Engadine, picking up a fair number of the "new" peaks and passes still uncaptured.'[1] Undoubtedly, though, the strongest member of the party was Adolphus Warburton Moore who, at the age of twenty-seven was already one of the leading Alpine pioneers. By 1865 he had made nine important first ascents, including the Gross Fiescherhorn, and culminating in the ascent, far ahead of its time, of the Brenva Spur on July 15, 1865. Climbers who attempt the Brenva Spur, still a serious and demanding climb today, will find the Col Moore at 3479 metres, just as those who climb the Tour Ronde by the South-East Ridge will pass the Col Freshfield at 3625 metres.

As was the custom of the day, the three 'gentlemen mountaineers' were joined by the great Chamonix guide, François Joseph

Dévouassoud, who attended Freshfield on almost all his mountaineer-ing ventures between 1863 and 1892. Freshfield often wrote in praise of his guide, and on his death accompanied his reminiscences of Dévouassoud with an execrable poem that began: 'Knight-errant of the glacier-cleaving blade'.[2] Elsewhere he wrote: 'He has taken tea with dignity with the Armenian patriarch at Etchmiadzin, has handed coffee at Jerusalem to a Turkish Pasha and paid his respects to the Archbishop of Canterbury.'[3] The accounts which Freshfield left of his expeditions, both in the Alps and in the greater ranges, leave no doubt that 'the gallant François' was treated more as a friend, companion and equal, than as a paid employee.

Freshfield, Tucker and Dévouassoud left London in January 1868 (Moore was unable to leave before the summer and joined them at Tblisi in June). Their objectives were not confined to the Caucasus. First they would make a general tour of Syria and the Near East, although there the only mountaineering effort was to attempt Mount Ararat, which by then had had two previous ascents – excluding that claimed for Noah. The final attempt was made by Tucker and Dévouas-soud. Freshfield dropped back, suffering from the altitude but still not lost for words: 'Above them stretched interminable snow-slopes, seamed here and there by rocks, but, unluckily, rocks of an utterly useless description to the climber. They were not ridges, but discon-nected crags of lava, suggesting by their fantastic shapes the idea that half the animals, after leaving the Ark, had been petrified as they came down the mountain. Here was an elephant, glissading elegantly, using his trunk for an alpenstock; there a tapir, or some antediluvian-looking beast, by whose untimely fate, now for the first time discovered, natu-ralists have lost a species'.[4] Dévouassoud cut steps up firm névé until he could go no further, and then Tucker pushed on alone, reaching a height which he estimated to be more or less that of Mont Blanc, before he too turned back.

From Ararat they went back to Tblisi where they met up with Moore before venturing into the Central Caucasus. After crossing the Kresto-voy Pass they descended into the valley of the Terek and found them-selves near the foot of Kazbek (5047m), the extinct volcano reputed to be the site of Prometheus' ordeal. The first ascent of Kazbek took place on July 1. It was not a great feat of mountaineering, and the major incident was a fall by Tucker as he was cutting steps downhill, fortunately held by Freshfield and Moore. The route was, however, too steep to reverse, and they descended, in some trepidation, down the northern flank, having come up from the south. A hero's welcome awaited them in Kazbek village where they had been feared lost.

They had been in the Caucasus only a week, and already one of their major objectives had been achieved. The next task they set themselves was a high-level traverse of the entire range, from the Terek valley at the extreme east of the Central Caucasus, to Elbrus, the highest and westernmost mountain in the range. The first week of their journey covered relatively straightforward ground, up the Terek valley, across into the Ardon valley, and then over the Mamison Pass and into the central part of the range. Their reception by the Ossetian villagers was not always welcoming, however, and they came to blows with their own porters in the village of Zacca over a disappearing cloak. 'In self-defence I was obliged to let go the cloak, and in a few seconds my friends came to the rescue, Tucker hitting straight into the eyes of the thieves, while Moore charged down the hill with the point of his ice-axe directed full at their stomachs, and François lent the weight of his elephantine bulk to the united onset.'[5] After the Mamison Pass the work of exploration proper began as they came within sight of the Adai Kokh group of mountains. They reconnoitred the southern approach to the group and decided against it, with Freshfield saying of what appeared to be the principal summit that 'its sides are of a steepness appalling to anyone who has ever allowed the idea of climbing them to enter his head'.[6] Undaunted, they crossed a new pass into the Uruch valley and explored the extensive Karagom Glacier on the northern side of the massif before descending back into the Rioni valley.

From there they crossed the Nöschka and Naksagar Passes and entered the province of Svanetia at Jibiani. Freshfield was not impressed by his first encounter with the Svanetians. He refers to the 'uncouth ferocity' of the men and describes the women as 'uniformly ugly'. The children fared even worse: they were 'wild-looking ragamuffins, with matted locks, and ran about half-naked, clad in one tattered garment of old cloth or sacking; some of the girls had the most savage faces, more like animals than human beings'.[7] The inhabitants of Jibiani then added to their sins by purloining a tent-pole and a volume of Tennyson! Four days later, however, the party caught its first sight of what was subsequently discovered to be Ushba:

> Due north, above the low wood of the adjoining hillside, shot up two towers of rock, one slightly in advance of the other, forming, as regards height, steepness, and outline, beyond all comparison the most wonderful mountain mass we had ever beheld. Tier above tier of precipices rose straight up from the valley, culminating in two tremendous towers, separated by a deep depression. The twin summits resembled one another in form, and appeared to be long roof-like ridges, falling away in slopes of mingled rock and ice of terrific steepness. The idea of climbing either of them seemed too insane to be so much as suggested, and even the lower slopes of the mountain above the meadows of Betsho are so tremendous that it looked as if a stone dropped from the top of either of the peaks would scarcely stop rolling before it reached the valley. There was no mistake about it, the Caucasian Matterhorn was found at last, only here we had one Matterhorn piled on another, and then multiplied by two.[8]

Unsurprisingly, they enjoyed the scenery and passed on without investigating any further.

They then turned northwards and crossed the Nakra Pass, arriving at the large village of Urusbieh. They were now within striking distance of Elbrus, whose twin summits, at 5633 metres and 5621 metres, are the highest in Europe. There was at the time some uncertainty about whether Elbrus had previously been ascended. In 1829 a surveying expedition led by the Russian General Emmanuel attempted the mountain. The general promised a reward of 400 roubles for the first ascent and claimed to have seen a solitary figure disappearing into the mist that he believed hid the summit. He duly handed over the reward, but future generations have been more sceptical and the matter has remained in doubt. (See Appendix II.) Freshfield and his companions certainly had little time for the story. They set off from Urusbieh on July 29 for what they, and almost all historians, believe was the first ascent of Elbrus. The climb itself was technically even less demanding than that of Kazbek. Freshfield refers to 'the final cone of Elbruz, which rose immediately before us, resembling in shape an inverted tea-cup'.[9] The summit was reached on July 31 after a single bivouac. Unknowingly, they had climbed the eastern, and slightly lower, of Elbrus' twin peaks. The view, however, was recompense enough for the extreme cold which they reported: 'Beginning in the east, the feature of the panorama was the central chain between ourselves and Kazbek. I never saw any group of mountains which bore so well being looked down upon as the great peaks that stand over the sources of the Tcherek and Tchegem. The Pennines from Mont Blanc look puny in comparison with Koschtantau and his neighbours from Elbruz. The Caucasian groups are finer, and the peaks sharper, and there was a suggestion of unseen depth in the trenches separating them, that I never noticed so forcibly in any Alpine view.'[10]

After Elbrus they went to the spa town of Pyatigorsk, a haven of civilisation and site of Lermontov's duel, where they rested for a few days before setting off to complete their circuit of the Central Caucasus by traversing the range to the north. The most significant event here was the opportunity for a close look at Shkhara and Koshtan-Tau, the third and fourth highest peaks in the range, which Freshfield misidentified as Koshtan-Tau and Dych-Tau respectively. Both mountains were previously unknown to British geographers, although they appeared on the Russian five-verst* map, and Freshfield was characteristically eloquent in their praise: 'While admiring, and endeavouring to carry away a recollection of, the noble outline of the group I have attempted to describe, we could not help regretting that such grand mountains should have been deprived of their legitimate honours by a mere volcanic accident like Elbruz. In Koschtantau [Shkhara] and Dychtau [Koshtan-Tau] the Caucasus would have had a worthy king and queen. Elbruz is at best a bloated monarch, and has little beyond size to recommend him.'[11] Even so, they prudently decided to leave the peaks for future visitors, and eventually arrived back at Tblisi on August 26.

*   *   *

---

* A verst is an old Russian unit of measurement, equivalent to .663 of a mile or 1.067 km (6 versts, therefore, are more or less 4 miles).

The 1868 expedition was primarily one of exploration. Freshfield and his companions crossed, and managed to make some sense of, the complicated topography of the Central Caucasus, covering enormous distances in the process, but their mountaineering feats were limited to the two easy extinct volcanoes at either end of the range. Freshfield himself, unlike Moore and Tucker, was primarily an explorer rather than a climber, and it is as such that he should be remembered. An amusing story illustrating this appeared in the *Alpine Journal* after his death. E. J. Garwood recalls climbing the Piz Bernina with Freshfield and Benjamin Wainwright. 'After lunching at the foot of the rocks we re-roped to continue the climb, and at one awkward point Freshfield, who was behind me, asked me to keep a tight hold of the rope. Shortly afterwards he called a halt and asked me to examine the rope as it was hurting him; on doing so I found he had tied himself with a slip-knot. "Well," he remarked smiling, "you see, I am accustomed to climb with guides who always roped me up; I do not profess to be an expert climber, but only a mountain geographer." '[12]

Freshfield published only a brief itinerary of the 1868 journey in the *Alpine Journal*, saving his full Victorian prose for the expedition book. Rather than reprint here accounts of the ascents of Elbrus or Kazbek to illustrate his contribution to Caucasian exploration, we have chosen, firstly, a description of crossing the difficult Karagom Glacier Pass between the Uruch and Riom valleys, an epic day of more than twelve hours' hard going. This has been taken from his *The Exploration of the Caucasus*. It is followed by the diary of his second visit to the range, made in 1887. Freshfield's daily jottings have an immediacy not found in his books and the prose flows easily. It is interesting to note the changes he finds in the nineteen years since his first visit. He was accompanied, as ever, by François Dévouassoud, but on this occasion they were joined by François' brother Michel and his nephew Joseph Désailloud, both also Chamonix guides. The party was completed by the Hungarian mountaineer and photographer Maurice de Déchy who had made three previous visits to the Caucasus.

3
Crossing the Karagom Pass

by Douglas W. Freshfield

In 1868, when the three young Englishmen whose travels are recorded in my *Central Caucasus* undertook to examine *ambulando* the nature of the chain between Kasbek and Elbruz, the second object of their journey was the exploration of this Adai Khokh Group. We had no trustworthy map to guide us at that date. Our information was limited to the notes, mainly archaeological, of Brosset, to a very confused notice in Klaproth of the snow-passes between Stir-Digor and Gebi,* and to the vague indications and blue smears of the five-verst map. The excursions of Dr Abich and Dr Radde had been limited to the lower ends of the two great frozen streams which, issuing from far invisible and unknown fountains in the recesses of the range, stretch their icy tongues down into the forest region. One of these, the Zea Glacier, flows into a glen some ten miles long that opens on the Ardon valley at St Nikolai. Beyond the paths of men or the tracks of hunters all was obscure.

Our intention in 1868 was to have gone up the Zea valley, and crossed from its head to the Mamison. But the difficulties we experienced with the inhabitants in traversing the deep and isolated basins that hold the sources of the Nardon made us give up a project which involved separation from our baggage. Consequently we carried out but half our plan, and were content, in the first instance, to cross the Mamison to the southern side. We found ourselves at Chiora in the Rion valley, at the foot of a native glacier pass, leading to the north side of the chain. It seemed, according to the map, to descend by a side glen on to the great glacier referred to by Abich. At that time passes were still as much in vogue with climbers as peaks. We saw pleasing prospects

---

* The best explanation that has been given of Klaproth's very curious description of the passage with horses of the Gebi Passes—the Gurdzivsek, and Gebivsek or Gezevsek (new map)—is that he took down hearsay information and turned it into a narrative in the first person.

of adventure and discovery in crossing the native pass, and finding a way for ourselves back over the unknown snowfields farther east. Our interpreter and luggage were abandoned, and we started in the lightest marching order.

Leaving Chiora before daybreak, we wandered over pastures where the birches waved their delicate branches in the first breath of dawn, while the moonlight still shone on the upper snows. Shepherds' fires shone at intervals through the dusk, and the native who was carrying our provisions up to the snow led us a long circuit in order to visit some of his friends who were camping out with their flocks. In the Caucasus the peasants take far less pains than in the Alps to make themselves at home in their summer quarters. They have more sheep and horses, and far fewer dairies. It is only rarely, and on the north side, that huts, answering to an Alpine chalet are found. In general, the herdsmen are contented with a slight shelter; an overhanging crag, a hollow under an erratic boulder, or a few boughs with a sheepskin thrown over them. Close at hand a forked stick is thrust in the ground, on which the owner, when at home, hangs his gun. Two more sticks and a crossbar support a pail. This is a Caucasian Kosh, a place where men sleep or rest, the *gias* or *gîte* of the Western Alps. That in so moist and variable a climate as that of the Central Caucasus the shepherds should not suffer more from exposure says much for the general healthiness of the highlands. Not long ago, similar natural shelters were used by Bergamasque shepherds in the Engadine.

Up and down, or along ridges, our track led us, till it descended into a beautiful meadow, surrounded by trees, where a bright spring bubbled up amongst flowery grass under a clump of alders. This spot, called on the one-verst map Notsanzara, lies not far from the foot of the steep zigzags that lead up on the side of the glacier that flows out of the basin west of Burdjula.

Flocks of sheep, led by men in sheepskin hats and long grey coats, and escorted by savage dogs, were hurrying down from the pass. After entering on the glacier, we missed, or rather abandoned, the tracks of the shepherds, which turned sharply to the left. Walking straight up to a gap at the head of the *névé*, we crawled equally straight down a snow-wall, which seemed to me at the time of appalling steepness.

Photographs have since confirmed my first impression. But the snow was in such perfect condition that the descent proved neither dangerous nor difficult. From the top we had the amusement of watching a second flock of sheep leap the *Bergschrund* on the true pass, which lay at some distance on our left.

A level glacier and a rocky glen received us on the north side. The glen soon opened on the great ice-stream we had come to encounter. The first view of it, admirably reproduced in Signor Sella's photograph, was exciting, but hardly encouraging. The ice-falls of the Karagom equal in beauty, in breadth and in altitude any that I know: not so steep or so formidable as the frozen cataract of the Adish Glacier, they are more singular in their surroundings, and the noble gateway in the mountains through which they pour adds to their scenic effect. We camped—if to light a fire and spread a mackintosh can be called to camp—in the fir-wood above the moraine. Nineteen years later I revisited the spot, coming up from the valley of the Urukh on the north side. The native track crosses the broad ice-stream, and in the hollow under the moraine, on the right bank, a substantial log-hut offers unexpected shelter to travellers.

The position of our 1868 bivouac, with regard to the glacier, was similar to that of the Montenvers Inn with regard to the Mer de Glace. Looking northwards over the great frozen billows, we could see, beyond the point where they plunged out of sight, the fir-forests and corn-land of the Urukh. In the opposite direction the great ice-fall closed the view, and gave no hint of the mysterious region from which it flowed.

Next morning at daybreak we set out on our adventure. For two hours a shepherd's track helped us as far as the highest grass on the west bank of the ice. Here we were close to the foot of the last and loftiest of the frozen cascades, and the work of the day began. At first all went smoothly; we found corridors between the great ice-blocks, and were able to avoid the chasms that seamed the slope. But when these chasms became more and more continuous and, running across the snowy dells, forced us right or left into the intricate labyrinth and among the crystal towers, our prospects of success began to look very questionable. We had to encounter in an aggravated form all the familiar difficulties and perils of an Alpine ice-fall. The aggravation consisted chiefly in the constant repetition. No sooner had one turret-staircase been hewn out in a crack of some imposing barrier than another castle appeared behind it. The glacier was something more than a mountain dragon: it was a very hydra. But our motives for perseverance were strong. To retreat meant a long tramp down to a distant village, where we should have to trust to signs to get provisions, and to run the risk of being arrested as suspicious characters, and sent down two days' journey to some Cossack outpost on the northern steppe.

I renounce any attempt to depict the individual difficulties—the 'bad places'—we encountered during the next few hours:

> The moving accident is not my trade,
> To freeze the blood I have no ready arts,

to quote Wordsworth—and climbers suffering under no such disability have frequently depicted their feats and those of their guides in similar emergencies, both with pen and pencil. One particular snowbridge or causeway remains pre-eminent in my memory. It was long and narrow and rotten, and it ended in nothing. The leader had to lean across and cut a precarious foothold in the opposite bank of ice, and then make a bold leap into his pigeon-holes. Dévouassoud leapt, and we followed. The rest was not quite so bad, but there was a great deal of it. We wearied of the exquisite beauty of the icicle-fringes and the blue ravines, of the fantastic forms of the sun-smitten towers and pinnacles. There was not a moment's pause in the battle; we halted neither for food nor rest. At last the clear ice turned to more opaque *névé*, the surface was less tormented, and we began to count on victory. But the final moat, at the point where the steepening of the slope caused the most severe tension, had still to be overcome. It held over us an upper lip which was not mastered at the first attempt.

It was half-past one, and we had been six hours in the fall, and nine hours from our bivouac, before we sat down on the level snows to consider our further course through the undiscovered country no human eye had ever before seen.

We were on a great snowfield, sloping gently towards us from the south; more steeply from the east. A low rocky mass divided the branches; to the right rose a conspicuous and welcome landmark, the crest of Burdjula. Behind us were wild rock-peaks, the Karagom Khokh of my map: the highest summit of Adai Khokh and its neighbours were no doubt seen to our left, but I did not identify them till long afterwards. We chose the southern bay, and again set out. The surface at this late hour of the day was soft, and it was not till after three hours of steady and heavy wading that the monotony of the white and blue world into which we had broken was suddenly relieved by the appearance, above the level snows that had hitherto formed our skyline, of the purple line of the mountains on the Turkish frontier.

The view from the pass towards Asia was of surpassing beauty. The whole basin of ancient Kolkhis, Mingrelia and Imeretia, the Racha and Lechgum, lay at our feet. Flashes of reflected sunshine showed where the waters of the Rion forced their way through a labyrinth of green ridges and dark forest-clad ravines to the pomegranate gardens of Kutais. Far away in the west we saw for the first time the snows of the Laila, the range that encloses Suanetia on the south. The mid-day vapours had disappeared early: it was a perfect late summer afternoon, and the rays of the sun, which was already sinking towards the west, transfigured parts of the landscape with a golden glory, heightened by contrast where the shadows thrown by the dark pikes of the range south of Gurshevi and the tower of Shoda fell across the lower slopes. One of the reasons that a want of picturesque effect is so generally complained of in high mountain views is that they are rarely seen early or late enough in the day. I have never been on a peak or pass more than four hours before or after mid-day without being astonished at the beauty of detail and colour, of light and shade, added to landscapes that, in the noonday glare, are apt to be impressive only by reason of their vastness. Thus, for example, the view from the Wetterhorn becomes superb when the great peaks of the Oberland fling their shadows towards the spectator who watches from that lonely pinnacle; the prospect over Suanetia from the Laila is exquisite when the first sunbeams touch its corn-fields and towered hamlets.

Over the details of the descent into the Rion Valley I need not linger. As first-comers generally do, we got into some needless difficulty, but before nightfall we had gained turf, and, conscious that Glola might be reached by breakfast-time next morning, lay down beneath the highest birches, with ice-axes driven in below us to prevent our rolling down the slope, as heedless as any Caucasian shepherd of the absence of supper or the showers that passed over us. We were conscious of having lived a day which would never fade from our memories.

From *The Exploration of the Caucasus*, 1896

A Skeleton Diary of Six Weeks' Travel in the Central Caucasus in 1887

by Douglas W. Freshfield

Left London by night mail on July 10, spent two days and a night at Vienna, a day at Charkoff, a night and morning at Rostoff on the Don. Otherwise travelled day and night, reaching Vladikafkaz [now Ordzhonikidze] on the afternoon of July 19. Russian first-class carriages equal to sleeping cars, and buffets excellent. Gaiters stolen from registered package. All goods registered in Russia should be under lock and key. At Vienna François Dévouassoud, his brother Michel, and his nephew, Joseph Désailloud, all guides on the Chamonix roll, met me. At Charkoff I was joined by M. de Déchy, of Budapesth, a member of the Alpine Club and Goegraphical Society, and a most skilful amateur photographer, who had made three previous journeys in the Caucasus, on the first ascending, with the guides A. Burgener and P. S. Ruppen, Adai Choch (15,244 feet) and Elbruz.

M. de Déchy undertook to provide his own tents and many other articles of equipment for the party. He also took on himself the labour of buying and forwarding our joint provisions of every sort, so that I only took out sleeping bags, saddle bags, and a few luxuries and instruments from England, some of which were kindly lent me by my friends Messrs. Tuckett, Blackstone, Dent, and H. Walker. Speaking Russian, and having acquaintances among the Russian officials, M. de Déchy was able to dispense with an interpreter, and to obtain some valuable facilities. But for these inducements I should hardly have revisited the country.

July 19.—Hills of Pätigorsk in sight early. Snows clouded. Caucasus meets steppe as Alps meet Lombard plain. Loftier snows and bolder peaks, but no cultivation or campanili; only riverbanks with thickets of reeds, expanses of mallows and wild sunflowers, and here and there on projecting knolls the remains of a primitive hillfort or the tumulus of some forgotten warrior. So the Alps must have looked to the Romans when Gallia Cisalpina was still a new province. Met in train the son of Ismael, the Urusbieh chief, returning for the Long Vacation from the University of Moscow, where he is sent at government expense. Also Professor Kovalevsky, who was good enough last year to send me his work on the Ossetes, and was now returning to prosecute his researches into primitive laws and customs among the Chetchens. Reached Vladikafkaz in afternoon.

20th.—M. de Déchy visited officials. Sent off two cases *viâ* Kutais to Suanetia. This proved a mistake, as the impetus of the Vladikafkaz officials did not carry the cases beyond Kutais, and we might, as it turned out, have taken them across directly from Urusbieh. Shops generally well stored, but preserved meats scarce and dear.

21st.—Rail back to Kotlorevska, where guides had been left to sleep in the waiting-room. Drove (six hours, two stages) to Naltshik in *telegas.* Steppe smooth, and jolting only a faint reminiscence of old tortures on the Armenian roads and rocks. Lodged at Naltshik in a squalid room in the post station, a bad beginning, as we were comfortable here nineteen years ago, and Dent and Donkin were well lodged last year.

All the chiefs of the district in town. Hamzet of Urusbieh asked by name after Moore and Tucker. Since I last saw him he has been to the Oberland to study dairy farming at the expense of the government – not to much purpose, I fear! Here also is the chief of Tchegem and the seven-foot giant of Bezingi, with several of his retainers figured in Donkin's photographs, copies of which I have happily at hand to present them with. The Nachalnik promised to expedite our journey to Urusbieh, and to forward our letters and a case of provisions in due time to meet us at Bezingi. He also provided us with a Kabardan Cossack, a gentle, intelligent, and serviceable attendant, who remained with us for three weeks.

22nd.—Clear view of snowpeaks over forest range. Dychtau and another great peak ('peut-être encore plus haut,' says François) in foreground. Second peak must be Dent's Guluku, my Unknown Peak. Conclusion, Guluku is Russian Koshtantau, 17,096 feet. This explains much.

Morning spent in dividing and repacking provisions and paraphernalia – an enormous task, in which M. de Déchy displays great enthusiasm, perseverance, and ability; and I the reverse. Drive in the afternoon across steppe to Baksan station. Splendid distant view of Kazbek, a slender pyramid of pure snow rising far above its neighbours in the east. Luminous atmosphere; distances clear and soft in colour, remind me of the Roman Campagna. Drive on beside the river to the straggling village of Atashutan. Overtake local Priestav sent to aid us. Received coldly at first by Kabardan chief; subsequently invited to sleep in his house, and served about midnight with a heavy supper.

23rd.—Two peaks of Elbruz visible a hundred yards above house. Fail to get off until 9 a.m. Forty miles (sixty versts) to Urusbieh. Drive about ten versts to first bridge, where Urusbieh chiefs have a house, the best sleeping-place to divide the journey. Heavy shower in afternoon. I enjoy a solitary two hours' starlight ride, meeting many belated Tartars on the road. At last, at 11 p.m., we reach Urusbieh, and occupy the old guest-house, now somewhat dilapidated.

24th.—The chiefs of Urusbieh have not prospered. Of the three brothers Mohammed has been killed, and his murderers having denounced – falsely in all probability – Ismael as the instigator of the crime, he was kept for a time under arrest. The family lawsuit with the government as to the forests is still dragging on, though the chiefs have succeeded on a preliminary point. Their influence is far from what it was, and the village is under no control.

In the morning I walked up hillside behind village; saw some earth-pinnacles and a waterfall. Landscape severe and arid but thoroughly alpine, snowpeaks in every direction promising fine excursions. Understood Grove's appreciation of Urusbieh, after walking over the low-level passes of the northern valleys in dull weather. M. de Déchy involved in intricate and interminable negotiations for the transport of our baggage across the chain. Settled at last that our Cossack shall cross the Dongussorun (Nakra Pass) to Betsho with donkeys, while we, with eight porters, cross the Adyr Su Pass, which is very seldom used and considered difficult by the natives.

25th.—Three hours' noisy wrangle in morning as to distribution of burdens. The porters seemed to me to have some reason on their side, and were most systematic in weighing and apportioning each man's load.

Steep ascent into glen of Adyr Su, which opens opposite village. Picturesque pinewoods, and fine glacier views. Glaciers on both sides as well as at head of valley. Long plain below glacier. Pitch tents (we have two) beside Kosh (shepherds' bivouac answering to alpine chalet, but rarely provided with any permanent shelter) 200 feet below ice. Excellent *airam*, not sour, but like Devonshire cream.

26th.—Porters all eager to start. Off at 5 a.m. Instead of taking the best line along flowery slopes E. of glacier, porters lead up moraine (Caucasians love moraine!) Fine icefall right with waterfall bursting out of it. Five glaciers meet at head of glen. Easy pass to Adyl Su westward;* said to be one also eastward to Tchegem. Obvious links in high-level route of the future from Koshtantau to Elbruz. Our pass lies deep and high in a recess, and at the eastern base of the peak, compared by Moore to the Schreckhorn. Ascent by hard snowbanks, which I hurried up, as every step brought fresh peaks into sight, to projecting rock with stoneman, where we breakfasted and roped. Then long soft slopes of névé to pass, a broad snow-col, 12,700 feet by aneroid – seven hours from bivouac. I gave the laden porters a lead through the heavy snow. On reaching the top their leader slapped me on the back and shook hands warmly, ejaculating, 'Djighite! Djighite!' – a word familiar to me from Tolstoi's 'Les Cosaques'.† Fine view of precipitous range opposite (S.), enclosing an enormous glacier flowing S.W.; Leila chain in distance. After short descent Tetnuld and Dent and Donkin's peak seen over gap at head of glacier. This gap probably leads to Thuber névé; another nearer us seems to be known as a pass from Tchegem to Suanetia. On reaching main glacier, Ushba comes into sight. Magnificent ice scenery. Great glacier pouring down from N., another

---

* The Adyl Su is the tributary of the Baksan flowing from the main chain next to the W. of the Adyr Su.

† 'Un véritable *djighite* doit avoir de belles armes. Quant à son uniforme il peut être usé et porté avec négligence.' I do not think it was my ice-axe won me the title! It was applied in old days to a successful warrior, Cossack or Tcherkess.

meeting ours from W. Comparable to Mer de Glace at Couvercle. Porters thought they saw bouquetin on wonderfully green slopes N. of glacier. Left ice for flowery hillside just above junction of glaciers; the united stream breaks through a narrow valley nearly due S. White rhododendrons still in full bloom. Very rough barely indicated track on slopes, then a mile or two of moraine, relieved at last by a bank gay with white and blush wild roses, yellow lilies, and strange blooms innumerable. Path cut off by lateral ravine; driven back to ice; recover track on further side. I run on and find good site for tents near a stream in hollow between old moraine and hillside, 200 feet above present end of glacier. Out fifteen hours, including many halts for photographing, &c. Two guides worse for *airam*; porters walked splendidly. Shower in night drove the porters for shelter into neighbouring pine grove.

27th.—End of our glacier, which I propose to call Gvalda Glacier (6,200 feet); of a second (Mestia Glacier) which has at one time joined it (6,000 feet), the lowest on the S. side of the Caucasus. This glacier is not so large, but steeper. It flows from two basins, one immediately under the N. peak of Ushba, the other leading to a pass to the Adyl Su valley, which our porters held worse than the one we had crossed. (This ice-stream is well seen from the Latpar Pass.) Fine view of Ushba from camp. The beauty of the descent into Suanetia more than realised my recollections. The enormous glaciers of the chain are met by the most luxuriant hillsides. There is no intervening zone of barrenness. Green things were growing even on the rubbish which covered the end of the glacier.

Below glacier path level and scenery tame to first houses on left bank; whence we crossed open sunny slopes, hay meadows and copses, with fine views of Ushba and the towered hamlets of Mestia, and the glaciers of the Leila in the distance. Met boy with dish of trout. Took up quarters (easy four hours) at Cancellaria (a small building used both as a court-house and travellers' bungalow. These shelters contain, as a rule, no furniture beyond a raised platform, though a bench and table are sometimes found). Starshina (village headman, appointed by Russians, and distinguished by wearing a chain), a huge wild man with a broad Babylonian physiognomy. A very small sharp boy interpreted for him. Bought a sheep and feasted the men of Urusbieh. One of them took a great fancy to me, and on parting shook hands most warmly, called me once more a 'djighite', and offered to remain with us as long as we liked. I return to my old opinion that the Urusbieh hunters are the raw material of glacier guides. They are far better on a glacier than most Tyrolese were twenty-five years ago, and they are untiring walkers and weight-carriers. I strolled in afternoon to junction of Mestia and Mushalaliz torrents. Past school-house; room decorated with prints of single Cossacks pursuing Turkish armies, charts of the heavens, and pictures of common objects of civilisation. Tetnuld's silver spear high in air over thickets of azalea and rhododendrons, now past bloom. Dent and Donkin's peak [Gestola] seen on N. flank of Tetnuld. Counted over seventy towers in neighbouring villages. Above Cancellaria is a very ancient birch tree, with several rude stone seats under it.

28*th.*—Rode or walked through Latal to Betsho (about 4 hours). Excellent path on right bank through the ripening barley-fields between neat wattled fences. Splendid scenery. Foreground of white towers, golden barley, and graceful birches. In middle distance slopes, on which the sombre groups of pines and firs show as shadows among the lighter foliage of the birch, beech, and poplar woods. Snow peaks brilliant behind defile dividing Mestia and Mushalaliz.

Curious church at Nendjar, built of carefully squared blocks of limestone. Bell (as in Corsica) outside on framework. Chancel hexagonal. Graves round church, others round an old pear tree some distance off. Seats under tree as at Mestia. D. and D.'s peak now becomes prominent. Lunched under great sycamore at Latal, under fire of the women's eyes, a most picturesque group. Two old churches or chapels here, one with arcade of arches round semicircular apse. All kept locked up and impossible to enter. Crossed well-remembered little pass to Betsho, whence Moore first caught sight of Ushba in 1868. On Betsho side, just below the top, there is a level shelf of hay-meadows, ringed with birches, poplars, and azaleas, one of the loveliest spots imaginable. Lost my way in the wood, and on coming out found myself above the government buildings, erected after the disturbances in 1875, and now half in ruins. Lodged in large, but comfortless, Cancellaria, and most hospitably entertained by the Russian Priestav and his wife. This is the centre of authority, and a post comes here, more or less regularly, every fortnight. Found our Cossack had arrived the day before by the direct Betsho pass (compared by M. de Déchy to the Alphübel), with the luggage on two donkeys! Prince Wittgenstein, an Austrian who has spent his life in the Russian service, and an Abkhasian noble, Prince Shervashidze, arrived with a numerous retinue in search for gold. Their train gave some idea of the picturesqueness of the ancient mode of travel. Prince W. speaks English fluently. He told me that there are horse-passes by the valley of the Dal, from Suanetia to the Kodor, but that the paths nearer the great chain, between the Neskra and the Kodor, used formerly by the Baksan Tartars, are no longer passable except on foot.

Fireflies and glow-worms at night. Height 4,500 feet. Radde saw fireflies 2,000 feet higher, near Adish.

29th.—I started at 5 a.m. with Michel and Joseph to reconnoitre Ushba. Long grass walk up valley, then good steep horse-path through fir forest, and up flowery slopes to foot of Gul Glacier* (*circa* 9,000 feet). Loitered at first owing to doubtful weather. Sky clearing, pushed on fast up glacier, avoiding icefall by rocks on E. bank. Determined to make for rock peak opposite Ushba, forming E. end of ridge, descending from N. peak, and separating the small Betsho, or Gul, Glacier from the great Mestia Glacier. Steep upper slopes of névé in horrible condition. Took to rocks. 'Sped not our feet without the aid of hands.' Steep, but no real difficulty. More than two hours' hard climbing brought us to the ridge. Nasty ice-filled gully between first and second peak; three hours from glacier, ten hours from Betsho. Height about 12,500 feet (aneroid unluckily left behind), yet only the Hörnli, or foot-stool of Ushba.

Wonderful and most interesting (to a climber) view of Ushba, its twin peaks, and the great snow-ladder between them. Snow avalanches constantly falling over the cliffs and sliding down the slopes. The whole mountain hissing with snow, like a snake surprised by an enemy. Wish I could stamp on its head. *Faciam per alium, spero.* On other side stones go bounding with a sulphurous reek down a very great precipice into

---

* I take this name from M. Iljin. See Petermann's *Mitteilungen*, vol. xxx.

the S. basin of the Mestia Glacier, a noble curve of ice. At its head, opposite us, rise two noble peaks, of steep writing desk form, the sloping W. side being snow. Crests of Tetnuld and neighbours clouded. All upper Suanetia in sunshine. Leila opposite, higher than ourselves (13,500 feet?). Built stoneman.

Loose rocks and snow on ice treacherous in places. After one hour's careful descent took to névé, and slid down on young avalanche to foot of ice-fall. Found gold-digging princes building a birch-tree hut in the glen above Mazer. Got back to Betsho in four hours' sharp walking from top, just avoiding night and a thunderstorm. Friendly Priestav provided supper. Very stiff in the shoulders.

30*th*.—Rain or cloud most of the day. Glad to rest. Priestav ordered horses.

31*st*.—Priestav provided us a Suanetian Cossack to act as interpreter. He proved almost useless. No horses until 1 p.m. Ushba coated with fresh snow. Examined carefully 'Burgener's route', up southern peak. I and François went with luggage by Mestia and low pass to Ipari, the rest of the party by the route which I had followed in 1868. Baggage horse overloaded and much delay. One of M. de Déchy's barometers unfortunately broken. We crossed pass by splendid moonlight, arriving long after the others, at 11 p.m. Slept in rough Cancellaria.

August 1*st*.—Rode up narrow, but most picturesque, glen of Adish torrent, stream easily fordable. Glimpses of white crest of Tetnuld and one splendidly framed view of Ushba. Emerged suddenly (3 hrs) upon barley-fields of Adish.

(This isolated hamlet is attached to Ipari, and has no Starshina, or priest. The people were pagans until 1865, when they were officially converted and baptised. In 1864 Dr von Radde passed through the place by night to avoid dealings with its inhabitants. Ipari, Kalde, and Ushkul are the three wildest communes of Free Suanetia, formerly the wildest part of the Central Caucasus. This year I have visited all three.)

Halted by shed at top of village. Villagers asked high prices for provisions, and quarrelled noisily among themselves for our custom. All joined amicably in a photographic group. On parting, one man demanded money for our having rested on his land, and, when laughed at, had recourse to the traditional pantomime of fetching his gun.

Another laid hold of my ice axe, which I had stuck in the ground and forgotten while mounting, and when the Cossack rode back asked money for its return. Kabardan Cossack was indignant; the Suanetian impotent. We got out our revolvers for the only time in the Caucasus. A few copecks, however, settled all difficulties, and before leaving our Cossack bought a sheep. The whole affair was nothing more than an attempt at extortion, enforced by traditional violence of tone and gesture. Compared to our encounters in 1868 this was but a petty wrangle. Of real passion on one side, of danger on the other, I saw no trace. The marked improvement in the people generally in Suanetia during the past twenty years is creditable to the government and its local officers. Even in the faces of many of the rising generation one sees traces of less violent habits and civilising influences. Adish in its remote recess is naturally the last spot to reform.

Camped in a birch copse, 1 hr from village close to glacier. M. de Déchy found from marks made two years previously, that ice is sensibly advancing—11.30 mètres in two years. Purity and grandeur of icefall more than equal to my recollection.

August 2nd.—Pouring rain in night. Guides' tent pitched in hollow, and they consequently moist and miserable. Cossacks apparently quite dry under birch-bark shelter and bourkas. François opens tent and announces in a deplorable voice that the remainder of our sheep has disappeared. Further researches reveal that the waterproof cover over luggage pile has been disturbed; the lock removed from M. de Déchy's hand-portmanteau, and the clothes inside cleared out; the lid of the medicine chest lifted—and the contents left untouched. Some of the Steigeisen kindly procured for us by Viennese friends, a revolver and several minor objects stolen. No scientific or photographic instruments opened. Waterproof cover carefully replaced, so that we did not discover the more serious theft till long after we had missed the mutton. Thieves must have been daring and deliberate. The pile was not distant three yards from the Cossacks or our tent, and between the two!

(An exaggerated report concerning this theft and its consequences was published during my absence in some English newspapers – 'Standard,' August 24. I regret it, not only because of the needless anxiety caused to many of my friends, but also on account of the mischievous effect the report is likely to have in spreading completely wrong impressions as to the difficulties or even dangers of Caucasian travel. It would be a misfortune if intelligent travellers were, on the strength of an exceptional act of theft, the prompt punishment of which will be the best security against its repetition, frightened off from a country which is, in my opinion, now ripe for the better sort of Long Vacation tourists and Alpine Clubmen. I wandered by day and night, often alone and unarmed, on both sides of the chain without the slightest difficulty, meeting with nothing but pleasant greetings. Mr Peacock, H.B.M.'s Vice-Consul at Batoum, entirely confirms my opinion as to the general security of the mountain districts.* To readers of this diary it will not be needful to correct the statement that my journey was cut short by the 'robbery'. In fact, an arrangement to go with M. de Déchy to Basard-jusi was not concluded until a week after the robbery took place.)

Rain continues to pour pitilessly. Determine to descend to Mushal, and call up Cossacks from Betsho on the men of Adish. Struggle with wet ropes and canvas; and to preserve photographic cases from damp during packing. As we start sky clears. Village seems almost deserted as we pass. Beautiful afternoon stroll over the high path to Mushal. Tempted to camp at the exquisite spot where the view opens into the Mushalaliz. Luckily resist. Meet large party of haymakers (Caucasian hay-making seems independent of weather). Steep descent. Quarter ourselves on priest of Mushal, who has a good timber-house with a broad balcony running all round it, and a view of Ushba.

3rd.—Weather doubtful. M. de Déchy sends off Suanetian Cossack with letter to Priestav at Betsho, and priest's son to Adish with fifteen roubles (28*s*), to attempt to compound felony and recover stolen goods. He was unsuccessful. I with two guides make a false start for Tetnuld. We are soon brought to a standstill by a trackless forest and a rainstorm. Light a fire under an impenetrable pine, and wait until the rain rolls off. Return. Day of rainstorms and gleams, like English Lake weather.

4th.—More storms and rarer gleams. Day of arrivals. First, a grim

---

* This year there were five, or, counting my second visit, six, different parties of visitors in Suanetia, none of whom met with any difficulty that I have heard of.

old Cossack sergeant with three comrades come to look up the men of Adish. Then in many detachments, like a stage procession, the Bishop of Poti and suite, on an episcopal tour; a most picturesque cavalcade of mules, monks, and long-haired singing men. The Bishop has the best room, and we share the second with his secretary and chaplain, and a Mingrelian gentleman in his company. The ecclesiastics commence at dusk an interminable service. About 11 p.m. supper is served, to which all, except the Bishop, sit down. Cheese, mutton roast and boiled, fowls and pork, with very fair Mingrelian wine in abundance. The robes and long hair of the ecclesiastics make the scene a curiously vivid reproduction of a Cena by a sixteenth century master. Our host is exactly like one of Albert Durer's apostles.

5th.—The Bishop and his party ride off. I agree with M. de Déchy that I will start again for Tetnuld, undertaking to meet or catch him up on the Zanner Pass on the 7th, so that no chance of a fine day may be lost for the passage of the chain. He meantime kindly undertakes the very tiresome task of organising a band of porters and getting them under weigh. There is only one man in the village who has ever crossed the pass, which has fallen into complete disuse for twenty years.

(M. de Déchy's account of the rest of the day. Early in afternoon some villagers came in from Adish. After them the Priestav arrived, having lunched at Mestia with the Bishop. The villagers were summoned. First the two men who demanded money of us. 'What do you mean by asking money from my guests—honourable persons who are escorted by Cossacks?' Their side-arms were taken away, and their hands tied behind their backs. Then came the turn of the fifteen heads of families. They protested that the village was innocent; that the robber must have been a chance traveller. 'That cannot be,' said the Priestav. 'You know perfectly there is no road, and there are no travellers in your valley.' They were given two hours to produce the property. Nothing being forthcoming, their side-arms were, after some pretence of resistance on the part of one or two, taken from them, and they were ordered to remain in custody at Betsho until the goods were returned. 'I am anxious,' said the Priestav, 'to show Mr Freshfield as an Englishman that we can act with vigour in case of need.' And certainly no English officer could have come to the help of his countrymen with more vigour, good judgment, and, as the event proved, success than M. Aetovsky, the excellent Priestav, came to ours.

I started with the three guides, and a Suanetian to show us the path to the glacier, about noon. Very rough, and in places entirely obliterated, track on right bank of torrent. Picturesque ravine. In two hours reached foot of glacier; about 8,000 feet. Two streams just join; one, the Zanner, coming down in an icefall from an invisible upper region; the other descending steeply from the base of the pyramid of Tetnuld. Find at 9,000 feet on right bank of Tetnuld Glacier an excellent spot for bivouac under an overhanging crag among rhododendrons. Discover horns and bones of bouquetin (*Capra Caucasica*), probably killed by avalanche, close by. Sky clears at sunset.

6th.—Woke at 12.30 a.m. Started at 12.45 by cloudless moonlight, after comfortable evening in sleeping-bag. Up avalanche *débris* and moraine to top of lower icefall. François, with old instinct, charged straight in the moonlight at the vast slope of séracs; and we got through without serious delay, though as much by luck as skill, the bridges corresponding curiously. Wonderful ice scenery at sunrise on a great plateau. Streamers of light opposite sunrise from western horizon. Elbruz and Ushba flash out like beacons over the lesser mountains. Turkish ranges, still snow-streaked, far away to S.W. More crevassed slopes to little plateau, narrow but long, immediately under peak. This we have to traverse in its whole length. Snow heavy, despite cold. Very steep crevassed bank leads up to a last snow-plain only a few feet under the notch in the S. ridge we have been aiming at. Pushing our leader over a Bergschrund, we reach this saddle at 9 a.m. Glorious outlook. At our feet Adish and its glacier, at the head of its névé Djanga, and beyond it the five-crested peak I have hitherto called Koshtantau, the Shkara of the Russian map and Dr Radde. Our height 15,000 feet. Very long ridge between us and summit. Snow in perfect condition for safety, but too soft for speed. Precipitous slopes all the way on the Adish side. View down like that on the Scheideck from the Wetterhorn. Successive steeps in the ridge hide summit. Leader has hard work, and is constantly changed. At last, four hours after leaving saddle, step on to

top, a short level snow-ridge. Fronting us, beyond the hitherto unseen
Zanner icefields, stands Dent and Donkin's peak, holding its own well,
but I think a little (without having their measurement in my mind, I
put the difference at 100 to 200 feet) beneath us. Aneroid marks 16,700
feet. A snowy ridge, moated by huge ice-cliffs, divides the Zanner and
Adish névés, and connects Tetnuld with watershed. It abuts against the
secondary summit, shaped like a Tartar saddle, between Djanga and
D. and D.'s peak. Koshtantau looks well, but is almost completely snow-
coated. Dychtau is comparatively ineffective. The most distant point of
Shkara is the highest.

I put the peaks tentatively as follows:—Shkara, 17,200 feet; Koshtan-
tau, 17,096 feet (5-verst map); Dychtau, 16,925 feet (5-verst map);
Djanga, 16,900 feet; Tetnuld, 16,700 feet; Gestola (D. and D.'s peak),
16,550 feet. At any rate, these are the six giants of the central group,
and four, if not all of them, come between Elbruz (18,526 feet) and
Kazbek (16,546 feet).*

Elbruz, as we rose, lifted itself higher and higher above all the rock-
peaks of the main chain, and now stood up supreme, a great white
throne. Absolutely impossible to detect with the eye any difference in
height between its two peaks, or those of Ushba. As the E. peak of
Elbruz is nearer it may well be lower, and I do not wish to throw doubt

---

* I use, without hesitation, the name Tetnuld for the peak I climbed. It is
the peak conspicuous throughout Suanetia, and described by that name
by the visitors to that valley, from Dr Radde to M. de Déchy. It is also so
called by the natives. It is a curious accident that, on the watershed almost
in a line with it, and less than two miles distant, there should be another
peak very similar in form and almost equal in height. It was natural that
A. W. Moore should have thought that he recognised in the peak on the
watershed seen from the Bezingi Glacier the Tetnuld of Suanetia. But the
two mountains are quite as distinct as the Weisshorn and Dent Blanche.
Whether the peak on the watershed should be called Gestola is a question
of far more doubt. The name has no authority beyond that of the 5-verst
map, and I use it provisionally, knowing no better. I have omitted the prefix
Tau in the case of all the Suanetian mountains. I first used it through
reading a G (Gora) as a T on the map. Tau is Tartar, and is applied by the
Mohammedans N. of the chain to a high peak or pass, *e.g.* Minghi Tau,
Adyr Tau. Compare the Tauern of the Tyrolese Alps. Mr Donkin's map
requires correction as to everything S. of the watershed, except the actual
position of Tetnuld and the spur it stands on.

on the published measurements. I fancy the N. peak of Ushba is a few feet the higher of the two. Reach summit at 1.15 p.m., leave at 2. Descend to bivouac in five hours without difficulties, avoiding lower séracs by keeping to the left side of the glacier. No sign of our party on slopes beside Zanner Glacier. Sup on contents of one of Silver's admirable self-cooking soup-tins. Make guides pile up rhododendron branches, and sit beside the blaze watching Ushba fade into a shadow among the marvellously bright stars; but no answering signal according to agreement. Find guides sound asleep. Night cold.

7th.—Rouse guides, and get off by 5 a.m. Glacier surface hard-frozen, and hour's descent trying to stiff limbs. Succeeding steep ascent beside Zanner Glacier still more so for laden guides. François first discovers tracks of our party. At top of ascent (9,000 feet) find their camp. Fire had been lit behind a boulder where we could not see it. Huge glacier basin opened out, with Gestola N. and Tetnuld S.; the peaks both beautiful snow pyramids, their lower slopes cut off by tremendous séracs and icecliffs. After an hour and a half of level ice strike up rocks W. of lofty icefall, coming from higher basin N. Hard steep slopes, where a slip would be nasty. On reaching top, Joseph hails caravan, thirteen in number, sitting on snow on further side of icefall. They have mounted the opposite bank. Catch them up at about 10.30 a.m., and fall on provisions. Porters, an absurd group with blackened faces and all sorts of apologies for veils. They decline—not unnaturally—to relieve guides of their heavy loads. Third steep ascent to the upper snow reservoirs; immense undulations; snow growing soft. Hours pass in slow advance; porters begin to wander uncertainly. I insist on making for gap at base of rocks far ahead. Mists pass over. Porters sit down and pray: seem to have by heart a form of prayer suitable to the emergency; hailing the sun when it begins to pierce with a jubilant hymn or howl. I go ahead, and try to force the pace. Snow dreadfully soft. We are all fairly bemisted for a time, but rocks on left keep us straight. At last, at 6 p.m., thirteen hours after leaving bivouac, we stand on crest of the Caucasus, looking across to the great peaks and down on the basin of the Bezingi Glacier. All the range from Gestola to Shkara clear in evening light. What a prodigious array of snowy cliffs and crests! Opposite Koshtantau (Guluku) a huge rock-peak with two high shoulders; no mountain view

I have ever seen approaches this in sublimity. The hour, of course, added to its impressiveness.

We now found cause of disuse of pass. High cornice and Bergschrund on further side. Perfectly easy descent, however, from point 150 feet higher to our left by a rib of rocks and snow-slope. We descended. Porters refused to stir. They sat on the crest and screamed like pigs being put on board a steamer. The poor Cossack and we got hoarse in adjuring them. At last three tied themselves with the Cossack and ventured. They got down the rocks, and then tumbled all of a heap over the Bergschrund, which was not open enough to engulf a stick, much less a man. Cossack lost his dagger. The remainder followed with ludicrous precautions. I never saw men in such terror at so little. I should have liked some of the ignorant critics who think mountain people are necessarily mountaineers to have seen our Suanetian troupe. More than an hour was consumed in this five minutes' descent.

7 p.m.—Hastened across small soft névé to ridge of rocks marked by stonemen. Here, as it was already growing dark, we proposed to halt. Fortunately the porters insisted on going on, and as the wind was blowing bitterly we agreed. Ran down 1,000 feet over slopes of soft slate to the first level, about 1,800 feet below pass, and as much above Bezingi Glacier. Pitched tents rapidly in the dark, and warmed Silver's soups. Porters chanted triumphantly a ballad of Queen Thamara, borrowed our ice-axes to dig themselves beds, rolled themselves up in their bourkas, and were soon asleep.

8th.—Koshtantau clear early, but cloud on Shkara. Walk back to stonemen with Joseph to recover aneroid, see panorama once more, and in hopes of seeing a bouquetin. None visible, though fresh tracks abound. For the second time I saw no wild animal during my whole journey. Showers begin. Return to camp and determine to descend towards Bezingi. Grass slopes to great glacier. Find flocks and shepherds. Porters take to ice. Long laborious walk in drenching rain over a geological museum of boulders of every kind of gneiss, granite, and slates. Pick up small fragment half slate, half granite. We make a mistake in leaving glacier on left bank of torrent, and descending a long hour over stony ground, instead of camping on right bank at opening of Mishirgi glen. Pouring rain, no fire possible; two porters sent on to

Bezingi to order horses for next day. Michel confesses to suffering from a frostbitten foot since Tetnuld. Cossack nearly snow-blind, and in great pain.

9*th*.—At 7 a.m. mist; an hour later blue sky. I started at once back to Mishirgi Glacier with François. Crossed front of Bezingi Glacier; snowpeaks glorious. Left François opposite Kosh. Went on alone up grassgrown moraine on S. side of Mishirgi Glacier, a pleasant path, to spot where this abuts against the mountain-side. Then walked out and on into centre of glacier (10,000 feet). Full view of N. face of Koshtantau and extraordinarily steep range connecting it with Dychtau; latter peak out of sight at the end of a further bay of the glacier. Very warm; enjoyed invigorating bath in glacier pool, and returned delighted with my solitary ramble in this wonderful mountain recess.

The glaciers of the central group are generally advancing, after a period of retreat. Their advance is demonstrated in this way. In the Caucasus moraines grow quickly green. Fresh piles of rubbish have been shot in many places down the grass quite recently. This greenness—one of the characteristic beauties of the Western Caucasus—is, I fear, conclusive proof of a moist climate. However, I only had four wet days and two half wet days in six weeks.

Returned to camp. Grateful to find M. de Déchy with lunch and horses all ready. Strode and rode down to Bezingi over flowery pastures in little more than two hours (3 hours 15 minutes from Bezingi Glacier). Guest-house damp and squalid. Seven-foot chief produced a bundle of letters for me out of his sheepskin coat, and the box of provisions from Naltshik.

Looked at Michel's foot and did not like it. Foot generally inflamed.

10*th*.—Have to speak decidedly as to prices of provisions. Bezingi is in a transitional state. Old custom of hospitality breaking down, and new tariff very elastic. Chief sends us one loaf broken into fragments to make it look larger. Michel left in charge of chief's son. We take horses and go up side valley, which according to Russian map ought to lead to the noble peak the map-makers call Dychtau. (The Dychtau of the natives is probably the range over the Dychsu glacier; otherwise Shkara.) Dull scenery. Many pasturages. Buy sheep. Camp near good-sized glacier in E. branch of valley.

11th.—Ascend glacier to point commanding view of its head. Upper ridges of Dychtau apparently fenced in by icefalls and cliffs. M. de Déchy photographs. I suffer from a preconceived idea that the W. glen will furnish a way to Dychtau. Top of peak visible at its head I assert to be Dychtau, against the opinion of François and M. de Déchy. Main source of my delusion was not sufficiently disregarding topographical details of 5-verst map. I resolve anyhow to climb the peak.

M. de Déchy proposed that, in order to send back Michel by next steamer, and visit Basardjusi in Eastern Caucasus (which he had long been urging on me), we should give up Balkar; and offered to return himself at once to Bezingi, ride down to Naltshik and devote a day to repacking, so that on my arrival, twenty-four hours later, we might go on at once to Vladikafkaz. This arrangement I agreed to, mainly influenced by Michel's condition, which was a blow to my hopes of further climbing, and also a source of some anxiety.

François, Joseph, and I proceed up glen with small tent, camp on rock-strewn plain (10,000 feet), at junction of torrents from two glaciers. Cold night, guides not having brought enough wraps.

12th.—Start at 2 a.m. on glorious morning. François finds his way admirably, in the light of a waning moon, up steep rocks, over very rough ground, and across hard snow-slopes. By a golden dawn we enter a charming little glacier cirque, as flat as a cricket ground; ascend steep snow between green crevasses to northern ridge of peak (3½ hours). Large glacier on further side with broad snow-peak beyond it. Ridge barred by a rock-tower. Obvious breach blocked by boulders. Joseph tries right, and finds rocks difficult; I left, and discover practicable ledge. The crest beyond is long and steep, but nowhere difficult. Keep to rocks as much as possible, owing to detestable condition of snow. Reach summit 9.30 a.m. in about three hours' climbing from foot of ridge. Fine top and glorious panorama—Mishirgi Glacier at our feet; magnificent N. face of Koshtantau, seven thousand feet of Caucasian snow-cliffs, immediately opposite—a sight never seen before by mortal eyes—top of Dychtau only visible over shoulder of broad intervening snow-crest. Saw several avalanches fall from cliffs E. of Koshtantau. Ushba, Tetnuld, and Gestola in sight; Shkara and Djanga hidden; Kazbek in the E.; beautiful far-away views of the steppe beyond Vladikafkaz and Pätigorsk. Glacier group N. of Uruch makes a grand show, seems to have several peaks of about 15,000 feet. Elbruz enormous as usual. Complete and interesting sight of the long lofty spur between Tchegem and Urusbieh. Its peaks are, for the Caucasus, tame, and there are at least three practicable passes over its glaciers.

Our peak may be the Mishirgi Tau of Mr Donkin's photograph. Aneroid gives it over 15,200 feet. M. de Déchy thinks the villagers at Bezingi (it is the highest summit on the E. side of the valley visible from the village) call it Uku.

Rested a long time on the top and on the ridge, enjoying the view, the beautiful colours of the distances, and the magnificent snowcliffs opposite. Descended easy but long tiresome slope to the E. glacier. 'Tire' perhaps in ourselves partly, for we had done a good week's work. Glacier sloshy or stony. Bread ran short. Were successful in getting horse left at Kosh recaptured and loaded. Got back easily to Bezingi by 7 p.m. Found provisions left out for us, asked for samovar, and cooked our supper. Chief's son distinguished himself by making me understand that if he 'sped the parting guest', M. de Déchy had promised that I would give him an English knife.

13*th*.—Up at 4 a.m. Horses caught and saddled by 6, so young chief got his knife. Beautiful day and pleasant ride. Valley scenery in morning lights an agreeable surprise. Castle on opposite hill, above upper end of defile. Beautiful glimpses of our peak, then of Djanga and Koshtantau from gorge; lunch by stream at foot of ascent—four hours. Splendid views all the way up of the lawns and forests to the E., and the snowpeaks behind us. Cross ridge and enter Naltshik forest; halt on its edge in glade paved with wild sunflowers; wood romantic but interminable; path execrable at first, then improves and follows stream bed. To avoid wetting his boots one of our horsemen jumps up behind me; becomes a nuisance when he begins to chant Tartar melodies into my ears; shake him off and wind up with a brisk canter into Naltshik.

I suffered from streaming cold in the head for twenty-four hours, the only indisposition I had in the Caucasus; guides also were in excellent health except on first pass. Mountain climate is most healthy and invigorating.

On arrival M. de Déchy announces that, owing to a change in his family arrangements, he intends to return next morning to Odessa.

14th.—No sleep, revolving plans. Decide, chiefly on Michel's account, still to go to Tiflis, and thence either to Basardjusi or back by the Mingrelian valleys to Suanetia—if I can find an interpreter. There is no one at Naltshik this year who speaks any tongue but Russian. Start in telegas at daybreak. At station I and the guides leave for Vladikafkaz, and M. de Déchy for Rostoff. Out of thirty-five dozen plates he brought out he takes home nine dozen negatives of Caucasian glaciers and groups. Thanks to M. Boichevsky, the governor's secretary, arrangements for crossing Dariel are speedily made. Diligence tickets for guides. I find at hotel a Russian colonel and his wife, with whom I share a carriage. Doctor sees Michel, and advises complete rest. Comfortable bed, after twenty-three nights of substitutes.

15th.—Over Krestowaja Gora to Mleti, 10 hours' posting. The scenery of this road—even the Dariel gorge—struck me as insignificant. Travellers who think that by driving over it they see 'the Caucasus' are grievously deluded.

16th.—Reach Tiflis 3.30 p.m., in time to pay calls and visit bazaar. Dr von Radde dissuades me from Basardjusi, on the ground that the mountains are more interesting geologically than for their scenery, and hardly worth the long journey except as part of a Daghestan-Kakhetia circuit.

17th.—Despatch Michel home *viâ* Batoum and Constantinople.* Inspect Dr von Radde's most interesting and artistically arranged Caucasian Museum. In the afternoon one of the thunderstorms Tiflis is famous for burst. I was imprisoned while making purchases in the Persian khan and forced to take refuge on upper floor. Extraordinary sight; shops turned into waterspouts and streets into raging torrents.

18th.—Train to Kutais; Bakou line broken by storm.

19th.—Interview three interpreters; showy Mingrelian, apathetic young Swiss, and wiry middle-aged German. Secure the German. Capture in government offices two boxes sent off from Vladikafkaz. Set up in provisions. Cloudless weather sets in. Two young Germans in the

---

* He got home without difficulty, and has completely recovered the use of his foot.

hotel with a Kals (Tyrolese) guide and an interpreter, slowly preparing to start for Betsho and Urusbieh.* Get off in light marching-order without tents in afternoon, and ride 20 versts up Rion on the Mamisson carriage-road.

20th.—By Rion valley and low sunny pass to Zagiri. Sleep at Duchan (wine-shop). Meet our Suanetian Cossack and hear of the recovery of M. de Déchy's effects stolen at the Adish Glacier. The culprit was a native of the village.

21st.—Difficulty in getting horses owing to desultory officials. Nachalnik absent. Picturesque parties of church-goers pour in. Fine ride up narrow valley of Skenes Skali to Lentechi. After further delay our interpreter distinguishes himself by engaging fresh horses to Ushkul. Above Lentechi superb forest scenery. Pines and beeches of an 'unbelievable height'. Night falls and the woods are lit up with multitudes of fires, and noisy with the sound of small gongs and answering shouts. All the male population are afield to keep off the bears from the maize crops. Halt at the first house in Tcholur. The female garrison refuse us admission in the absence of their protectors, and we sleep under an open shed.

22nd.—The ascent to the Latpar pass is long and steep but picturesque. On the pass we find Herr Zumstein, of Gressoney, and Mons. R. Lerco, with an Oberland guide and an interpreter, bound for Elbruz, Kazbek, and Ararat.† Glorious panorama of southern side of central group, with all its peaks and glaciers. The path descends along a projecting spur commanding the loveliest prospects over the hills and valleys of Suanetia, swimming in sunshine, to Ushba, Tetnuld and Shkara. Tetnuld closely resembles N. face of Weisshorn, and looks noble between the birch branches. Halt at the guest-house of Kal, a solitary loghut, clean and comfortable. Villagers bring us provisions. Ushba clear at sunset. Day of memorable splendours.

---

* I learn from the *Œster. Alpenzeitung* that this guide reports that his party were driven back by storm from Elbruz on September 1 'without being able to ascertain whether they had reached the top', and that they also failed in two attempts on Kazbek.

† According to a letter of M. Lerco (*Rivista* of the I.A. Club for Sept., p. 292), this party succeeded in ascending Elbruz and Kazbek.

23rd. – Glorious morning. Noble view up Kalde glen of Djanga and Shkara. See the stumps of the razed towers of Kalde, where two Russian officers were murdered in 1876. Ride up to Ushkul. On entering Tshubiani (300 yards below Jibiani, our old quarters in 1868), greeted by a gentleman in civilised costume and offered hospitality. Our host proves to be M. Bussarion Nichoradse, a native of the village, now a schoolmaster at Kutais, and here only for his summer holidays. He provided me with a bed and many comforts, and gave me much valuable information. The two castles, one close to Tshubiani, the other high on the hill S. of it, are popularly held to have been the summer and winter residences of Queen Thamara. No one at Ushkul can read Russian, and the Starshina keeps all the official papers unopened in a locked chest. There is a priest paid 40*l.* a year by the government; he enjoys a sinecure. Rode on to the source of the Ingur in the Shkara Glacier (2 hours). My horse nearly carried off its legs in the torrent. Climb grassy ridge opposite Shkara. Find on brow (9,500 feet) two stonemen. The stupendous precipices and five peaks full in front; two glaciers meet at my feet. A tiny blue tarn close by. The Belvedere Alp of the Caucasus. Reluctantly turn back. There is no direct way practicable for native porters, either from here or the next valley eastwards to the Dych Su Glacier, as I had hoped.

24th. – Engage fresh baggage horses, which are not ready till 9 a.m. Spend two hours on the castle hill of Tshubiani in view of the snows. Path over great hay downs to the Naksagar pass. A few yards left there is a grand view of Shkara and the peaks round the Scena valley. Pleasant descent through rampant flowers. Scenery culminates where, at the meeting of two valleys, four families from Ushkul have made a settlement. Their barley fields and loghuts give life and a centre to the landscape. Magnificent woods of various foliage, pine-forests, rock-peaks. Shkara, resembling Monte Rosa from Val Anzasca, fills the background.

Good path ceases. Where two ravines deepened by rains cut the hillside we lose the track. Great difficulty in hauling the horses out of the second gulley. Track has to be dug with the axes. Recover faint path leading up and over spur into valley of W. Skenes Skali. Horses perform incredible feats; one irremovably large fallen tree lifted sufficiently by united effort for them to pass under. Finally, by cleverness of beasts and goodwill and handiness of their drivers, reach at dusk commodious beech grove within reach of water of Skenes Skali. Roaring fire and luxurious night in sleeping-bags, broken only by a false alarm of a bear among the horses.

25th.—Wonderful wade through a valley of flowers from 6 to 12 feet high, which entirely conceal a laden horse. Path at times hardly traceable. Great difficulty in torrent beds. The final climb to the Noshka pass is so steep that a man would naturally use his hands; yet the horses got up, though without their loads. From height N. of pass I obtained an admirable view of chain. Two bold rock peaks and small glaciers, then sudden breakdown to a pass like the Monte Moro, which must lead on the N. side onto the glacier in front of my sketch of view from the Stuleveesk pass. Descent short and comparatively easy; reach at 6 p.m. birch-bark shelter on bank of E. Skenes Skali after twelve hours' very slow and toilsome progress.

26th.—Reach Gorlbolo ridge a mile N. of its lowest point by easy track. Magnificent panorama from the grass crest over which the path passes. Ushba, Shkara, Dychtau, and top of Koshtantau on one hand, two passes (Edenis Mta and Pass Mta) opposite with Rion sources. E. the great peak of the Upper Uruch, at the head of the glaciers of the Sopchetura, the first tributary of the Rion; Burdjula and Adai Choch. The mountains descend in curved ridges to the woods of the Rion basin. Shoda, a very imposing isolated glacier-capped summit in S. lateral chain. Resolve to climb it from Gebi, in pursuance of A. W. Moore's intention in 1868. In that year, owing to broken weather, we had only glimpses of the chain from Gebi to Betsho. I have now seen in perfection the wonderful landscapes I thought I had missed for ever, and secured rough outlines of both sides from the Karagom pass to the Zanner, which, with M. de Déchy's and Donkin's photographs, ought to settle the relations of the glaciers S. and N. of the watershed.

Descend leisurely over pastures bright with golden crocuses to the Rion. Herds of horses and cattle from the N. side feeding. One Karatchai Tartar, on being asked how many horses he had brought over, replied '*Sto*'—a hundred. Four hours down valley from Sassagonelli to Gebi; thirteen hours in all from bivouac.

At Gebi new church and guest-house, but old, inquisitive crowd; count over fifty in close circle in small room, and then employ François and Joseph as 'chuckers out.' A ragged ancient is discovered in inner room, and his cloak on the sleeping-bench. He asserts his right to stay there as guardian of the local archives, which are deposited in a padlocked cupboard. Forward his cloak out of window and himself out of doors, and send a decided message to the Starshina that I mean to be left alone. These measures succeed. An intelligent villager is appointed our purveyor, and procures meat, poultry, good wine, potatoes, and even sugar. Parted the best of friends with our Jibiani horsemen and their admirable beasts. Two of the men were thoroughly good fellows, and their pink tunics, black bashliks tied up in turbans, and handsome faces, will remain a pleasant foreground in my memories of our forest wanderings and camp-fires.

27th.—Festival. Village green bright with groups of women in red or blue robes, with long white scarves falling from the head over the back, and many rows of amber beads. Where do they get the amber? Some very handsome girls. Found churchyard full of basketfuls of eatables— the fruit of the earth. Priest blessing them inside. Recognised and shaken hands with often, which shows that if the Gebi folk stare hard it is to some purpose! One of our old porters inquired after 'Paul and Franski'.

Set off in afternoon to sleep out for Shoda. Pleasant path through beech forest to pasturage at foot of limestone crags in glen on E. side of mountain. Grand sunset view of Adai Choch group. Two peaks new to me visible N.W. of Adai Choch; probably near head of Skatykom valley—one a doubleheaded rock-peak, the other a blunt snowy crest, which holds the sunset last of all. They appear to be as high as, if not higher than, Adai Choch itself. Cold wind drives us into well-built birch-bark hut; but we pay dearly for our shelter.

28th.—Morning doubtful. Up steep freshly-mown slope to ridge springing from Shoda; traverse rough ground under crags to base of chimney between them and the peak. Crumbly shale chimney to ridge, and easy climb along it up to the glacier-cap. The ice falls in avalanches down inaccessible cliffs into the glen W. of ours. About 600 feet of snow-slope to the top. Mists unluckily prevail, and the panorama is lost—the only view lost in this year's journey! The Russian measurement, 11,128 feet, seems to me low. The aneroid showed 7,400 feet of difference between the top and Gebi, which would make the peak what it looks—11,900 feet. It has, I believe, been reached by natives. We found hay, obviously from a hunter's shoes, on the ridge below the glacier. Descend directly steep slopes from ridge to head of glen. Fine views as mists clear; seven hours up from Gebi, five from Kosh.

29th.—Ride to Oni. Great, but light sun-heat in middle of day. No horses at Oni. Arrange with an old Shylock-like Mingrelian to bring them next morning at daybreak. Fine view of our old Karagom Pass from bridge. Warm night. Sleep in balcony of wretched Duchan. Disturbed by dogs.

30th.—Horses not collected till 7 a.m. Down Rion valley for four hours. Large gangs of natives at work on road. Carriages are to pass the Mamisson next year! They will not continue to pass it for many months unless the engineers pay more attention to the protection of the road from floods. Long dull ascent to Nikhortsminda. Farewell view of Adai Choch group, followed by a delightful ride through the romantic Nakarala forest; gigantic pines and planes and beeches, with an undergrowth of bay, box, laurel, and azalea; rocks and pools, like Fontainebleau. Sudden view of the lowlands and mists under sunset glow from gap at the south-western edge of this great limestone plateau. Steep and long descent down a streak of boulders called a road; then by zig-zags in forest. 'Gostinitza London' and railway station of Khibouli at 9 p.m. Gale at night rocks house.

31st.—Line made for coal traffic; not yet open for passengers. Ride of 35 versts over hills and commons to Kutais. Visit monastery of Ghelati. Farewell view of Shkara and Tetnuld from last hill above Rion. Through pomegranate hedges and dusty streets of Kutais to Hôtel de France. Part from our interpreter, who had served me admirably throughout.

In this second portion of my journey I fairly tested the chances of the traveller with no government papers or special advantages. We got on excellently. I come to the conclusion that the prospect of pay, something in excess of Russian prices, is often quite as efficacious as official documents in procuring speedily horses or provisions; and that *as a rule* the private traveller with a competent interpreter is under no disadvantage. The exception is in such a journey as that from Naltshik to Urusbieh, where official help doubtless saved us delay. In *fine weather* sleeping bags are an excellent substitute for a tent.

Left, in a thunderstorm, by the evening train for Batoum.

September 1*st.*—Mists low on hills. Hothouse atmosphere. Embarked on Austrian-Lloyd steamer for Constantinople. Guides went on by sea to Venice. I returned by Varna and the Orient Express.

I have left myself, I find, too little room for the generalisations from my recent experiences with which I had meant to conclude. I can state but a few. I do not think much of the necessary difficulties and hard-ships of Caucasian travel. M. de Déchy has conclusively shown the possibility of transporting backwards and forwards, even across the most icy and formidable portion of the great chain, baggage largely exceeding in bulk that necessary to the ordinary mountaineer. We found the natives, on the whole, good travellers when once on the road. I believe, and Mr Peacock, H.B.M.'s Vice-Consul at Batoum, who knows the mountains of the Caucasus better perhaps than any Englishman, entirely confirms me, that most of Dent and Donkin's difficulties were owing to their worthless interpreter. And my enquiries in the country all lead me to the conclusion that the attack of fever, from which the second party of Alpine Clubmen in 1874 suffered, was an unfortunate accident, due mainly to their having been entirely off their guard. This was A. W. Moore's own opinion. Soukhoum Kaleh is, no doubt, the most dangerous point of entrance and exit; but my German interpreter had made several journeys from that port into Abkhasia in which neither he nor his companions had suffered.

The Caucasus, in my opinion, has in many ways advanced in the last twenty years, and is now ripe for Alpine Clubmen. *Alpine Clubmen* I have written; but I mean men of the stamp of the early explorers of the Alps, accustomed to rough lodging and living—travellers as well as mountaineers. To climbers who have seldom been beyond the 'three centres', who consider Cogne and Pontresina far off, who delight in *tables d'hôte* and depend upon huts, who have made a 'record' by being nursed by two great guides up some twenty great, and perfectly well-known peaks, it would be cruel to recommend the Caucasus. Caucasian explorers must, like the early explorers of the Pennine Alps, the Tyrol, and Dauphiné, be men able to take care of themselves in difficulties, ready to take their share of petty privations and of hard work, even to exercise their own judgment in critical moments. I lay stress on the last point, for I feel sure that the majority of guides will at first be inclined to reason from their past experience without making sufficient allowance for the altered conditions of a new field of action, and that their decisions will need the revision of men on their guard against the possible danger of trusting to what Mr Dent has called 'acquired instinct', where it is no longer applicable.

I had great good fortune in weather and health. Ill luck, first and worst, in the condition of the peaks and passes, owing to an abnormal winter and unsettled early summer; next, in my strongest guide being frostbitten, and in the want of a climbing companion.

The winter, I was assured by good observers, such as Dr von Radde and Mr Peacock, had lasted two months longer than usual. There had been no heat in Tiflis up to the middle of August! The consequence was that the glaciers were coated, and the rock-peaks laden with snow in the worst possible condition, such as one sometimes finds in the Alps in June. In an ordinary season and with the support of all my companions, we might have fairly hoped to conquer not one but three of the great peaks. As a climber (and among virgin snows I found the old passion as strong as ever) my share of success does not satisfy me; but, on the other hand, I saw more scenery in perfection, acquired more topographical and general information, and suffered less from fatigue or hardship than I had imagined possible. My first object was to enjoy myself. In that I succeeded. My second was to remove some bugbears, and to show the younger members of the Alpine Club where, if they have the same tastes and energy as its founders, their work now lies; and how they should set about it. Whether I shall succeed in this or not it is for them to decide.

From *The Alpine Journal* 13, November 1887

4
A Peak in the Bag

Freshfield's 1868 expedition, although much talked about, did not open the floodgates to the Caucasus, and it was six years before another party ventured out. This time it was Moore who provided the impetus. Encouraged by improvements in the Russian railway system which reduced the 2500 miles from London to Odessa to four days and made it possible to reach Tblisi by train, he persuaded Horace Walker, Frederick Gardiner and F. Craufurd Grove to join him, together with the Swiss guide Peter Knubel. Once again the members of the 1874 party had excellent Alpine records. Walker had been with Moore on the Brenva Spur in 1865 and had made the first ascent of the Ecrins the previous year, as well as the highest summit of the Grandes Jorasses in 1868. Gardiner was a pioneer of guideless first ascents, including the Ecrins in 1878 and the Meije in 1879, while Grove's tally of first ascents included the Dent d'Hérens (1863), the Zinal Rothorn (1864) and the Aiguille de Bionassay (1865).

Unfortunately, however, little opportunity arose for the members of the party to put their experience into practice in 1874. Their major mountaineering achievement was to ascend the Western Summit of Elbrus (5633m), no more technically demanding than the Eastern Summit climbed on the 1868 expedition. Moore was absent when the top was reached, having decided to wait for two Russian friends. He attempted to repeat the climb the following day, only to be beaten back by a storm from high on the mountain. Moore's private and posthumously published diary reveals his unspoken disappointment: 'The moment was one of the bitterest of my life. The dream of the past six months was dissipated, an unlooked for opportunity gone, never to recur. The reflection that I had led my party to victory, though an active share in it had been denied me, consoled me not one jot.' Nor was his sense of mortification in any way relieved by the knowledge that the Western Summit was now recognised as slightly higher than the East: the first ascent of Elbrus which he had so confidently believed belonged to himself, Freshfield and Tucker had been wrested from them forever.

Perhaps the expedition's most lasting achievement was the exploration of glacier approach to the Bezingi basin, at the foot of what has now come to be known as the Bezingi Wall and which provides some of the most sustained and demanding climbing in the range. The Bezingi basin contains eleven of the fourteen peaks over 5000 metres in the Caucasus, including Shkhara, Dych-Tau, Jangi-Tau and Gestola. Moore and his companions, however, wisely left them to future parties, merely noting that 'a more glorious spectacle was never displayed to mountaineers'.[2]

Ten more years passed before the Central Caucasus received its next climbing visitors. The Russo-Turkish War of 1877–8 was partially fought in the Caucasus, and the Moslem population of Daghestan took advantage of the disorder to stage an uprising. It was a year or two before the Russians managed to reimpose central control, and during the late 1870s and early 1880s the Caucasus probably didn't seem an ideal holiday destination. By 1884, however, things had settled down enough for mountaineering activity to recommence. The Hungarian mountaineer and photographer Maurice de Déchy, who was to make a significant contribution to the exploration of the range, made his first visit that year. Accompanied by the guides Peter Joseph Ruppen and Alexander Burgener, he repeated Elbrus East and traversed the range, making the first ascent of Mamison-Khokh in the Adai Khokh group.* He returned in 1885 and again in 1886 but made no further ascents until he joined forces with Freshfield in 1887.

In 1886, however, the assault began in earnest on the remaining unclimbed major peaks in the Caucasus. The easiest summits, Elbrus and Kazbek, had been climbed and those that remained were of a completely different order of difficulty, more akin to the harder technical routes then being pioneered in the Alps. The first mountain to succumb was Gestola (4860m), known at the time as Tetnuld-Tau, and the party which succeeded on it was led by Clinton Dent, elected

---

* He claimed, however, the first ascent of Adai-Khokh itself. Harold Raeburn identifies the mountain in 'The Highest Peak of the Adai Kokh Group, Central Caucasus' (*AJ* 30, 1915).

President of the Alpine Club the following year. Dent was a man of character, what we would consider a typical Victorian: principled, staunch, unquenchably energetic. 'Vigorous' is a word that recurs in writings about him. He was born to ample means, having no obligation to earn a living, yet he chose an arduous profession and through diligence and ability rose within it to a position of eminence. Tom Longstaff, remembering him nearly fifty years after his death, wrote of Dent: he was 'a peerless climber; a most cultivated writer; a great surgeon; very much a man of the world; his malice was delicious without a trace of anger . . . altogether the most intriguing character I have ever known.' Dent had been associated since 1870 with the celebrated guide Alexander Burgener, who had already visited the Caucasus with de Déchy. The high point of their Alpine partnership was the first ascent of the Grand Dru in 1878 (it was Dent's nineteenth attempt on the peak). Burgener joined Dent on Gestola, as did the Swiss guide Basil Andenmatten, and the party was completed by William Frederick Donkin who, as well as being a good mountaineer and an Honorary Secretary of the Alpine Club, was one of the finest mountain photographers of the nineteenth century – and a colleague of Dent's at St George's Hospital in London.

The piece which we have chosen to reprint here is Dent's account of the ascent of Gestola. It is a stirring tale, very much in the tradition of Victorian mountaineering literature. Brave men, accompanied by even braver guides, battle against the elements, the outcome always in doubt until the party finally staggers back to camp. Modern readers will perhaps find Dent's prose pompous and overstated. And certainly it has little of the black humour and self-mockery which mark much of the finest writing about mountaineering in English. He does, however, have a fine eye for detail and, at times, a dry wit which alleviate the general tone of manly heroism. It is worth noting as well that Dent, like Freshfield, makes no bones about attributing the success of the venture almost entirely to the efforts of his guides. Less creditable, however, is what appears to be his almost infinite disdain for the inhabitants of the range. Perhaps he was less lucky than Freshfield in the ones he happened to meet, but there seems to be little curiosity about the people of what was still a relatively unexplored area, or desire to treat them as anything but packhorses and food-providers. This attitude, sadly, is hardly confined to British mountaineers in the nineteenth century.

Dent's account of the expedition provides an example of the complexities of identifying quite which Caucasian mountain the pioneers were climbing at the time. He climbed Gestola under the impression that it was Tetnuld-Tau. As a long footnote to his article makes clear, the peak in question was known at the time under a variety of different names – Tetnuld-Tau, Totonal-Tau, Tötönar and Tötönald. All the authorities and maps available at the time put it in different places. Freshfield and Radde thought that Tetnuld and Totonal were identical, but neither recognised the existence of the mountain which now goes under the name of Tetnuld-Tau. The Russian five-verst map also gave only one summit. Dent himself added to the confusion by calling Gestola Tetnuld, and Tetnuld Totanal. The only one to get it even approximately right was the Russian ten-verst map which correctly identified Gestola as the northernmost of the two summits, but then placed Tetnuld on the wrong side of the Adish glacier! In any case, nobody paid that much attention, as it had the rest of the area almost completely wrong.

As Dent recognised, the main problem was that nobody had yet explored the Bezingi region properly from both sides, or reached adequate heights in weather that permitted taking bearings. In the absence of scientific evidence the early explorers were positively anecdotal in their information-gathering techniques. Donkin, in his account of the expedition after the ascent of Gestola, is completely unabashed on the subject: 'Before starting we asked the men what they called the great peak above us, and the head policeman – the only one of them who could boast any literary attainments or had the smallest appreciation of what we had come for – wrote down Guluku in my notebook. The hunter agreed, so the name was adopted.'[4] The peak in question is now known as Dych-Tau and is the third highest summit in the entire Caucasus.

In view of the confusion over nomenclature we have edited Dent's article to bring it into line with modern usage.

5
The Ascent of Gestola

by Clinton Dent

In future years, when Europe has been rearranged, and wars and rumours of wars have ceased to be, M. de Déchy's rather sanguine expectations may be realised, and the Caucasian snow-fields may become the regular haunt of the mountaineer. Then may the village of Bezingi, situated on the north side of the chain at the foot of these mighty giants, develop into a Grindelwald or Zermatt, and assume an importance which up to the present seems rather wanting. Giant hotels may rise, crowds of knickerbockered climbers may throng what represents its streets, and—last stage of development—cricket matches may be played on its central platz, the natives assembling to watch the local eleven contending against the champion team of all Urusbieh; this may happen, but there are few signs of it as yet.

On the evening of August 21 we picked our way along the Western Terek valley *en route* for Bezingi, a little anxious as to the possibility of discovering the hamlet before nightfall. No lights are ever to be seen in the villages, but certain signs raised our hopes and led us to believe that we were nearing civilisation, for the amount of garbage in the path increased at each step. Presently we stopped and were told that we had arrived. No village could be seen, however, but the path lay high, and the difficulty was easily explained. Bezingi is beautifully situated on a brown and barren slope, and is unpretending, even modest, in its nature. When the natives wanted in the old days to construct a house (there are no modern buildings) they cut out a large wedge-shaped piece of the side of the hill to save trouble, so that one wall consisted of the vertically cut soil. As the roofs were covered with turf, and their inclination was nearly uniform with the slope of the hill, the village was almost invisible from above.

The caravan consisted of Mr Donkin and myself, the guides, Alexander Burgener, Basil Andenmatten, and an imbecile interpreter whose name ought scarcely to be mentioned in the same breath with those just given. A tattered boy, whose company we eschewed, as he was a perfect menagerie, and two other natives, completed the party. This boy, we trusted, was not such a fool as he looked, but Providence had not so ordained it. He was said to be possessed of great topographical acumen, but did not fulfil expectations. He certainly chose the right path once, while it was light, but guided us systematically wrong after sunset. Familiar now with the manners and customs of the country, we reined in at a promising-looking outhouse, and entering boldly, demanded, like the Knight of Snowdoun,—Rest and a guide, and food and fire.

Another stage had been reached, and at last we were within touch of the great snow mountains. The wearisome journeys across the steppe in the crawling trains were things of the past; our tossing on the Black Sea was forgotten; the toilsome ride in a baking sun, perched on the exquisite instruments of torture called saddles, were done with for the time. They are terrible things, those native saddles; but they are easy to ride on in the sense that it is difficult to fall off. The rider retains his position on the same principle that a clothes-peg sticks on an airing line. The horses are weedy, melancholy animals, afflicted with chronic thirst. They have little energy save when they shake themselves. This they do with astounding and distressing vigour. We were among a new, and to us a strange people: the motley crowds that we used to see at the railway stations, the Jews, Turks, Circassians, Mongrel—I mean Mingrelians, and others, were replaced by a purer race, that is, in point of descent only. One Caucasian village is very like another, and the manners and customs and characteristics of the natives in all the parts we visited were much the same. The general design of the house in which we were lodged was severe in its simplicity—*simplex munditiis*, unless the latter word implies cleanliness, as I have an inkling it does. It comprised one room, which was situated, rather literally, on the ground-floor. The front wall was of stone plastered over with mud, the chinks stopped up with anything that came handy. The floor was such as nature provided. The roof, constructed by the art of man, was of wood, decorated with prodigious festoons of cobwebs, and covered externally with turf. The single apartment in the town that boasted a glass window was reserved for the use—this I knew only by hearsay—of the ladies holding official positions in the prince's household, but ours was the next best. A hole, some three feet square, boarded up at night, admitted at once into our apartment air, light, and the perfume of an adjoining stable yard. The room was furnished with an uncompromising seat, an uncertain table, and the framework of a suspicious bed. We were hospitably received, and invited to seat ourselves. Mindful of our lengthy ride, we were impelled only by the strongest sense of the proffered courtesy to do so. We were given to understand that refreshments were being prepared, and while waiting composed ourselves in preparation for the ordeal which invariably awaits the traveller during his sojourn at a Caucasian village. There was no delay. Almost immediately on our arrival we held the customary levée, a function for which there was no need to issue any invitations. In an astonishingly short period of time, considering the lateness of the hour, many natives straggled in and occupied standing positions near the door. Distinctions as to morning or evening dress were superfluous, for it is not customary, so far as I know, for the Caucasian to vary his apparel during the summer in any manner at any period of the twenty-four hours. For what conceivable purpose, indeed, should a Caucasian take off his clothes at any time. To wash? Bezingi has not been washed since the Deluge.

Of the natives that we met on this north side of the chain I may say at once that we found them simple, curious, dirty, and lazy. Their favourite and most habitual exercise is talking. They have no taste or aptitude for thieving. Like most other people, they are born liars. They have an undeniable talent for petty swindling. We were told afterwards that they have the character in the parts of being treacherous. This, I think, is far from the case. They are said not to value human life. So much the better for the traveller; people are not likely to take what they do not value.

Our business lay in other and higher regions, and we were not desirous of staying a moment longer than was necessary in the village. But, as in other parts of this strange country, the difficulty of getting into a given place is only equalled by that experienced in getting away from it again. In Russia there is usually difficulty in getting passports back from the police offices. In the Caucasus the delay is occasioned by the almost equally important article of food. The natives do not understand provisioning a party, and their views as to what are proper charges are unduly elastic, or rather extensile. The traveller, it is true, pays nothing for the rest and refreshment which the native creed enjoins shall be supplied to him. There is something fine, dignified, and touching in such chivalrous hospitality; but the Caucasians, while preserving the traditional spirit, are a practical people, and of course a good deal of swindling has to be done in order to make a profit. We longed, too, for the solitude of the mountains, and for purer air than the village afforded. Let me do justice, however. In one respect Bezingi might teach a lesson to more civilised towns: its drains are never out of order. The natives get over the difficulty which so perplexes sanitary engineers in a manner masterly in its simplicity. There are no drains.

The whole of the next morning was spent in a prolonged wrangle with the horsemen, who wanted to be paid three days' return journey. This we held to be exorbitant. Our interpreter made us understand with a good deal of difficulty that we might have three horses and a donkey as beasts of transport. Such a cavalcade was utterly unnecessary, but there appeared to be no help for it, so we concluded the arrangement. Our interpreter generally mismanaged everything for us, and this transaction was but a type of many others conducted through his agency. Nearly all our troubles were either due to or aggravated by this imbecile, and in a strange country the importance of an interpreter can hardly be over-estimated. The creature could only communicate with such of the natives as were able to speak Russian, which few of them were able to do. He could speak a few words of French, which was the language in which we addressed our remarks at him, but when he consented to listen was almost incapable of understanding. He was not a good cook; indeed, his sole performance in this direction con-sisted in once boiling an egg wrong. There were moments when we were so aggravated that we could have brained him, and were restrained only by the reflection that it was too complimentary a form of homicide. Let me dismiss him at once. When we parted from him at the end of our tour, he asked about five times more than he was entitled to. I feel bound, in justice to him, to add that he did not get it. He desired that his name should be mentioned to any of our friends who might be travelling in the Caucasus. Very well. His name was Constantine Tsoulai.

Between the Bezingi and Mishirgi Glaciers are some grass slopes, but to reach these we had to ford the torrent descending from the Mishirgi Glacier. Here, for the first time, the horses were of use; the little donkey, which was christened 'Garlic,' on the ground that it was very strong, and that a very little of it went a very long way, carried very nearly the whole of the luggage, together with a native weighing about twelve stone who jumped on his back at the last moment, across the river in the most extraordinary way. If the little animal had once lost its footing on the round loose boulders it must infallibly have been swept away, and there would have been an end of our mountaineering. We could have spared the native driver without regret, but we could not have spared our tent and provisions. It was almost dark by the time we reached the slopes. Having repelled, without much formality, a wild onslaught made by three dogs, the tent was hurriedly pitched and the blankets spread. Now the natives were quick enough; in a very few minutes a fire was lighted, and a sheep, for which we afterwards paid three shillings, was brought in, killed, and cut up with a rapidity and dexterity for which the Caucasians are famous. The prospects for the morrow seemed gloomy, for the clouds were low down on the mountains around. Still we were near them, and that was something. After a while the meat was pronounced to be ready. Our enjoyment of the repast was somewhat modified by the fact that the whole of the cooked meat had to be spread out inside the tent to cool, partly because the natives would have eaten it all if we had not kept it under observation, and partly because the threatening rain would have spoilt it. As an anatomical study the arrangement was interesting; but the presence of numerous steaming lumps of meat in the somewhat limited space afforded was not exactly appetising.

It was not till August 26 that we had fought our way up to the camping-place which we ought to have made days before, a little desperate, and determined to start for Gestola the next morning whatever the weather might be. The prospects were rather gloomy. We had, indeed, our tent; without it we could not have remained up at this height of about 10,000 feet; the natives had refused to carry it and Burgener had done so himself. In addition to the greatest part of our other necessaries.

The morning of August 27 was dull and threatening when we got up at 3 a.m. for our long-deferred expedition. We made a hurried toilet after the native fashion, which consists, as is well known, in a shake and a scratch of the head. Reminiscences of civilisation deterred us from coming up to the scratch, but we did get ready in a brace of shakes. I doubt if in the Alps we should have started at all under such unfavourable conditions. The way led up by the moraine on the left bank of the Bezingi glacier, and across some loose rocks, which, without a lantern, were rather troublesome; our lanterns had been broken some time previously. We crossed a small glacier which takes its origin in a snow basin lying north of our camp, and runs downward in a W.S.W. direction, terminating in the crevassed ice-fall of the Tetnuld glacier. The crevasses were large and troublesome, and occasioned much delay. A wide sweep across a loose small-stoned slope brought us back to the névé. This would be the right route for the Adine Col, leading down to Mujal, perfectly simple in both sides. Bearing to the left across the upper snow-fields below the Adine Col, we made straight for the great snow wall lying right in front of us, the N.W. termination of the huge Shkhara ridge. This gigantic wall extends continuously from the Adine Col to the east side of Shkhara. Gestola towers up from this wall, but Djanga [Jangi-Tau] and Shkhara rise from it in more massive proportions. The height of the latter peak can best be appreciated from the Stuleveesk Pass lying S.E. of the range, about twenty-five miles distant. At the point we made for, the wall, measuring from the glacier, is perhaps a thousand feet in height. The snow was in fair order, and but few steps had to be made as we ascended, but here and there the crust of snow was plastered but thinly on the hard blue ice beneath. Above, an enormous cornice hung over on our side. By making a wide sweep to the right we were able to attack the cornice at a favourable spot, and about nine o'clock burst through the snow crust and felt the keener air on the top of the ridge. It was like an introduction to celebrities of whom we had heard much, but whose acquaintance we had never made. Close by, on the S., Gestola towered above us. 'There is Elbruz,' said Burgener, pointing to the distant mass as excitedly as if it were a royal stag. The double-peaked Uschba nearer at hand was unmistakable. Far away over the green valleys of Suanetia rose the range of the Tau Leila group, and as we faced eastwards the great mass of Dych-Tau reared up before us, while beyond again could be perceived the form of perhaps the finest mountain we had ever seen, the mighty Koshtan-Tau. We turned southwards, and a startling vision met our gaze. A stately snow peak, half concealed and half revealed by wreaths of clouds, seemed to overtower. An immense ravine of snow and glacier intervened, but the northern arête of the newly seen peak could be just made out through the mist abutting on the great Djanga ridge. Was it Gestola? Burgener would not have it. 'Tau Totonal' (Tetnuld) it might be called, but in his opinion the peak we were making for was not only higher, but, further, was known as 'Tetnuld' wherever he had been on the south side of the chain. We were at the time under the impression that Gestola was visible from the north side of the chain, and it was evident that the mountain which had so suddenly started into prominence could not possibly be seen from this side without ascending to a height sufficient to see over the Djanga ridge. Even had time allowed, we should not have changed our plan of ascent. The peak in question should of course be attacked from the south side. It appeared accessible enough.

Woven in between all these peaks lay a wilderness of crevassed slopes, jagged rock ridges, and stretching glaciers, bewildering in their beauty and complexity. To see the wondrous sights that were crowded into those few minutes while we remained on the ridge, we would willingly have gone five times further and fared ten times worse. In high spirits we turned to the left (S.S.E.), and began our journey along the ridge which was to lead us to Gestola, ever keeping an eye on the snowy form of Tetnuld, and marvelling whether it would over top our peak or not. For a few steps, and for a few only, all went well. The snow was in good order on the ridge, but we had to leave this almost immediately and make S.W. in order to skirt the heights which still intervened between us and our peak. The ice began to change its character; two or three steps were cut with a few strokes of the axe, and then all went well again for a time. Then more steps, and a more ringing sound as the axe fell. We seemed, too, however we might press on, to make no impression on this first slope. Our doubt returned; the leader paused, drew up the rope, and bit at a fragment of ice as he gazed anxiously upwards over the face. No! we were on the right track and must stick to it if we would succeed. For an hour and a quarter we kept at it in silence, save for the constant ringing blows of the axe. Our courage gradually oozed out, for when we got back to the ridge again at the Tetnuld col we seemed to have made no progress at all. The top of the mountain far above was already swathed in cloud, and a distant storm on the south side was only too obvious. Another little peak was won before we looked about again, but the summit seemed no nearer. The exertion had begun to tell and the pace became slower. Some one remarked that he felt hungry and we all thereupon realised our empty state, so we fortified ourselves for further efforts on an Ant-Alpine repast of steinbock, black bread a week old, and water—invigorating victuals and exhilarating drink rather appropriate to the treadmill kind of exercise demanded. It is under conditions such as these that strange diet tells on the climber; but even more trying and more weakening than the poor quality of the food was the want of sleep from which we had suffered for a good many nights. In the language of science, our vital force and nervous energy was becoming rather rapidly exhausted, or, to put it more colloquially and briefly, we were awfully done. Three hours more at least was the estimate, and meanwhile the weather was growing worse and worse. Reflecting that all points fall to him who knows how to wait and stick to it, we pressed on harder to escape from the dispiriting thoughts that suggested themselves, and almost of a sudden recognised that the last of the deceptive little tops had been left behind us, and that we were fighting our way up the final peak. Better still, Tetnuld, which for so long had seemed to tower above us, was fast sinking in importance, and there really seemed now, as we measured the peak with the clinometer between the intervals of step-cutting, to be little difference between the two points. The air was so warm and oppressive that we were able to dispense with gloves. One of the guides suffered from intense headache, but the rest of us, I fancy, felt only in much the same condition as a man does at the finish of a hard-run mile race. The clouds parted above us for a while, mysteriously, as it seemed, for there was no wind to move them; but we could only see the slope stretching upwards, and still upwards. Yet we could not be far off now. Again we halted for a few seconds, and as we glanced above we mentally took stock of our strength, for there was no question the pleasure had been laborious. Some one moved and we were all ready on the instant. To it once more, and to the very last victory was doubtful. True, the summit had seemed close enough when the last break in the swirling clouds had enabled us to catch a glimpse of what still towered above; but our experience of Swiss snow mountains was long enough to make us sceptical as to apparent tops, and possibly the Caucasian giants were as prone to deceive as the human pigmies that crawled and burrowed at their bases.

Still anxious, still questioning success, we stepped on, and the pace increased as the doubt persisted. It is often said to be impossible, by those who don't try, to explain why the second ascent of a mountain always appears so much easier than the first; some explanation may be found in the fact that on a virgin peak the uncertainty is really increasing during the whole time, and the climax comes in the last few seconds. Every step upward makes success more probable, and at the same time would make failure more disappointing. In fact, the only periods when we are morally certain of success on a new expedition are before the start and when victory is actually won. Still we could hardly believe that any insuperable obstacle would now turn us back; yet all was new and uncertain, and the conditions of weather intensified the anxiety. The heavy stillness of the air seemed unnatural, and made the mind work quicker. The sensibility became so acute that if we ceased working and moving for a moment the silence around was unendurable and seemed to seize hold of us. A distant roll of thunder came almost as a relief. A step or two had to be cut, and the delay appeared interminable. Suddenly, a glimpse of a dark patch of rocks appeared above looming through the mist. The slope of the ridge became more gentle for a few yards. Our attention was all fixed above, and we ascended some distance without noticing the change. Another short rise, and we were walking quickly along the ridge. We stopped suddenly; the rocks we had seen so recently had sunk below us on our left, while in front the arête could be followed with the eye, sloping away gradually for a few yards and then plunging sharply down to a great depth. It was all over; through fair weather and through foul we had succeeded; and there was yet another peak to the credit of the Alpine Club.

It was not a time for words. Burgener turned to us and touched the snow with his hand, and we sat down in silence. Almost on the instant as we took our places a great burst of thunder rolled and echoed around—a grim salvo of Nature's artillery. The sudden sense of rest heightened the effect of the oppressive stillness that followed. Never have I felt the sense of isolation so complete. Gazing in front into the thin mists, the very presence of my companions seemed an unreality. The veil of wreathing vapour screened the huge panorama of the ice-world from our sight. The black thunder-clouds drifting sullenly shut out the world below. No man knew where we were; we had reached our furthest point in a strange land. We were alone with Nature, far from home and far from all that we were familiar with. Strange emotions thrilled the frame and quickened the pulse. Weird thoughts crowded through the mind—it was not a time for words. Believe me, under such conditions a man will see further across the threshold of the unknown than all the book-reading or psychological speculation in the world will ever reveal to him.

Coming back to considerations more prosaic and practical, we found that it was 1.15 p.m. We realised, too, that the ascent had been very laborious and exhausting, while there was no doubt that evil times were in store for us. There were no rocks at hand to build a cairn, but we reflected that the snow was soft and that our footsteps would easily be seen on the morrow. The aneroid marked the height we had attained as 16,550 feet. A momentary break in the mist gave us a view of Shkhara, and we had just time to get a compass observation. After a stay of fifteen minutes we rose and girded ourselves for the descent. I think we all felt that the chief difficulty was yet to come, but we had little idea of what was actually to follow. Directly after we had left the summit a few puffs of wind began to play around and some light snow fell. Still, it was not very cold, and if the storm would only keep its distance all might be well. Down the first slope we made our way rapidly enough, and could have gone faster had we not deemed it wise to husband our strength as much as possible. In an hour and twenty minutes we reached the place where we had left the provisions and the camera. The feast was spread, but did not find favour. Never did food look so revolting. The bread seemed to have turned absolutely black, while the steinbock meat looked unfit to keep company with garbage in a gutter; so we packed it up again at once, more from a desire to hide it from our eyes than from any idea that it might look more appetising later on. Andenmatten's headache had become much worse, and he could scarcely at starting stand steady in his steps. Possibly his suffering was due to an hour or two of intensely hot sun, which had struck straight down on us during the ascent. I could not at the moment awaken much professional interest in his case, but the symptoms so far as I could judge were more like those experienced by people in diving-bells—were pressure effects in short—for the pain was chiefly in the skull cavities. I may not here enter into technical details, and can only remark now that though Andenmatten suffered the most it by no means followed on that account that his head was emptier than anybody else's. In due course we came to the ice slope up and across which we had cut our way so laboriously in the morning; here, at least, we thought we should make good progress with little trouble; but the sun had struck full on this part of the mountain, and all the steps were flattened out and useless. Every single step ought to have been worked at with as much labour as in the morning, but it was impossible to do more than just scratch out a slight foothold, as we made our way round again to the ridge. Below on the west side the slope plunged down into the Ewigkeit, and our very best attention had to be given in order to avoid doing the same. It was one of the worst snow faces I ever found myself on, perhaps under the conditions the worst. The direction in which we were travelling and the angle of the slope made the rope utterly useless. Close attention is very exhausting: much more exertion is required to walk ten steps, bestowing the utmost possible care on each movement, than to walk a hundred up or down a much steeper incline when the angle demands a more accustomed balance. Not for an instant might we relax our vigilance till, at 5.30 p.m., we reached once more the ridge close to the place where we had forced our way through the cornice in the morning.

We had little time to spare, and hurrying up to the point, looked anxiously down the snow wall. A glance was sufficient to show that the whole aspect of the snow had entirely altered since the morning. Burgener's expression changed suddenly, and a startled exclamation, which I trust was allowed to pass unrecorded, escaped from him. Andenmatten brought up some stones and rolled them down over the edge; each missile carried down a broad hissing band of the encrusting snow which had given us foothold in the morning and swept the ice-slope beneath as black and bare as a frozen pond; here and there near rocks the stones stopped and sank deeply and gently into the soft, treacherous compound. The light had begun to fail and snow was falling more heavily as we pressed on to try for some other line of descent. A hundred yards further along the ridge we looked over again: the condition of the snow was almost the same, but the wall was steeper and looked at its very worst as seen through the mist. Some one now suggested that we might work to the north-west end of the ridge and make our way down to the pass by the ice-fall. We tramped on as hard as possible, only to find at the end of our journey that the whole mass seemed abruptly cut away far above the Adine Col, and no line of descent whatever was visible. We doubled back on our tracks till we came within a few yards of the summit of a small peak on the ridge, the height of which was probably not less than 15,000 feet. Already the cold was numbing and our wet clothes began to stiffen; again we peered over the wall, but the rocks were glazed, snow-covered, and impossible. The leader stopped, looked right and left along the ridge, and said, 'I don't know what to do!' For the moment we seemed hopelessly entrapped; the only conceivable place of shelter for the night was a patch of rocks close to the summit of the peak near at hand, and for these we made. It was an utter waste of time. Apart from sleeping, we could not have remained there an hour, for we met the full force of the wind, which by this time had risen considerably, and was whirling the driving snow into every crack and cranny. What might have begun as a temporary rest would infallibly have ended in a permanent occupation. Indeed, the cold would have been far too intense that night for us to have lived on any part of the bleak ridge. The situation was becoming desperate. 'We must get down off the ridge and out of the wind.' 'Ay,' said Burgener, 'we must, I know; but where?' The circumstances did not call for reasonable answers, and so we said, 'Anywhere! To stay up here now means that we shall never get down at all.' Burgener looked up quickly as if to say no, but hesitated and then muttered, 'That is true. Then what will you do? There is no way down anywhere along the wall with the snow as it is now. There are great ice-slopes a little way down.' As he spoke he leant over and looked along the wall for confirmation of his opinions. A little way off a rib of rock, blacker than the rest, showed through the mist. We both saw it at the same time; Burgener hesitated, looked at it again, and then facing round glanced at the prospect above. The wind was stronger and colder and the snow was driving more heavily. There was no room for doubt. We must put it to the touch, and take the risk. We turned again, in a few minutes had squeezed ourselves through the cornice and were fairly launched on the descent.

We were now on a much higher level on the ridge than at the point we had struck in ascending. It was only possible to see a few yards down; the rocks looked appallingly steep, glazed, and grizzly, and we knew not what we were coming to. But at any rate we were moving, and in a stiller atmosphere soon forgot the cold. We went fast, but only by means of doing all we knew, for the climbing was really difficult. It was a case of every man for himself, and every man for the rest of the party. Now was the time to utilise all that we had ever learned of mountain craft. Never before, speaking for myself only, have I felt so keenly the pleasure of being united to thoroughly trustworthy and good mountaineers; it was like the rush of an eight-oar, where the sense of motion and the swish through the water alone are sufficient to make every member of the crew put all his strength into each stroke. The mind was too active to appreciate the pain of fatigue, and so we seemed strong again. Now on the rocks, which were loose and crumbly in parts, elsewhere big and glazed, now in deep snow, now on hard crusts, we fought our way down. So rapid was the descent that when the opportunity offered we looked anxiously through the mist in the hope of seeing the glacier beneath. We must have hit on a possible line of descent to the very bottom. But there was not a moment for the grateful repose so often engendered by inquiring minds on the mountains. We were racing against time, or at least against the malevolent powers of darkness. Down a narrow flat couloir of rock of no slight difficulty we seemed to go with perfect ease, but the rocks suddenly ceased and gave way to an ill-favoured snow slope. The leader stopped abruptly and turned sharp to the right. A smooth ice-gully some thirty feet wide separated us from the next ridge of rock. The reason for the change of direction was evident enough when Burgener pointed it out. As long as the line of descent kept to the side that was more sheltered during the day from the sun, so long was the snow fairly good. Our leader judged quickly, and with the soundest reasoning, as it proved directly afterwards, that the line we had been following would infallibly lead, if pursued further, to snow as treacherous as that with which we were now so familiar. Across the ice-slope then we must cut, perhaps, a dozen or fifteen steps. The first two or three Burgener made vigorously enough, but when within ten or fifteen feet of the rocks the extra effort told. He faltered suddenly: his blow fell listlessly, and he leant against the slope, resting hands and head on his axe. 'I am almost exhausted,' he said faintly, as he turned round to us, while his quivering hands and white lips bore evidence to the severity of the exertion. So for a minute or two we stood in our tracks. A word of encouragement called up what seemed almost a last effort: some little notches were cut, and we gained the rocks again. A trickling stream of water was coursing down a slab of rock, and at this we gulped as eagerly as a fevered patient. Standing on the projecting buttress, we looked anxiously down and caught sight at last of the glacier. It seemed close to us: the first few steps showed that Burgener's judgment was right; he had changed the line of descent at exactly the right moment and at the best possible place. Down the last few hundred feet we were able to go as fast as before. The level glacier beneath seemed in the darkness to rise up suddenly and meet us. We tumbled over the bergschrund, ran down a short slope on the further side of it and stood in safety on the glacier, saved by as fine a piece of guiding as I have ever seen in the mountains. We looked up at the slope. To our astonishment all was clear, and I dare say had been so for long. Above, in a blue black frosty sky, the stars were winking merrily; the mists had all vanished as by magic. No doubt the cold, which would have settled us had we stayed on the ridge, assisted us materially in the descent by improving the snow.

There seemed still just light enough to search for our tracks of the morning across the glacier, and we bore well to the right in the hope of crossing them. I fancy that the marks would have been really of little use; but anyhow, we could not find them, and so made a wide sweep across the upper part of the snow basin. As a result we were soon in difficulty with the crevasses, and often enough it seemed probable that we should spend the rest of the night in wandering up and down searching for snow bridges. But we made at last a patch of shale and rock, which we took to be the right bank of the little glacier we had crossed in the morning. Our clothes were wet, and the cold was becoming so sharp that it was wisely decided, against my advice, to push on if possible to the tent at once. For some three or four hours did we blunder and stumble over the moraine, experiencing not a few tolerably severe falls as we did so. Andenmatten selected his own line of descent, and in a few minutes we had entirely lost sight of him. It was too dark to find our way across the glacier, and we could only hope by following the loose stone ridge to make our way to the right place. So we stuck to the rocks, occasionally falling and nearly sticking on their detestably sharp points. Even a Caucasian moraine leads somewhere if you keep to it long enough, and as we turned a corner the huge glimmering mass of Dych-Tau towering up in front showed that the end of our journey was not far off. Presently the little white outline of the tent appeared, but we regarded it with apathy and made no effort to quicken our movements, although the goal was in sight; it seemed to require, in our semi-comatose condition, almost an effort to stop. As we threw open the door of the tent the welcome sight of divers packets neatly arranged in a corner met our gaze. The head policeman had proved himself an honour to his sex, an exception to his compatriots and a credit to the force. There was bread, sugar, rice, meat, and firewood—yet we neither spoke nor were moved. Andenmatten spurned the parcels with his foot and revealed the lowermost. A scream of delight went up, for they had found a packet of tobacco. The spell was broken, and once more all were radiant. Such is man. A strange compound—I refer to the tobacco—it proved to be, that would neither light nor smoke, and possessed as its sole property the power of violently disagreeing with the men. It was past midnight before the expedition was over. There were few preliminaries observed before going to bed. I don't think that even Donkin took more than a quarter of an hour in arranging a couch to his satisfaction, and placing a very diminutive air-cushion on anatomical principles in exactly the right place; while Andenmatten was fast asleep in two minutes, his head pillowed gently on some cold mutton, and his boots reposing under the small of his back. Something weighed on our minds as we too lay down and tried to sleep. The towering cone of Gestola, the distant view of Uschba, Elbruz, and the giant Koshtan-Tau, the rock and snow-slopes pictured themselves one after another as dissolving views on the white walls of the tent. The expedition was over, but the pleasure and the impressions it had evoked were not. Faster and faster followed the visions as in delirium. I sat up, and in the excitement of the moment dealt a great blow at the nearest object, which, as it chanced, was Andenmatten's ribs. I shouted out to my companion. A muffled 'hulloa' was the response, and he too rose up. 'What is it?' 'By Heavens! it is the finest climb we have ever made.' And so it was. Then we fell flat back and went to sleep.

My readers, I fear, have long since been tempted to do the same, and the account of this single expedition must have seemed interminable. My tale has no moral, and I scarcely dare hope that it has been in my power to give even a glimpse of the fascination of these scenes. Would that I were able to tempt some to visit them! Others have endeavoured to lure climbers to these wondrous mountains with but little practical result. Why should I succeed?

To those who have the health, strength, experience and energy, I can but say—THERE, in that strange country, those giant peaks wait for you—silent, majestic, unvisited. Would you revive in all their freshness the pleasures which the founders of our Club discovered thirty years ago? If the old feeling still is as strong as I think, as I know it to be, go there. If you love the mountains for their own sakes; if you like to stand face to face with Nature where she mixes sublimity of grandeur and delicacy of beauty in perfect harmony; if these sights fill and satisfy you of themselves—go there! If you prefer the grandeur, with some of the rough edges knocked off (and carried away in tourists' pockets); if you choose rather to play at travelling and roughing it, you will stay at home in the Alps. You will have missed much, and your mountain education will have been imperfect. If you think your temper is perfectly equable—go there; you will be undeceived, and your family circle may derive benefit therefrom. If you wish to be far from the madding crowd, far from the noise, bustle, and vulgarity of the buzzing, clustering swarms of tourists—go there. Nature will, as it were, take you gently by the hand and seem to say, 'I am glad to welcome you; come, and you shall look upon sights that I don't choose to show to everybody. Yet more, I will make a present of them to you; and in after times you shall call up in memory recollections of me, as I can be when in the mood, and you shall hug these memories with delight and even dream on them with enthusiasm.' If you wish for this—go there. To the end of your days you will remember it with pleasure. Go there!

From *The Alpine Journal* 13, May 1887

6
Annus Mirabilis

Dent's rousing exhortation to his fellow Alpine Clubmen was well heeded. In 1887, as we have seen, Freshfield's party climbed Tetnuld and several minor peaks. By the end of 1888, one of the most dramatic years in the history of the Caucasus, successful ascents had been made of several of the great peaks which previous expeditions had contented themselves with admiring from afar. Dych-Tau (5198m) was climbed by two different routes in a matter of weeks. In the main Bezingi basin Katyn-Tau (4970m) was climbed, as were Shkhara (5200m) and the Eastern Peak of Jangi-Tau (5030m). Further to the west, climbers ascended the North Peak of Ushba, Freshfield's 'Caucasian Matterhorn'. But it was also a year of tragedy. Four men disappeared without trace in the vicinity of Koshtan-Tau. Their disappearance and the subsequent investigations will be the subject of the next chapter. Here we will confine ourselves to the triumphs of the other two British parties active that year in the Central Caucasus.

Unlike most of the pioneers in the Himalayan ranges, the climbers who explored the Caucasus did so in small groups, climbing quickly and with a minimum of support. They were, in effect, applying the techniques of Alpine mountaineering to an area far higher, wilder and more remote than the Alps were even then, let alone now. Speed and boldness gave the only security of success in mountains notorious for their changeable weather, and the parties active in 1888 possessed both in good measure. The smallest was composed of just two climbers, Albert Frederick Mummery and his guide Heinrich Zurfluh. Mummery was without doubt one of the most significant mountaineers of the nineteenth century. His visit to the Caucasus was the last he took before being converted to guideless climbing – an activity in which he was to shine between 1889 and his tragic death on Nanga Parbat in the Punjab Himalaya in 1895. Like Clinton Dent, he was closely associated with the great Alexander Burgener. Their first coup was the Zmutt Ridge on the Matterhorn in 1879, but it was the first ascent of the Grépon in

1881 which marked the beginning of a new era in Alpine climbing. The majority of climbers during and for the first few years after the Golden Age of Alpine mountaineering were happiest on snow and ice, avoiding rock where possible and resorting to it only when their favoured terrain ran out. The Grépon, however, was a rock-climbing route – and a technical one at that. The celebrated Mummery Crack (actually led by Burgener) is still given the respectable Alpine grade of IV and was a remarkable achievement for men in nailed boots, with a dubious hemp rope and no means of protecting themselves to speak of. With the ascent of the Grépon the bounds of possibility were expanded to include the vast acreage of steep Alpine rock which earlier climbers had studiously avoided.

In the Caucasus too Mummery climbed a route with a considerable amount of technical rock-climbing. It was the first ascent of the formidable Dych-Tau (5198m), the third highest mountain in the range. We have reprinted his account of the climb from his *My Climbs in the Alps and Caucasus*, and there is little to add beyond mentioning that Freshfield described this ascent of the South-West Ridge as 'one of the most brilliant rock-climbs ever effected'.[1] The route remained unrepeated until 1935 and remains one of the great Caucasus classics, the enormous, hard rock ridge swinging upward – as it says in a recent guide – 'like a celestial ladder from the Bezingi Glacier to the summit'.[2] Today the 'control time' for its challenging 3000 metres is two to three days. Mummery and Zurfluh took just eleven hours for both ascent and descent, an incredible achievement for its period – and an acknowledged tribute to Mummery's vision coupled with Zurfluh's skill. In addition, the party made crossings of several important passes, greatly contributing to the solution of the intricacies of Caucasian topography.

Mummery's relations with the British climbing establishment were at times rather strained. He had been blackballed by the Alpine Club in 1880 and was not elected until his return from the Caucasus in 1888. There is still debate over why the Victorian mountaineering community should have taken such a dislike to him. According to some it was a social matter. Mummery was rumoured to be a bootmaker in Dover, when to be 'in trade' carried little social cachet. In fact his family ran a flourishing tannery business. More than anything, it was probably a simple matter of jealousy and resentment. Mummery's achievments had been considerable, and he had accompanied them with vigorous criticism of the prevailing mountaineering orthodoxy. Even in 1888 Coolidge reported that he had had to falsify the results of the ballot to secure Mummery's election. In any case, Mummery acted very much as an independent agent, both in the Alps and elsewhere, and the second of the three parties active that year in the Caucasus found itself unwittingly following in his footsteps. When they arrived at the Misses-Kosh, where Mummery had camped a few weeks before, the hunter who had been there at the time informed them, much to their dismay, that Mummery 'had slept out one night and climbed Dych-Tau; had slept out two nights and climbed Koshtan-Tau; and had slept out again one night and had climbed Gestola'.[3] It says a lot for Mummery's reputation that this extravagant tale was actually believed.

This second party consisted of Henry Holder, Hermann Woolley and John Garford Cockin, together with the Swiss guides Ulrich Almer and Christian Roth. None of the three British climbers had spectacular Alpine records, and they are principally remembered for their activities in the greater ranges, particularly in the Caucasus which all visited several times. They began their trip by attempting Dych-Tau, news from Mummery's hunter notwithstanding. A first attempt was unsuccessful. It did, however, succeed in teaching them the obvious: 'What had we gained? We had learnt, what Mr Donkin had tried to teach, but which only such an experience would make us realise, how great were the distances and how deceptive the appearances amongst these huge mountains of the Central Caucasus. We had learnt something of the character of the work before us. We had discovered that mountaineering in the Caucasus, at least under existing conditions, was a different thing from mountaineering in the Alps.'[4] Undaunted, however, they set off again two days later. This time they decided to attempt the North Ridge from the west – they had originally tried to continue the route from which Dent and Donkin had retreated the previous year, not realising that Mummery had already climbed it. The change of route brought success and they reached the summit in the early afternoon of the second day, after a long snow climb with a single steep rock step. On the summit they found the cairn which Heinrich Zurfluh had left. Refusing to be outdone, they left their own sardine tin.

A few days later they all, except for Cockin, made an uneventful although difficult ascent of Katyn-Tau (4970m) which lies between Jangi-Tau and Gestola. An infected cut in his wrist prevented Woolley from taking part in any further climbs that year, but Holder and Cockin took advantage of the fine weather to make three further outings. They reached the Shkhara Col between the Bezingi and Dychsu Glaciers; made an attempt on Mishirgi-Tau (4928m), and climbed the steep and pyramidal 'Salananchera', which they understood to be 4348 metres. (Today we call it Salinan and have elevated it to 4510 metres.) After this Holder and Woolley returned to England, while Cockin stayed behind with the guides.

Cockin's first coup was the ascent of Shkhara (5200m). The chief difficulties were concentrated on the summit ridge, but it was in many ways a much more typical ascent for the times than Mummery's route on Dych-Tau. Cockin himself noted, 'We were not on rocks more than fifteen minutes all the way. The guides had at least five, probably six, hours' step-cutting.'⁵ Five days later Cockin, Roth and Almer climbed from the Bezingi Glacier to the Eastern Summit of Jangi-Tau, noting to their disappointment that it was the lowest of the three summits. They then left the Bezingi basin, and headed west to turn their attentions to Ushba.

Although lower than the principal peaks of the Bezingi basin, Ushba was certainly the mountaineering prize of the Caucasus. A mountain of astonishing symmetrical beauty, justly compared to the Matterhorn, it struck the earliest pioneers as being impregnable on all sides. There is, however, a single line of weakness – relative weakness, anyway. From the south an obvious couloir leads from the Gul Glacier to the col between Ushba's twin summits. It was this route which they attempted. The first attack was made on September 22, but Roth developed severe arthritic pains, doubtless as a result of his step-cutting exertions, and they were forced to retreat. Two days later Cockin and Almer tried again. They got tangled up in the icefall on the Gul Glacier, found their way blocked by a difficult bergschrund and turned back after cutting steps for five hours. There followed two days

of bad weather with a heavy snowfall. The conditions were not particularly auspicious for climbing a long snow couloir which is prone to
avalanche even at the best of times. Nonetheless, Cockin and Almer
set out again on September 28. Avalanches had removed much of the
new snow and they were able to follow the steps cut on their previous
attempt. They reached the foot of the couloir after seven hours' climbing through the icefall. The snow in the couloir was soft and, although
steep, relatively easy to climb. A further three hours took them to the
col:

> At 1.10 Almer broke through the edge on the neck. We were near
> to the south peak, but as the ridge leading to the top of this had
> much frozen snow and ice on it, whilst the rocks of the northern
> peak looked easy, we turned at once to our right. Almer had some
> step-cutting before we could get off the neck and reach the rocks
> of the north peak. These were not difficult. The top, which we
> reached at 3.45, was snow, the highest point being an overhanging
> cornice; this we looked over but did not venture to tread upon.
> Almer put up a small stone man a few feet below. We stayed on
> the top till 4.22, but were in mist all the time and could not ascer-
> tain whether the north peak was the higher or lower one. We had
> only a short look at the ridge from the neck to the top of the south
> peak, but were both inclined to think it would go, at any rate when
> clear of ice. At 4.22 we began the descent and reached the tent at
> 11.20 by lantern-light.[6]

The North Peak is in fact the smaller by some fourteen metres. The
South Peak, at 4710 metres, is considerably more difficult and it was
not climbed until 1903 in what was even then an outstanding performance.

This is not, however, to belittle Cockin and Almer's achievement.
The ascent of Ushba, like the other great ascents of 1888, was a tour-de-
force of speed, boldness and endurance. This is universally recognised,
although the route has rarely been repeated due to its objective
dangers. The century since then has seen an enormous improvement
in equipment and in technical ability, but few modern climbers, even
with crampons making step-cutting unnecessary, can match those
early pioneers in the Caucasus. And it was of course the guides, so
often omitted in mountaineering histories, who were the real heroes,

finding the route, leading it and then organising a safe descent. One can only wonder what would have happened had Heinrich Zurfluh, Ulrich Almer and Christian Roth not been at the head of their respective parties.

7
Dych Tau

by Alfred Mummery

Though the faithful climber is, in his essence, a thoroughly domesticated man and rarely strays from his own home, the Alps, a spirit of unrest occasionally takes hold upon him and drives him forth to more distant regions. Seized with such a fit of wandering, the first days of July, 1888, found me camped on the right bank of the Bezingi glacier, where, in the cool air of the snow fields, on slopes white with rhododendron and with the silent unclimbed peaks above, I could rest from the rattle and roar of trains, the noise of buffets and the persecutions of the Custom-houses.

My sole companion was Heinrich Zurfluh, of Meiringen. The experience of ten days' continuous travel, culminating in two and a half days on the peculiarly uncomfortable Tartar saddle—we had ridden from Patigorsk to Naltcik, and thence to Bezingi and the foot of the glacier—had sufficed to make him a confirmed pessimist. 'Es gefällt mir nicht' was the burden of his song, 'I don't like it'. And though this phrase may, perhaps, be regarded as summarising the conclusions of modern philosophy, it struck me that it was scarcely a fitting watchword for the mountaineer face to face with the hugest of unclimbed giants.

Our camp was of a most Spartan simplicity, for we had outwalked our baggage, and Zurfluh's knapsack, which I had fondly imagined contained sleeping-bags and soup-tins, proved to be mainly filled with a great pot of most evil-smelling boot grease—brought with much labour all the way from Meiringen—a large hammer, an excellent stock of hobnails and a sort of anvil to assist in their insertion. These various articles were doubtless of great value, but hardly useful as bedding for, whatever may be the case with rose-leaves, a man need scarcely be a sybarite to object to crumpled hobnails as a mattress. Luckily various portions of a sheep, a large loaf of Russian bread, and a load of firewood had been piled on an active native whom we had met and appropriated before leaving the rest of our caravan.

The night proved remarkably cold, and we were glad to turn out at 4 a.m. and start on a preliminary examination of our peak. I soon discovered, however, that Zurfluh had more ambitious views, and was possessed of the wild idea of taking a mountain 17,054 feet high, as a training walk! It was, however, desirable to see what lay behind the Misses glacier, so I limited my protests and followed the rapid advance of my leader. We kept up a long couloir which was separated from the Misses glacier by a low ridge of rock. Reaching its head we ought to have crossed over on to the glacier, but we disliked the long snow slopes leading up to the ridge amongst which we thought, I believe erroneously, that we detected the sheen of ice. In consequence, we kept up the rocks to our left, and, about eight o'clock, reached a point where it was, perhaps, possible to traverse on to the great slope, but the whiz of the train was still in my ears, and the limpness of English life still ached in my muscles, and I failed to give my leader the moral support that was needed. He looked at the traverse and did not quite care for its appearance. He looked at the slope above and thought it very long. He gazed at the ridge leading to the summit and denounced it as interminable. A confident Herr and he would have hurled himself at the difficulties, and his great skill, quickness and strength would, I verily believe, have enabled us to reach the summit; but for the nonce I adopted the destructive rôle of critic. I pointed out that it was already late, that a night on the ridge would be chilly and that the traverse and the slope beyond had every appearance of being stone swept. My mind, however, was as flabby as my muscles, and instead of declaring for a prompt and immediate retreat, I followed Zurfluh languidly up the cliff to see whether a second and easier traverse could be found. There proved to be no such possibility and about 9 a.m. we abandoned the ascent.

On the way back we glissaded the couloir, spinning down a thousand feet or more in a single slide. A few weeks later when Messrs Woolley, Holder, and Cockin reached the Misses kosh, the Caucasian sun had stripped almost every atom of snow from this gully.

We found to our sorrow that the camp had not yet arrived, and a second cold and comfortless night ensued. The next morning, as a consequence, Zurfluh was too unwell to start, so with the energy of an amateur I explored the approaches to the southern face of the mountain. In the course of my solitary wander I scared a herd of seventeen Tur, and subsequently reached the extreme south-western buttress of the peak, a point almost worthy of a distinctive title, as it is separated from the mass of the mountain by a broad col, and is only to be reached by a long and not wholly easy ridge. Its height is about 13,500 feet, or possibly more, and one looks over the Zanner pass into Suanetia and across the Shkara pass to the mountains on the further side of the Dych Su glacier. The face of Dych Tau, however, had all my attention. The peak seen from this side has two summits, and I found it quite impossible to decide which was the higher, the great tower to the right and apparently behind the main mass of the mountain looking as if it might be the culminating point. This doubt, and the fact that much snow was still lying on the huge rock face, determined me to cross the passes I was anxious to see before attempting the ascent, so that by distant views the doubt as to the true summit might be settled, and by the lapse of time and the Caucasian sun the snow might be, in a measure, melted from the rocks. On my return to the Misses kosh I found that fortune was smiling on me, the camp had arrived and Zurfluh was once more ready for work.

The next two weeks were devoted to excursions in the valleys of Balkar, Suanetia, the Bashil Su, and Cheghem. Returning from the latter by a grass pass to Tubeneli, we once more made our way toward the Bezingi glacier. Near the foot of this latter a thick and wetting mist, combined with the offer of new milk, induced us to halt at a cow kosh and we pitched our tent by the side of a great boulder. During the night a goat mistook the tent for a stone and jumped off the boulder on to the top of it, subsiding amongst its startled inmates. Though I am quite willing to guarantee the behaviour of this make of tent on an exposed ledge in a gale of wind, it must be admitted that it is wholly unequal to the attack of a daring goat. After many efforts Zurfluh and I succeeded in extricating ourselves from the tangled *débris* and rebuilt our mansion, though when morning dawned, it exhibited a miserably baggy and disreputable appearance. During breakfast our Tartar porter gave us to understand that a palatial kosh, replete with all the luxuries of life, was to be found on the left bank of the glacier nearly opposite the Misses kosh. The weather looked so threatening that Zurfluh urged me to go to this Capua of the mountains where, as he wisely said, we could wait till sufficiently fine weather set in for our great expedition. This seemed so excellent a proposition that we at once packed up the camp and started. Zurfluh and the Tartar soon began to exhibit symptoms of rivalry, and gradually lapsed into a walking match for the honour of their respective races, creeds, and foot-gear. I had no ambition to join, and the men quickly disappeared from sight. Injudiciously following some directions which Zurfluh had given me, and which he averred were faithful interpretations of the Tartar's remarks I tried to get along the left moraine. This latter, heaped up against the cliffs and scored by deep water-channels, soon demonstrated Zurfluh's inefficiency as interpreter. After some trouble, not to say danger, I succeeded in reaching the glacier, and tramped merrily over its even surface. Before long, however, a thick mist settled into the valley and suggested the possibility that I might fail to find the kosh, for unluckily. I had only the vaguest idea of its whereabouts. Fearing to miss it, I felt my way through some tangled crevasses to the left bank and explored a tenantless alp. Beneath a great boulder I found a most excellent cave. Where natural walls were lacking, it had been skilfully built in with stones, and the whole was roomy, clean, and dry. It undoubtedly affords the best shelter to be found anywhere above Bezingi. However, there were no sheep on the pasture and no sign of Zurfluh, shepherd, or porter, so I had to betake myself to the ice again, here crumpled and torn into the wildest confusion. After some protracted struggles and much hewing of steps I reached a second oasis. This likewise appeared tenantless, and I was beginning to think I should have to return to my previously discovered cave when, rounding a big rock, I heard the welcome bleating of sheep and walked almost into Zurfluh's arms. He had been much alarmed for my safety. Owing to more erroneous interpretation, he had gone considerably out of his way to take the séracs at exactly their worst and most broken point. Believing this worst passage to be the only one practicable, he not unnaturally concluded that I should come to untold grief.

Having mutually relieved our anxieties, I asked Zurfluh to take me to the much vaunted kosh. We found at first some difficulty in locating it, but the shepherd came to our help and led us to a black mark against a perpendicular cliff; this black mark defined the place where he lit his fire on the rare occasions when he had any firewood. At the present moment, he explained, he had not got any. Other pretence of habitation or shelter there was none. Even our small tent which had formed part of the Tartar's load had disappeared and the Tartar himself had vanished into space, Zurfluh, indeed, was inclined to think a crevasse his probable resting place, but my experience of his skill made me pretty confident that he had not chosen that particular method of joining the houris in Paradise. The misty rain pervaded everywhere; the lee side of the rocks was as wet as the weather side, and we gradually lapsed into that soddened condition which depresses the spirits even of the most cheerful. Moreover, we had depended on one or other of the active sheep we saw around us for our dinner; but the conversion of live sheep into cooked mutton is difficult in the absence of firing. We bitterly regretted the Misses kosh, where a Willesden canvas tent and a good store of wood were securely packed in the cave. I even suggested crossing, but Zurfluh absolutely refused to have anything more to do with the séracs while the fog lasted. An hour later, however, our mourning was turned into joy, for we beheld the broad shoulders of the hunter, buried beneath a pile of wood, struggling up the grass slope. He had, it seems, on learning that there was no wood, concealed his baggage in a dry hole under a stone and crossed to the Misses kosh to fetch our supply from thence. A bold and kindly action, done without thought of reward, for men who had little or no claim upon him.

A lamb was promptly pursued and slain, and soon we were sitting round a roaring fire watching portions of the aforesaid lamb sizzling on long wooden spits. The contemplation of these succulent morsels shrined in a halo of dancing flame rapidly raised my spirits, and I regarded as inspired the hunter's favourable reply to my query as to the weather. Zurfluh, however, was not to be comforted; he repudiated my translation of 'Yak shi', and cast bitter contempt on my efforts to speak the Tartar tongue.

The next morning his pessimism seemed justified, for the mist was thicker and wetter than ever. Yet the hunter still replied 'Yak shi' to all inquiries, so, somewhat contrary to Zurfluh's wishes, the camp was packed, and about mid-day the hunter led us through the mist along an excellent path. The shepherd had also consented to join our party, so I had the rare and delightful privilege of walking unloaded. As we ascended, the source of Zurfluh's troubles on the previous day became obvious. The hunter had evidently wished him to ascend the glacier till beyond the séracs, and then to return to the kosh by the path we were now following. Zurfluh, however, recognising the fact that he was getting too far up the glacier, had turned to the right, and in the impenetrable fog forced the passage at the worst possible point. The hunter naturally refused to show the white feather before an unbeliever, and followed.

We walked past the séracs and reached the level glacier without difficulty. On the way across we picked up some fine horns—which had once belonged to a Tur—and which I believe now ornament Zurfluh's abode at Meiringen. After ascending the short slope that leads to the long level moraine which here forms the most convenient pathway, we halted whilst the hunter sought to rearrange his foot-gear. This latter was, however, hopelessly worn out by our previous expeditions, and the contemplation of his bleeding feet roused him to much wrath. Finally he chucked the *débris* of his hide sandals into a crevasse and expressed his intention of returning home. I confess he had reason on his side; I have known a moraine try the temper even of a well-shod member of the Alpine Club, what then could be expected from a 'poor benighted heathen'? We endeavoured to coax him forward, but he was obdurate to the most artful flattery—possibly because he could not understand a word we said. The suggestion, conveyed by appropriate gestures and an occasional word, that he would not be paid if he did not do the work merely elicited the reply, also expressed by gestures and a large mass of wholly unintelligible sound, that he did not at all expect to be. These conversational efforts proved unsatisfactory to all concerned and consumed much time. It was in consequence a good deal past four before the luggage was redistributed. Happily the mists were by now obviously clearing, and through rifts and rents we could see the long ridges of Shkara glittering in cloudless sunshine.

Quitting the moraine, we swung round to our left and began ascending interminable slopes of séracs and stones. The shepherd here took pity on my struggles, and seizing my knapsack, insisted on adding it to the vast pile of luggage he was carrying. Despite his burden, he was still able to show us the way and strode upwards, a splendid picture of muscle and perfect balance. About six o'clock we reached the highest point at which it appeared likely we should find water. Above, long slopes of snow and screes led up to the little glacier which lies below the col separating the peak from the great buttress I had climbed two or three weeks before.

We dug out the screes with our axes and made an excellent platform for the tent, then the fire was lit and we rejoiced over hot soup, English biscuits and Caucasian mutton. Before us was the great ice-embattled wall of Shkara and Janga, rising high into the warm tinted air, whilst below the silent glacier gloomed dark and cold, as the gathering mists of evening crawled slowly along its slopes. Behind our tent towered the great cliffs of Dych Tau. There is something in huge unclimbed peaks, especially when seen by the light of ebbing day, which is strangely solemn. Jest and joke are pushed aside as profanation, and one gazes on the tremendous cliffs with feelings closely akin to those with which the mediaeval pilgrim worshipped at some holy shrine. The lengthening shadows fell athwart its face and showed deep gullies and jagged ridges, ice-glazed rocks and vast pitiless slabs of unbroken granite. From crack to gully and gully to ridge we traced a way till it emerged on a great smooth precipitous face where, as Zurfluh piously remarked, we must hope that 'Der liebe Gott wird uns etwas helfen'. We watched the last flicker of sunlight play round its topmost crags, and then crept into the shelter of tent and sleeping bags. The hardier Tartar refused the proffered place beside us, and having washed his head, his feet and hands, in due accordance with the ritual of his creed, laid down in the open beside a great rock (not impossibly the same as that beside which Messrs Woolley, Holder, and Cockin camped a few weeks later). Zurfluh regarded these proceedings with much sad interest, feeling certain that the bitter wind would freeze him to death before morning.

At 1 a.m., Zurfluh, who had kept awake to bemoan the Tartar's slow and pitiable decease, crept out of the tent to investigate how this process was getting on. A few minutes later, with his teeth chattering, but none the less with real delight in face and voice, he told me that not merely was the Tartar still alive, but, bare feet and all, appeared to be enjoying a refreshing sleep! Zurfluh's mind relieved on this point, he engaged in a protracted struggle with the fire. The Bezingi wood always requires much coaxing, but at 1 a.m. it would try the patience of a saint and the skill of one of his Satanic majesty's most practised stokers. Unluckily the little stream, on which we had counted for a perennial supply of water, was frozen to its core, and the weary process of melting ice had to be undertaken. My boots were also frozen, and putting them on proved to be the most arduous and by far the most painful part of the expedition. However, these preliminary difficulties were at length overcome and we were able to rejoice over hot tea and biscuits in the warm shelter of the tent.

Soon after half-past two we began the ascent and tramped steadily up the crisp snow to the little glacier. We crossed it, and ascended the slopes to the col by the route I had previously taken when on the way to the south-western buttress. Reaching this we turned sharply to the right, and, scrambling round one or two crumbling towers, were fairly launched on the face. Working upwards but bearing ever well to the right, we reached a shallow couloir still plastered in places by half-melted masses of snow. One of these, smitten by Zurfluh's axe, broke away bodily, striking me very severely on head, knee, and hand. Luckily I was almost close to him, but even so, for a minute or two, I scarcely knew what had happened. Had there been three or four of us on the rope the results could scarcely have failed to be serious. I am aware that two men are usually regarded as constituting too small a party for serious mountain work. None the less, on rotten rocks, or where much frozen snow loosely adheres to the ledges and projecting crags, it has advantages which, so far as I am able to judge, make it almost an ideal number.

Happily, five minutes' rest restored my scattered senses, and we quitted this ill-behaved gully, bearing still further to the right over disintegrated rocks and loose stones. Going fairly fast, we reached the great mass of red rock, referred to by Mr. Donkin as marking the limit of his and Mr. Dent's attempt,* at 7 a.m. Without halting we still pushed on,

* After Gestola in 1886. Eds.

bearing ever to the right in order to reach the smaller of two long couloirs that had been very conspicuous from our camp. This couloir runs up the face of the peak towards the south-western ridge in the near neighbourhood of the summit. Zurfluh had, the previous evening, diagnosed its contents as snow, and the rocks being mostly ice-glazed and distinctly difficult, we thought it desirable to reach it as soon as possible. When we at length gained its brink we saw at a glance that it was much steeper than we had imagined, and that, if I may be pardoned the Irishism, the snow was ice. In consequence we clung to the rocks as long as any sort of decent progress could be made, and it was only when each foot of advance was costing precious minutes that we turned into the gully.

Hypercritical climbers have occasionally suggested that I am in the habit of cutting steps rather wide apart. I only wish these cavillers could have seen Zurfluh's staircase. He has a peculiar habit of only cutting steps for the left foot, his right having the faculty of adhering firmly to absolutely smooth ice and enabling him by a combination of jump and wriggle to lift his left foot from one secure step to another six feet above it. He kindly showed me how it was done and urged me to imitate his procedure, pointing out the great saving of time thus rendered possible. Since, however, any trifling error would have resulted in an undue acquaintance with the glacier below, I preferred to cut intervening steps; even then it was a most arduous gymnastic exercise to climb from one to another. Happily, some twenty minutes of these violent athletics brought us to a point where we could quit the gully for the slope on our right. Hard, solid rock then led us merrily upwards to a great secondary ridge. This ridge divides the south face of the peak into two well-marked divisions, to the east is the great couloir which reaches from the col between the two summits to the very base of the mountain, and beyond are the interminable series of buttresses and gullies that stretch away towards Mishirgi Tau; whilst to the west is the less broken cliff reaching to the south-western ridge. We worked up the secondary ridge, now on one side, now on the other, till we were pulled up at the point where it bulges outwards and towers up into the great crag which, like the hand of some gigantic sun-dial, throws long shadows across the face of the mountain. It was evident that the work would now become very much more serious, so we halted and made a good meal. We packed the remainder of the provisions into the knapsack and stowed it away under a large stone.

After prospecting the cliff on our right, Zurfluh came to the conclusion that nothing could be done on that side. We therefore turned our attention to the rocks on our left, and were soon traversing a huge slab by the aid of various minute wrinkles and discolorations. Happily it soon became possible to turn upwards, and, trusting mainly to our finger tips and the sides of our boots, we forced our way back on to the ridge at the very top of the sun-dial projection. For a short distance it was almost horizontal and extraordinarily sharp. So much so, indeed, that we were fain to accept the attitude much affected by foreign climbers in foreign prints, and progress was made on our hands whilst a leg was slung over each side as a sort of balancing pole. A gap fifteen feet deep separated this razor edge from the mass of the mountain beyond. Zurfluh jumped down on to a convenient bed of snow and cheerily went on his way. Shortly afterwards I reached the gap, and, as I fondly imagined, similarly jumped, but the bed of snow did not take the impact kindly and slid away into the little couloir on my left, a more or less breathless Herr being left clinging to a sort of banister of rock which projected from the gap. Happily this incident escaped the notice of the professional member of the party. I say happily, because the *morale* of the leader is frequently a plant of tender growth, and should be carefully shielded from all adverse influences.

We were now on the final peak. Gestola, Tetnuld and Janga were well below us, and even the corniced ridge of Shkara did not look as if it could give us much. Unluckily, over this great ridge an evil-looking mass of cloud had gathered, and from time to time shreds and strips were torn from it and whirled across the intervening space by a furious southerly gale. Some of these shreds and strips sailed high over our heads, shutting out the welcome warmth of the sun; others less aerially inclined now and again got entangled in the ridges below, blotting out their jagged spires and warning us that at any moment the cliffs around might be veiled in impenetrable mist.

The wall immediately above was evidently very formidable. Though I sought to keep up an affectation of assured success, I was quite unable to see how any further advance was to be made. Zurfluh, however, is a man who rises to such emergencies, and is moreover an exceptionally brilliant rock climber. He proved equal to the occasion, and vowed by the immortal gods that we would not be baffled a second time. Whilst he was looking for the most desirable line of attack, I replied to the shouts of the shepherd who had climbed to the col early in the morning, and, greatly interested in our proceedings, had spent the rest of the day on that bleak spot in a biting and furious wind.

Zurfluh, after a careful survey, determined that we must again traverse to our left. We crawled along the face of the great cliff, clinging to outward shelving and most unsatisfactory ledges, till we reached a place where strenuous efforts just enabled us to lift ourselves over a sort of bulge. Above this the angle was less steep, and a few cracks and splinters enabled us to get reliable hold. A short distance further, however, a second and, if possible, nastier bulge appeared. After contemplating Zurfluh's grateful attitudes and listening to his gasps as he battled with the desperate difficulty, it was 'borne in upon me'—as the Plymouth Brethren say—that the second* peak in the Caucasus ought not to be climbed by an unroped party. Would it not be contrary to all the canons laid down for the guidance of youth and innocence in the Badminton and All England series? Might it not even be regarded as savouring of insult to our peak? I mildly suggested these fears to Zurfluh. He asked me whether I would come up for the rope or whether he should send the rope down to me. For some hidden reason a broad grin illuminated his face as he strongly recommended the former course, pointing out that the ledge on which I was huddled was not a convenient place for roping operations. Despite this advice I unhesitatingly decided on the latter alternative, and when the rope came down, successfully grappled with the difficulty of putting it on. And now a strange phenomena must be recorded: a moment earlier I could have sworn before any court—and been glad to do it, provided the court was, as courts usually are, on level ground—that the cliff in front was absolutely perpendicular. Yet no sooner was the rope firmly

---

* Actually, the third, after Elbrus and Shkhara.

attached than the cliff tilted backwards till it barely exceeded a beg-
garly sixty degrees!

We were now able to get round the square corner of the peak on to
the face fronting the lower summit, and could look across to the ice-
swept cliffs of Koshtantau. The gap between the two peaks was well
below us—indeed, we were almost level with the lower summit. I had
always had misgivings about this section of the ascent, and it was,
therefore, with no small delight that I perceived a long crack up which
a way could almost certainly be forced. Apart, however, from the accident of this crack or fault, I am not sure this wall could be ascended.
With our elbows and backs against one side and our knees against the
other, we worked our way quickly upwards. The lower peak sank
rapidly, and the appearance of distant snows above its crest was hailed
with triumphant shouts. Then Zurfluh dived into a dark hole behind
a stone that had wedged itself in our narrow path, and desperate were
the wriggles and squeezings necessary to push his body through the
narrow aperture. Then we had to quit the crack for a yard or two and
scramble up a great slab at its side. Once more we got back into our
crack and on and ever upwards till at length we emerged on the ridge.
On the ridge do I say? No; on the very summit itself. Every peak in
Europe, Elbruz alone excepted, was below us, and from our watch-
tower of 17,054 feet we gazed at the rolling world. Turning to the left,
a few steps brought me to the culminating point, and I sat down on its
shattered crest. Huge clouds were by now wrapping Shkara in an ever
darkening mantle, and the long ridge of Janga was buried in dense,
matted banks of vapour white and brilliant above, but dark and evil
along their ever lowering under-edges. Koshtantau shone in its snowy
armour, white against black billows of heaped-up storm. Elbruz alone
was clear and spotless, and its vastness made it look so close that
Zurfluh laughed to scorn my statement that our passes from Mujal to
the Bashil Su were between us and it. He maintained and still believes
that Elbruz is situated close to Tiktengen, and I defy all the surveyors
of the Holy Russian Empire to convince him of error. A yellow look
about the snow suggested, it is true, considerable distance, but the
huge size and height of the enormous mass so dwarfed the intervening
space that I am not surprised at his mistake.

As I declined to give up my seat on the highest point, Zurfluh was constrained to build the cairn, on which his heart was set, on a point slightly lower. Under his fostering care this point grew and waxed strong till it proudly looked over the crest of its rival that, for the last few thousand years, had topped it by a foot. After three-quarters of an hour's halt the furious blasts of the hurricane made us quite willing to move, and at 11.30 a.m. we left the summit. We rattled down the crack, and got back on to the south face without much trouble. Then, however, I distinguished myself by losing the way, and was relegated to the nominally, more important post of last man. Zurfluh with brilliant skill picked up the line of ledges and cracks by which we had ascended, and we duly reached the horizontal ridge. Elated by our success, we strode boldy along its narrow edge instead of adopting the undignified procedure of the morning. Shortly afterwards Zurfluh imitated my bad example and lost the right line of descent. We could see the rock by which our knapsack was securely stowed, and our footprints were on a small patch of snow just above the wall, but we could not discover the line by which we had connected these two points. Ultimately we were compelled to make a sensational descent by a tiny cleft or crack just wide enough for toes and fingers. Its lower end opened into space, and a long sideways jump was requisite to reach footing. Zurfluh, aided by the rope, got across, and said he could catch and steady me as I came over. I have a keen remembrance of descending the crack, of leaning forwards and down as far as I could reach, and just being able to rest the point of my axe on a small excrescence; then leaning my weight upon it, I swung over sideways towards Zurfluh. An instant later he was clasping my knees with such devout enthusiasm that I felt like a holy prophet ejected from the shining mountain into the arms of some faithful devotee.

This practically ended our difficulties. A few minutes later we reached the knapsack and soon demolished its contents. Our porter was still sitting on the col watching us, and Zurfluh, mindful of the habits of the Swiss when in high places, averred that he would certainly have finished every scrap of provision in the camp. None the less we greeted his shouts with loud jodels and much triumphant brandishing of ice-axes. Our lunch being brought to a summary conclusion by the total exhaustion of the supplies, we stuffed the rope into the empty knapsack and turned once more to the descent. We got on rapidly till we reached the couloir. The ice was here so rotten, and much of it so ill-frozen to the rocks and underlying ice, and the whole gully was so obviously swept by falling stones, that we unanimously refused to follow our morning's track. My own impression is that, apart from other objections, even Zurfluh did not quite like descending the remarkable staircase by which we had scrambled up. Crossing the couloir we struck on to the rocks, and soon discovered some precipitous ice-glazed chimneys down which we managed to crawl. Regaining our route of the morning, we sped merrily downwards to the belt of red rocks. The summit of a new peak in one's pocket lends strength and swiftness even to the clumsy, and I shuffled after Zurfluh in most active fashion. Our porter soon came to the conclusion that the interest of the play was over, and we saw him pick himself up and go warily down the slopes. A little later, Zurfluh, perceiving that even a Herr could not go much astray, was seized with a desire to show the Tartar how easy slopes should be traversed, and dashed towards the col with the speed and graceful ease of the well-practised chamois hunter. When a man is being hopelessly outpaced by his companion, he always experiences great pleasure in seeing that same companion miss the easiest line of descent. This pleasure I experienced on seeing Zurfluh, after reaching the col, keep to the line by which we had come in the morning. My previous exploratory climb had made me aware of a convenient snow-filled gully in which an exceedingly rapid standing glissade was possible. Reaching this highway, I spun down to the little glacier. Having run across this, I sat myself comfortably on my hat, and slid down the long slopes almost into the tent, where Zurfluh was still busy emptying the snow from his pockets.

The porter met me with loud shouts of 'Allah il Allah! Minghi Tau, Allah, Allah!'

We soon discovered that, instead of consuming the whole of our provisions, the porter had not even had a crust of bread. We urged him to take a preliminary lunch, or rather breakfast, while the soup was cooking, but he refused, and seemed in no hurry for dinner. He manipulated the fire with much skill, making the vile wood burn in a really creditable manner, and only pausing from his efforts to award me an occasional appreciative slap on the back. It being early, 4 p.m., Zurfluh expressed a strong desire to strike camp and descend, but the delights of the kosh did not rouse my enthusiasm, and I refused to move. Indeed, it is one of the great pleasures of Caucasian travelling that the weary tramp over screes, uneven glacier, the horrors of the moraine, and, too frequently, the reascent to the hotel, are unknown. A camp at one spot is practically as comfortable as at any other, and in consequence, so soon as one feels inclined to sit down and laze, the day's work is over and one postpones the screes and moraines to the sweet distance of to-morrow. It is, indeed, a rare delight to sit at one's ease in the early afternoon and gaze at the huge cliffs amongst which one has been wandering, free from all the thought of hurry, of moraines, or of darkness.

Towards evening the gathering clouds burst in thunder, and the screes below us, right down to the glacier, were powdered with hail and snow. As the moon rose, however, the curtain was rent apart, and the great ridges, shining in the brilliant whiteness of fresh-fallen snow, gazed at us across the dark gulf of the Bezingi glacier. The evening, being windless, was comparatively warm, and it was nearly midnight before Zurfluh's peaceful slumbers were disturbed by the struggles of a shivering Herr with his sleeping bag.

The next morning we went down the glacier to the Misses kosh, packed up our belongings, and tramped to Tubeneli. Fresh stores had arrived from Naltcik and the old chief feasted us on chicken and cakes, but these delights failed to comfort the melancholy Zurfluh, and he flatly refused to do aught but return straight home. On Dych Tau the excitement of the climb had aroused all the vigour and strength he possessed, but now that the spurt was over he broke down completely. He was undoubtedly very poorly, and looked the mere ghost, and a most thin and melancholy ghost, of his former self. 'Es gefällt mir nicht', may be good philosophy, but it undoubtedly tends to a pre-Raphaelite condition of body.

From *My Climbs in the Alps and Caucasus*, 1895

8

'Herr Gott! Der Schlafplatz': the Tragedy of 1888

Mummery's and Cockin's triumphs were only one side of the story in the 1888 season. As so often in climbing, success and tragedy came together. Mountaineering then was still too young for either its practitioners or the general public to have become as blasé as we are now about death in the hills. When William Donkin, Harry Fox, Kaspar Streich and Johann Fischer disappeared in the vicinity of Koshtan-Tau at the end of August, the shock-waves were international. It was the first major accident since the dramatic deaths of Michel Croz, Lord Francis Douglas, the Reverend Charles Hudson and Douglas Hadow while descending after the first successful ascent of the Matterhorn twenty-three years earlier. On the Matterhorn a rope broke, saving the lives of Edward Whymper and the Taugwalders, father and son, and sealing the fate of the other four. Nobody has explained this mysterious accident satisfactorily, although accusations have been hurled around ever since. The Caucasus tragedy of 1888 was even more mysterious. Donkin, Fox, Streich and Fischer disappeared almost without a trace.

William Frederick Donkin was a lecturer in Chemistry, a widower, and by the time of his second expedition to the Caucasus in 1888, was widely recognised to have revolutionised mountain photography. He was, as anyone who looks at his photographs today will recognise, an artist who could employ the bulky equipment of the day to communicate a personal vision that few other photographers, and still fewer painters, have matched.

He was not the first to take a camera into the hills, by any means. Photographs had been taken above the snow-line since the 1850s. But in the early days of mountain photography the logistical problems were overwhelming. The only available negatives were wet-plates that had to be processed on the spot. For this the photographer needed a portable darkroom and considerable quantities of water, as well of course as the necessary chemicals. All this equipment was extraordinarily bulky. In the case of Aimé Civiale, who was taking mountain photographs at the end of the 1850s, his equipment weighed over half a ton. Added to this, there were technical difficulties. The whole procedure of taking a photograph took literally hours. The plates had to be prepared in the darkroom tent, coated with collodium and then sensitised in a silver bath, before exposing the photograph and beginning the process of developing. When the Bisson brothers, the greatest of the early mountain photographers, returned in 1861 from a multi-day expedition to Mont Blanc with the first photographs taken from the summit, they had only three successful pictures to show for it. Each glass negative was enormous by today's standards, with sixteen by twenty inches a common size, and very fragile. The Bisson brothers' first attempt on Mont Blanc was foiled when a clumsy porter dropped the box containing the plates. They managed, however, to take some truly remarkable pictures, including an imposing portrait of the Chamonix Aiguilles from the Brevent, and some famous and frequently reproduced scenes on the Mer de Glace.

Mountain photography gradually became easier. When the Reverend Hereford George, first editor of the *Alpine Journal*, embarked on a photographic tour of the Alps in 1865 he invented a darkroom tent with a cupboard inside, enabling the photographer to keep the plates wet for several hours, thus avoiding the trials of having to develop the negatives immediately on exposure. His camera was also much smaller and lighter, its plates six inches by eight, or less. Both tent and camera could be carried by one man, compared to the twenty-five porters employed by the Bisson brothers.

The greatest change came in 1869 with the invention of dry-plates. No longer was it necessary to develop the plates on the spot or within a few hours. They could be exposed and then left indefinitely before developing. Donkin took full advantage of this new-found freedom to wander far from the familiar panoramas. He was, of course, a skilled mountaineer in a way that none of the other early mountain photographers were (although Whymper had taken to carrying a camera, he used it more to help him with his sketches than as an end in itself). Donkin's preferred plate size was seven inches by five, and this, together with his use of the carbon developing process and his skills as a chemist, produced prints of a quality and clarity of definition that continue to impress. His best photographs, like the 1880 portrait of the Aiguille du Géant, have never been surpassed and it was only his tragically early death that led to his being overshadowed in the history of mountain photography by his friend and protégé, Vittorio Sella.

In the two years since their first ascent of Gestola Donkin and Dent had become recognised as authorities on the Caucasus. Indeed, they had published a set of guidelines for visitors to the range, declaring the greatest requisite of all to be 'infinite patience'. When they returned in 1888 the third member of their party was rather less experienced, though well known as a sportsman. Harry Fox came from a West Country Quaker family that produced several generations of mountaineers, but he only started climbing in the summer of 1884, at the age of twenty-eight. Under the tutelage of William Graham and William Cecil Slingsby he made rapid progress, fulfilling the entrance requirements for the Alpine Club by the following year and making some impressive unguided ascents, including Dent's old adversary, the Aiguille du Dru. Slingsby thought very highly of him. 'I have no hesitation in saying that he was the best amateur climber I have ever met. He was as equally at home on difficult rocks as in forcing a way on an intricate glacier or in step-cutting upon a steep snow-slope, in planning a difficult expedition as in executing it. In physical strength and endurance, which were largely owing to his extreme temperance and perfect self-control, few were his equals.'[1] Fox worked in the family woollen business in Wellington (famous for its fine worsteds and durable puttees), where it was said most of the newest and most interesting developments were in 'Harry's department'. He was a popular and familiar figure, riding the streets in his dog cart; on his disappearance, the local newspaper wrote that it was no exaggeration to say that Wellington mourned as a town the loss of one of her most promising sons. As was usual at the time, the party was completed by two guides. Kaspar Streich was prominent in the Oberland, thirty-eight years old and very well thought of by his many British clients. His assistant, Johann Fischer, was from a famous guiding family, son of the Johann Fischer who was killed on the Brouillard Glacier in 1874 and, although only twenty-one, clearly had a glittering career in front of him.

The expedition had relatively modest aims. Surveying and photography were to be as important as mountaineering, with theodolites, sextants, clinometers and aneroids featuring in the baggage, as well as Donkin's camera equipment. In particular, they hoped to get high enough on Ushba to work out how it stood in relation to the main ridge of the Caucasus, as well as to chart the complicated glacier systems that surround it. In the Bezingi area, the minute topography of what they called 'Dych-Tau' was to be the main target. They meant Koshtan-Tau, as we know now, one of the mighty 5000-metre Bezingi peaks, which seemed the best place for Donkin to exercise his photographic skills, and for Fox to employ his surveying equipment. Dent maintains that they spoke more of making a high tour of the peak than a first ascent. Dongusorun, on the other hand, a mountain resembling a huge Breithorn, he felt 'was not likely to be difficult and the camera and surveying equipment would easily be carried to the top'.[2] Clearly they would have liked to settle some unfinished business from two years before by bagging the real Dych Tau (which they had then called 'Guluku' and now considered to be 'Koshtan-Tau'), but they could hardly hope it would still be virgin if Mummery got there first.

As so often, when they found themselves close to the mountains the lure of the virgin summits proved irresistible, and their plans became more ambitious. A letter which Donkin wrote to his brother on August 15 tells the tale of their attempts on Ushba, as well as of their successful ascent of Dongusorun.

> I sit in the blazing sun at a rough wooden table outside a wooden sort of barrack called a Cancellaria, one room of which we have, in a small valley which you may roughly compare with the Zermatt valley on a smaller scale, but with an enormously larger Matterhorn at the head of it, towards the left – the great Ushba. It is still unclimbed. We have been here nearly a week, 4 days of which we spent in camp high up by the moraine under the mountain, and had two hard tries to get up the two twin peaks, but were beaten; the first time we tried the N.E. and slightly higher peak, by going up the great snow couloir between them; the weather was fine but too warm, so the snow was not hard enough, and it became

dangerous from avalanches. We had to keep upon the rocks at the side which were very difficult, and at last it was a choice between the steep snow and its risks and a defeat; so, though you may imagine the disappointment, we turned back and came down again. Even then we were not free from risk; huge avalanches had already fallen, and we had to run and slide down the slopes as fast as we could, tumbling through the masses of snow and ice débris till we were clear of avalanche tracks and could take it easy. Even so we were out for 13 hours and hard at work all the time.[3]

This first attempt on Ushba was by the route on which Cockin and Almer would succeed six weeks later. The dangerous conditions which they encountered were typical for the route. Cockin and Almer benefited from exceptional conditions and very long necks when they made their ascent, and it is probably because the route is so objectively implausible that the Russians were for so long unwilling to accept that it had actually been climbed in 1888. Donkin, Fox and their guides were too sensible to try it again, so, rather than give up altogether, they transferred their attentions to the South Peak.

On Sunday we rested, and on Monday we had a try at the S.W. Peak from the S. arête. This avoids all risk of avalanches and we hoped for success. The telescope had shown that most of the route was easy except for one hard bit below the top. It was an enormously long climb over the lower rocks and snow gullies, nowhere very steep, but very tiring just because it was easy enough to go fast. At last however we were brought up against a cliff; the great cliff which guards the top, and such a tremendous wall of forbidding precipices I never saw before. It is nearly half a mile wide, and a magnificent and spotless field of snow hangs below it, sweeping down at a fearfully steep angle into the valley below.

This 'wall of forbidding precipices' was only to succumb to the talents and bravery of Schulze fifteen years later. It is indeed, as Dent and Donkin had seen through their telescope, the key to Ushba South.

We were on a ridge abutting against the right-hand edge of the cliff, and anxiously did we scan it for a possible way up. In the middle was a great crack from top to bottom, full of icicles; immediately over our heads the rocks went almost sheer up, solid and firm, but such little projections as there were sloped the wrong way and gave no hold whatever. Streich was not very well and obviously did not think it possible. However, we put down all the baggage and had a try at the lowest rocks. We got up a little way, a very little way, and then got hopelessly stuck. Fox, who is a most enthusiastic climber, wanted to try the ice gully, but merely to get near it involved getting up an overhanging slab of vertical rock which I declared was impossible; indeed, I had mentally given it up on first inspection. Once up those 400 or so feet of precipice, all would have been easy, as the top slope is gentle; but it was hopeless, so once more we had to accept defeat and turned downwards. Before doing so, however, we built a little cairn and I took a boiling point to determine the height we were at – nearly 15,000 feet. As we descended the interminable ridges of broken rock the clouds swept up and a little snow fell, but lower down we got into fine weather again. Ushba is its proper name – the rain peak.

After the failure of the second attempt on Ushba the party left the area. Dent, who had been ill since the first days of the expedition – his companions suspected a heart condition – started on the journey back to Britain. The remaining four set off as planned for Dongusorun on August 16. Dent recalled the parting.

> The picture of the open valley of Betsho one August day rises up before my eyes, perfect in every detail. The events of that morning revolve again and again in an unceasing order in the memory. Unbidden the recollection comes of the busy preparations for the start, and the merriment over the morning meal, for by tacit agreement we would anticipate even for an hour. Of a sudden we seemed to realise that the moment had arrived, and that all was ready for departure. Little was spoken. A silence seemed to gather around us. Strange that nothing was said of meeting again soon, yet so it was. The time had come. A shake of the hand, a pressure on the shoulder that meant more than words could express. The guides and then Harry Fox moved on a few paces. Donkin was before me – ay, as he is now as I write. I can see him, I can almost feel his grasp.[4]

The ascent of Dongusorun proved as straightforward as anticipated. The four men climbed the South-East Peak and made the observations they wanted from the summit. They then crossed a new pass between the Adyrsu and Chegem valleys and made their way over to the Bezingi area. They passed close by Holder, Woolley and Cockin and, although the two parties never met, Donkin sent Holder a letter on August 24.

Having arrived here this afternoon from Chegem, and hearing from your interpreter that you are in camp on the glacier, and that someone is going up to you tomorrow, I send a line to say how much interested I am to hear that you have had some success, and I hope that the weather may mend and that you may be able to do all you wish. I am here with Mr Fox only; Mr Dent was unfortunately obliged to leave us at Betsho, not being very well, and is returning home via Moscow. We have climbed Dongusorun, and traversed a new and splendid pass from Urusbieh to Chegem – both in perfect weather. We are bound for Balkar and Gebi, and thence home by Batoum, hoping to see something of the Dych-Su glacier on the way.[5]

Once again, Donkin and Fox were more ambitious than they had planned to be. They left Bezingi on August 25, bound for the Doumala valley. Their interpreter was sent round to Balkar with the heavy baggage, instructed to wait for them there. From the Doumala valley they went south up the Ullu-Auz Glacier towards Koshtan-Tau, bivouacking on the second night high on the glacier below the mountain. The weather had been windy and cold all day, deteriorating in the afternoon to a full-blown snowstorm with thunder and lightning. Fox wrote in his diary on the night of August 26:

Fischer searched for a sleeping place and found a cleft in the rocks that sloped upwards. A poor hole but affording shelter from snow and wind somewhat. The top was so narrow that one could only just squeeze oneself inside. Below it widened out a little. The angle was about 30 degrees. We managed to take down about a ton of rock and loose stones with which the crack was filled and made a sort of platform where Streich and I lay. I hollowed out a seat above and made a footstool of my iceaxe below. We curled ourselves in our sleeping bags and tried to be thankful for shelter. Everywhere was wet and clammy and a slow drip came over my knees. Position had to be changed every ten minutes, each change sending down a handful of pebbles on Donkin's head.

The wind was boisterous. Gusts of snow pattered in and whistled on the sleeping bags. I was just dozing off when I was awoke by a handful of stones from above which clattered about my ears followed by a large rock which I had thought secure. It came bang on my head and made me see a thousand stars so that for a moment the hole seemed full of light. In endeavouring to move it on one side I shifted the ice axe and sent a wheelbarrow of stones down

on poor D's head. His patience and endurance can only be likened
to that of Job.

I had to get down and share the platform. Fischer was already
ensconced in another crack outside so that room was found. The
guides were pretty wretched and had long abandoned all hopes
of a mend in the weather. I reminded them of previous experiences
but gloomy thoughts prevailed. The stones were hard to lie on but
by this time we are fairly accustomed to hard beds.[6]

Despite the miserable bivouac they made an attempt on Koshtan-Tau
the following day (August 27). They went up the North Ridge until
brought short by a tower of rock too difficult to climb. Streich suggested
that they try to turn it by descending a few hundred feet from the ridge
towards the Kunjum-Mishirgi Glacier and then climbing back up a
prominent rock rib to rejoin the ridge on the other side of the tower.
This they duly attempted, but it proved more difficult and time-
consuming than they expected. Fox described it in his diary:

> We left the col at 9.10. The descent took a long time and there was
> much step-cutting. We then tried the rib and found the rocks, as
> we expected, quite smooth. We cut up between them and forced
> our way up slowly, the fresh snow making everything most diffi-
> cult, but at 11.40 had made little progress, and as it was obvious
> we had not time to make our peak that day (the arête alone would
> take at least four hours), and as clouds were gathering, we reluc-
> tantly ordered a return.[7]

This initial failure did nothing to dampen their spirits. Fox wrote in
his diary the next day:

> A beautiful night. All slept like tops ... At 5.30 I woke up and read
> *Midsummer Night's Dream* till about 7.30, when the sun came
> out.

They had obviously decided what to do next for he went on to
describe their plans in some detail.

> Weather permitting we hope to start again tomorrow very early
> and take three or four days' provisions. Make the Dumala-Dych-Su
> Pass first day and camp near its head. Climb Dych-Tau [ie Koshtan-
> Tau] if possible from the south side the next and descend to the
> Dych-Su Glacier. Thence to Karaoul.

As he said, it all depended on the weather, which had been decidedly whimsical so far. Already clouds were welling up, with the promise of more rain before nightfall. Still, they enjoyed their rest-day, making such preparations as they could:

> Guides are busying themselves nailing boots; drying clothes, cooking meat, etc. Donkin is practising with a revolver at imaginary enemies (11.30) ... The man has gone for milk and cheese with a rouble note (much too high pay, but we do not want to be stinted). I have written up my notes. Donkin has worked out boiling point observations. We have read much Shakespeare. Gathered wood for tomorrow. Streich and I have had a good bake of bread. He would not believe in baking-powder until he saw its effects. The best bread we have eaten since leaving Batum. Feasted largely of it. Weather looks bad. Clouds down on to glacier (3 pm), will soon be over our camp. Hope for best. There is no understanding 'Caucasian meteorology'.[8]

A message (written in German) was sent round to their interpreter, Rieger, waiting in Balkar.

> We have been across the mountains towards Karaoul. We start early tomorrow, and hope to be in Karaoul (again) on the 30th, or 31st, where you must meet us. If bad weather should come on, or the descent on the other side prove impracticable, we may have to return to Bezingi and ride round. But, anyhow, wait for us at Karaoul. We send back our tent and some things we shall not need on the mountain. Pay the bearer for five days.[9]

The messenger who took this letter was the last person to see any of the four mountaineers, alive or dead.

The interpreter waited as instructed at Karaoul until he realised finally that something must have gone terribly wrong. He went from Karaoul to Naltchik and there he sent a telegraph to England on September 26, saying that he had had no news from any member of the party for twenty-eight days. Nobody who knew the area could doubt that an accident had befallen Donkin, Fox and the two guides. They had almost certainly perished somewhere in the mountains. The questions were how, where – and why.

By a stroke of good luck the noted explorer and hunter Clive Phillipps-Wolley was in the Bezingi area at the time. He was an expert on the region, familiar with the language and the author of a book, *Savage Suanetia*, which had been published four years earlier. He immediately volunteered to lead a search party. The Russian authorities took the disappearance very seriously, and material support was provided by Prince Dondukoff Korsakoff, Governor-General of the Caucasus and, closer to the scene, by the Russian surveyor N. Djukoff who had run into Donkin and Fox a few days before they disappeared. Phillipps-Wolley and Djukoff led one search party of nine locals. Three others were organised by Russian officials. But none of them found any traces of the party except a line of footprints in the moraine beside the Ullu-Auz Glacier.

By the first week of October it was clear to even the most optimistic that there could be no hope of finding the four men still alive. Harry Fox's mother gave up all hope of seeing her son again, and sent Dent a cheque for £500 to be forwarded to Kaspar Streich's widow who had just had her fourth child. Dent took upon himself the unpleasant task of writing to *The Times* to quell any future speculation.

> Unhappily, there exists no longer any doubt that Messrs W. F. Donkin and Harry Fox, with the Swiss guides, Kaspar Streich and Johann Fischer, have all lost their lives by a mountaineering accident. The disaster probably occurred about September 1 last, either on the mountain now known as Shkara or, less probably, on one of the neighbouring peaks. A thorough search, furthered, as we learn through various sources, by all the local and other authorities, is in active progress. An English traveller, who happens to be in the country, and who has an intimate acquaintance with the country, the natives and the language, is assisting in the search. While I am writing, a telegram from him comes to hand informing me that 'traces have been discovered on – glacier'. The name of the glacier I am unable to decipher.[10]

The tracks referred to are the solitary line of footprints mentioned earlier. Phillipps-Wolley also found the tracks of an avalanche across the obvious route to the pass leading to Karaoul, but without any evidence that the party had succumbed to it.

As Dent's letter shows, the British mountaineering community was convinced that Donkin, Fox, Streich and Fischer had fallen victim to the perils of the mountain, although at the time no-one could guess what sort of accident or on which mountain. But the Russians were more suspicious. Perhaps they remembered the difficulties which Freshfield had reported on his first visit, and which other travellers had occasionally encountered. More likely, they still distrusted the unruly Svanetians who had been so troublesome after the Russo-Turkish War of 1877–8 and who must still have seemed a recently subdued and wild tribe to the officials sent from Moscow to a bleak outpost of the Russian empire. Whatever the reason, foul play was suspected. The local villagers were accused of murdering and robbing the foreign climbers. A regiment of Cossacks was sent to the village of Bezingi to try to find and punish the perpetrators. Of course, they found not even the most tenuous shred of evidence, but their presence during the lean winter months was still a tremendous burden on the villagers who were forced to find food for both the men and their horses.

At the end of the second week in October the first snows of winter fell, making any further search impossible. There had been some talk of sending a party out from England (and Switzerland), and many offers of help were received. The more experienced Caucasus hands realised, though, that an expedition at that time of year would be able to do little except confirm what Phillipps-Wolley and the other searchers had already found – namely, very little. It was decided instead to wait until the next season, when the snows would have melted and whatever clues there might be would be revealed.

The search party that arrived in the Caucasus in July 1889 was probably the strongest expedition to visit the range in the nineteenth century. Dent was there, of course, anxious to find traces of his friends and to find out the truth about the fate that he had so fortunately been spared. Freshfield also joined the party, in his capacity as the Grand Old Man of Caucasian exploration. Hermann Woolley had been in the Caucasus with Cockin and Holder the previous year. Captain Charles Herbert Powell, the youngest of the three mountaineering Powell brothers, had not climbed in the range before, but was a fluent Russian speaker. The five Alpine Club worthies were accompanied by four guides: Christian Jossi, Kaspar Maurer (who had been with Dent and Burgener on the first ascent of the Dru), Andreas Fischer (Johann Fischer's brother and a schoolteacher by profession who had joined the expedition as a volunteer) and Johann Kaufmann.

The searchers had little to go on, although Phillipps-Wolley had retrieved the expedition's main luggage, which contained Fox's diary. And two pieces of information from the diary made their task much easier. First, they were pretty sure that the accident had taken place on or around Koshtan-Tau (which they still called Dych-Tau), rather than further west towards the main part of the Bezingi basin, as they had originally thought. Second, they knew that Donkin and Fox's last journey had taken them over the Ullu-Auz Pass that separates the Ullu-Auz and Tiutiun Glaciers. This is the pass that Fox in his diary referred to as the Doumala-Dykh-Su Pass.

The most sensible way to proceed was to try to retrace as much as possible of the ground covered by Fox, Donkin and the guides, in the hope of finding some clue that would tell them where, if at all, they had left the glacier to climb, but they had only a very sketchy knowledge of the terrain (which, of course, the missing expedition had been hoping to explore and map in detail). They decided against going up the Ullu-Auz Glacier where Phillipps-Wolley had seen the footprints which could only have been made by Donkin, Fox and the guides. Phillipps-Wolley had also reported traces of a large avalanche there. With what is perhaps a touching faith in mountaineering judgement, Dent and his fellow-searchers refused to believe that their friends could possibly have perished in anything so vulgar as an avalanche.[11] Instead they decided to go round to Karaoul and approach the Ullu-Auz Pass from the south, hoping to meet the line which Donkin's party had taken the previous year.

They took ten days to travel from Vladikafkaz to Karaoul, reaching it on July 25. From there they proceeded up the Tiutiun valley until they reached the Tiutiun Glacier. On July 28 they camped in a *kosh* on the right bank of the glacier. The next day they left at 4.30 to reconnoitre the south side of the Ullu-Auz Pass. The weather was perfect.

> The conditions were not merely of good omen, but were also in the highest degree fortunate, for the object of our search seemed very minute in the presence of such gigantic surroundings. The air was clear and soft, and the snow in perfect order for walking.

We worked our way due west, and gradually as we turned the buttress of rock a steep and broad ice gully came into view leading up to the pass ... our plan of action was clear and we set off without delay to ascend the wall. Two long ribs of rock lying on the right of the ice gully offered the best means of access. Both looked feasible, but it was only after a moment's hesitation that the left-hand one was selected, as it seemed more broken, was broader and ran up slightly higher. If the right-hand rib had been broken we might conceivably have missed the object of our search altogether. We made our way up the rocks without any great difficulty. Half-melted masses of snow constantly hissed down the ice gully as we ascended, and the great chasm that extends along the base of the cliff was choked for the most part with avalanche snow. The rocks were steep, but so broken as to offer good hand- and foot-hold. Still the mind was sufficiently occupied in attending to the details of climbing to prevent the thoughts from wandering. Insensibly we began to think little save of the view that would be revealed from the top of the pass. From time to time an opportunity would be found of gazing to the right or left, but progress was tolerably continuous.

Maurer, who was leading, looked upwards now and again as he worked out the best line of ascent, but the rocks were so steep he could only see a few feet. Just about midday, as he stopped for a moment to look upwards, I saw his expression suddenly change. 'Herr Gott!' he suddenly exclaimed, 'der Schlafplatz!' I think I shall never forget the thrill the words sent through me. We sprang up, scrambling over the few feet that still intervened, and in a moment were grouped on a little ledge just outside the bivouac. There was little enough to be seen at the first glance save a low horseshoe shaped wall of stones, measuring some six feet by eight, and carefully built against an overhanging rock. The enclosure was full of drifted snow, raised up into a hump at the back, where it covered a large rucksack. On a ledge, formed by one of the stones, a little tin snow-spectacle caught the eye as it reflected the rays of the sun. For a few moments all was excitement as the presence of one object after another was revealed. 'See here,' cried Maurer as he scooped away the snow with his hands, 'the sleeping bags!' 'And here a rucksack,' said another. 'Look, they made a fire there,' called out a third, 'and here is the cooking kettle and the revolver.' Then came somewhat of a reaction, and for a few minutes we could but gaze silently at the place that told so clear a tale and endeavour to realise to the full the evidence that had come upon us with such overwhelming suddenness.[12]

Freshfield, Woolley and Jossi continued up to the col a few hundred feet above. Freshfield left a magnificent and rather moving description of the scene.

> The silence of the upper snows was broken only by the constant ring of the axes and the voices of our comrades, which rose clearly through the thin air as they still laboured in their sad task of seeking all that might be found under the icy coverlet. Their figures were thrown out on the edge of the crags against the surface of the Tiutiun snowfields, as are those of sailors on a masthead against the sea when seen from some high cliff. The day was cloudless, the air crystalline, space was for a moment annihilated or shown in a scale by which we each seemed to stand, not 6 feet but 14,000 feet high. The many passes and heights of the central ridge of the Caucasus lay literally at our feet. We looked over them and past the clustered peaks and vast snow-reservoirs of the Adai-Kokh group to innumerable indefinite distances, amongst which I recognised the horn of Shoda, green heights of Racha, blue mountains of Achalzich, opalescent Armenian ranges fading into a saffron sky, on which hung the far-off amber cloudlets which often mark the position of Ararat. Every detail was as distinct as on a mapman's model, yet the whole was vast and vague, wonderful and strange, creating an impression of immeasurable shining space, of the earth as it might appear to a visitant from some other planet. The splendour of nature on this day of days seemed not out of harmony with the sadness of our errand. It affected the mind as a solemn and sympathetic Music. While I gazed, four white butterflies circled round the little monument, and again fluttered off. An ancient Greek would have found a symbol in the incident.[13]

But what had happened to the four men? The equipment left behind in the bivouac site suggested that they had left early in the morning and planned to return that evening. Their sleeping bags and provisions were there, but not their ice-axes and climbing equipment. Everything was laid out in readiness for a late return, carefully arranged so that they could quickly cook and collapse into their sleeping bags.

Their destination was clear enough from the place they had chosen to bivouac in. The summit of Koshtan-Tau could be reached by its East Ridge, which extended down as far as the Ullu-Auz Pass. The upper part of the ridge was a snowy crest that seemed to lead without much difficulty to the top of the mountain. It was obviously this that they were aiming for. But the lower part of the ridge immediately above the pass was composed of a series of huge rock pinnacles. The crest of the ridge could not be followed all the way. The rock pinnacles would have to be turned. There were two possibilities. Donkin and his party could either have gone back over the pass and tried to traverse past the pinnacles on the northern side. Or they could have gone directly from the bivouac site on the southern side. Neither seemed promising. 'The northern side is a series of forbidding ice slopes. The southern face consists of cliffs traversed by small slopes and steep ledges covered with ice and snow.'[14] Dent thought that the south side looked marginally easier, but still very treacherous ground. Whichever way they had gone, he and the other members of the search expedition concluded that a fall must have led to the mens' deaths. Assuming that they were roped up, this seems the most likely explanation. All it needed was a single slip, and the whole party would have fallen thousands of feet down the steep cliffs to an inevitable death.

No trace was found of the bodies. 'Save for some chance discovery, we must wait until, twenty or thirty years hence, the downward movement of the glacier may reveal that the story we have founded on this circumstantial evidence is accurate. For my own part I hope that the secret may be preserved.'[15] The glaciers, of course, have moved since then. But they still hold the remains of William Donkin, Harry Fox, Kaspar Streich and Johann Fischer.

The search expedition did not, then, manage finally to unravel the mystery of what had happened to the four climbers. In one respect, though, it was completely successful. By finding the final bivouac site in a place which no native of the Caucasus could conceivably have reached, even accompanied by skilled mountaineers, the expedition succeeded in dispelling the suspicions directed at the local population by the Russian authorities. However Donkin and his party had met their end, it was certainly not at the hands of the region's villagers and herdsmen.

A couple of days after finding the last bivouac, Dent sent a full report to Prince Dondoukoff-Korsakoff, Governor-General of the Caucasus, in which he emphatically scotched all the rumours and accusations. And in every village the expedition passed through the story of finding the bivouac site was ritually told and heard with great relief.

> As usual in the Caucasus the natives all crowded into our apartment soon after arrival. Powell would then select some Russian-speaking man in authority, and announce through him that the results of our expedition would be made known to whoever cared to hear them. The whole story was then told, and admirably Powell used to narrate it, winding up by pointing out how the people of the district were now exonerated from any suspicion that may have lain on them. Such suspicion, he used to add, had never been entertained by any English people. The account was always listened to in breathless silence. At the conclusion it was repeated by the chief to the natives in their own language. Then the ruck-sack was brought in and the articles found shown. These were always instantly accepted as absolute proof, the rusty revolver especially exciting attention. Expressions of sorrow and brief interjections were always heard from all sides. Then the chief spoke to some such effect as follows: 'we are indeed rejoiced that you have found these traces. It relieves our people from an irksome and unjust suspicion. It is well that Englishmen came to our country for this search, for we believe that no others could have accomplished what you have done. We are all very grateful to you. Englishmen are always most welcome in our country. We are glad to receive them. Our houses are theirs, and the best we can do shall always be done for your countrymen.'[16]

Dent's account of the gratitude of the local villager was borne out nearly seventy years later when the first British expedition after the war visited the Bezingi area in 1958. Arriving in the Bezingi valley late at night, they camped in a field. The next morning they woke up to encounter a bearded old man who was rather displeased to find them on his land. His anger disappeared, though, when he learnt from their companion Eugene Gippenreiter that the foreigners were English. His father, so he told them, had helped the search party in 1889 and could, in fact, remember the first Britons to visit the Bezingi valley. Gippen-reiter was told the story of how Cossacks had been sent to the village after the disappearance of Donkin, Fox and the guides, and how much had hung on Dent's insistence that the locals could not have had any-thing to do with the tragedy. As a sequel, ten years later Gippenreiter was given a *bourka* (a homespun woollen cloak) by the very same man to present to Sir John Hunt, the leader of the 1958 expedition, which he duly did at the 1969 General Assembly of the International Union of Alpine Associations. Accidents like that which befell Donkin and his companions can hardly have happy endings, but this perhaps is as close as they can come.

9

The Second Invasion

The tragedy of Donkin and Fox was the beginning of the end of British domination of the Caucasus. In the last decade of the nineteenth century the range ceased to be an exclusive playground for the more ambitious members of the Alpine Club, and by the first few years of the twentieth century it would be fair to say that the significant ascents were being undertaken and carried out by Austrians and Germans. It was, however, a slow process and, for the first few years after Donkin and Fox disappeared on Koshtan-Tau, major climbs were still being undertaken by Britons.

One of the characteristics of mountaineers that non-mountaineers find most disturbing is their tendency not to be discouraged when close friends die in the hills. In this respect the search party that discovered Donkin and Fox's last bivouac was entirely typical. Of the four climbers who made up the search party three took the opportunity to climb and explore further in the range. They split into two groups. Hermann Woolley took his two guides, Christian Jossi and Johann Kaufmann, both from Grindelwand, while Freshfield joined forces with Captain Powell and the guides Andreas Fischer and Kaspar Maurer. Freshfield and Powell's team successfully climbed the North-Western Summit of Laila in a very short and straightforward day trip. More significantly, however, they crossed several new passes and explored the Shkhelda Glacier basin, noting that it seemed to offer a route to the formidable South Peak of Ushba.

It was Woolley, however, who carried out the most significant expeditions in 1889. A few days after discovering Fox and Donkin's last bivouac site he climbed the Eastern Peak of Mishirgi-Tau (4918m) with Christian Jossi. They took the prominent couloir which descends the Southern Face from the col between the two summits until falling rock and ice forced them out onto the rocks at its side. After reaching the col, the summit was easily gained. Only five days later Woolley, Jossi and Kaufmann set out for Koshtan-Tau. They bivouacked in the rocks below the head of the Tiutiun Glacier on August 8 and made the first ascent of this, the last of the Caucasian giants still unclimbed, in eighteen hours the following day. Only Woolley and Jossi reached the summit, Kaufmann being too weak to continue after reaching the South Ridge. The principal obstacle on the route was the rock tower where the South Ridge meets the East Ridge, but they managed to avoid it to the left. As expected, they found no trace of Donkin and Fox on the mountain, confirming the conclusion of the search expedition that they had fallen to their deaths relatively low down, their bodies hidden in the snowfields at the foot of Koshtan-Tau.

Mountaineering activity continued in the range for the next few years, but it was sporadic and there were few significant ascents. The great Italian mountain photographer Vittorio Sella made his first visit to the range in 1889 and made a couple of first ascents, including the Central Peak of Laila. Mummery returned the following year with William Petherick but climbed nothing. Cockin and Holder returned to the fray the same year and attempted Jangi-Tau from the south but without success. They did, however, explore in the Adai Khokh group and made the first ascent of its principal summit. Holder made no attempt to exaggerate the technical difficulties of the climb: 'There was no crevasse to stumble over; nothing to strain our energies, no demand on skill or previous experience: simply a steady tramp through the snow.'[1] He did, however, note that the group presented excellent opportunites for the guideless mountaineer, with a considerable number of technical challenges still to be met. Other outlying areas also received attention. G. P. Baker and George Yeld climbed Bazarjuzi in Daghestan in 1890. Woolley, Solly and Newmarch visited Svanetia three years later and failed on what was obviously the greatest prize left in the Caucasus, the South Peak of Ushba. Woolley returned in 1895 and 1896, climbing Pik Woolley in the Shkhelda area.

The 1890s saw the first major German expedition to the Central Caucasus. In 1891 Gottfried Merzbacher (on his second visit) and Ludwig Purtscheller, with the guides J. Kehrer and J. Unterweger, made a whirlwind tour of the Caucasus in which they managed to tick off Tetnuld, make the first ascent of the highest peak of Dongusorun, climb all three summits of Laila, Adyrsu-Bashi and a new route on

Jangi-Tau. Heavy snowfall foiled an attempt on Ushba but, even so, the Editor of the *Alpine Journal* was hardly being just when he described it as a 'fairly successful tour in the Caucasus'.[2] This, however, was only a taste of the things to come when German mountaineers turned their attention to the Caucasus in earnest.

The 'last great problem' in the Caucasus was the Southern Peak of Ushba, far more imposing and technically difficult than the Northern Peak which Cockin had ascended in 1888. The problems posed by an attempt from the southern side were obvious. As is apparent from Donkin's photograph, the two principal features of the South Face are snowfields, one giving easy access to the summit and the other a con-siderable distance up the face. Between them lies a formidable rock band. It was clear to all those contemplating the climb that it could only be achieved if, first, a way could be found to the lower snowfield and, second, the rock band barring the way to the summit snowfield could be climbed. The 1890s passed without the second problem being solved (Donkin and Fox had reached the rock band in 1888 but found it far too difficult), and it was not until 1903 that a strong German-led team made a serious attempt on a route that was far ahead of the standards of seriousness and technical difficulty acceptable at the time. The expedition leader was Willi Rickmer Rickmers, a merchant and shipowner from Bremerhaven, who had already visited the range twice, with Amilius Hacker in 1895, then again with his wife in 1900. On his first visit Rickmers had made an unsuccessful attempt on Ushba, and he reconnoitred it sufficiently carefully to realise that he would need to come back with some of Europe's finest mountaineers if he was to have any chance of success.

It was 1903 before he returned with nine companions. They arrived at the foot of the mountain in July. The first of the two great challenges posed by the mountain was quickly solved. Adolf Schulze, Franz Scheck and Heinz Ficker, accompanied by a local hunter called Muratbi, man-aged to reach the lower snowfield by climbing steep rocks beside an avalanche-prone couloir. They then returned to camp where Rickmers and Ficker's sister Cenzi, the 'Maid of Ushba', were eagerly awaiting them. Scheck remained behind, but the next day the four climbers, with Muratbi as their porter, set off to try to find a way through the rock band separating the lower snowfield from the summit snowfield. They bivouacked that night on the lower snowfield. Reminiscing about the climb, Rickmers waxed lyrical about the presence of the 'Maid of Ushba'. 'Rarely, if ever, have mountaineers lived so luxuriously at such an elevation. For had we not a lady, a housewife, who not even in these surroundings could restrain the womanly impulse to help others? She prepared delicious ices of jam and snow, and made us feel quite at home.'[3]

When dawn appeared the following morning Cenzi von Ficker was up before the rest of the party making the tea. They climbed to the top of the lower snowfield and stopped just above the Red Corner where South and East Faces meet. Rickmers, doubtless with the purest of motives, stayed behind with Muratbi and the Ushba Maid, while Schulze and Ficker disappeared up the rock wall. Rickmers reports spending the time of enforced leisure very profitably. 'How shall I ever forget that snow shoulder under Ushba's summit, where she and I sat many hours, forgetful of the world below and ignorant of the future ... There we sat on the little patch of snow and talked and drifted into the great problems that move humanity, and we shirked none, for in the mountains is truth ... To us, a man and a woman in earnest converse, these were but the fit surroundings in which to discuss the questions of life.'[4]

We can only assume that the Ushba Maid shared these fine sentiments. She was clearly a young woman of rare charm and spirit. The local Svanetian prince, Tartarchan Dadeschkeliani (described as a cross between an English knight and a robber baron) was so captivated that, as she left for home, he made over Mount Ushba to her as a gift! She treasured the presentation document with its royal seal into old age, but appears to have made no formal claim on her property.

Higher on the mountain, while their support team were engaging the big issues, Schulze and Ficker wrestled with more material problems on the lower snowfield. Above the Red Corner the rock wall was only a couple of hundred feet high, but by three o'clock they had already been repulsed several times. Ficker quite sensibly suggested turning back, but Schulze was determined to make another attempt. They abandoned the wall above the corner and traversed westwards

Ushba from the south-east

along the top of the snowfield looking for a breach in the defences. They began to climb and then summoned Rickmers to join them.

> Up I flew as fast as my comrades' hands could pull ... After the first thirty feet the rocks became very difficult and I wondered how any man could climb them unaided from above. Now and then, in long intervals, came a muffled shout from above, telling me to follow the tugging rope, and exerting my powers to their highest I gained the next pitch, out of breath and half strangled

by the indispensable help from hands working behind the scenes at a higher level. After each hot and frantic effort came the cold wait at the next stand, and these waits grew longer and longer. I had only two ideas in my mind – that of securing myself and fixing the rope as well as was possible and the question, 'What is this? Why am I here?'[5]

At the sharp end of the rope Schulze was engaged in a Promethean struggle. He fought his way up a chimney, around an overhang and arrived at a steep and holdless slab. Halfway up it he realised that he could go neither up or down and had to hang there until Ficker could reach him and lend a shoulder to help him down. Still refusing to turn back, Schulze traversed to the right along a small ledge and disappeared out of sight. And then disaster struck:

> Suddenly I shuddered, for I heard a curious grating sound, and, peering out from my recess, I beheld the soles of two hob-nailed boots, toes upturned, facing valleywards. I knew enough to make me sick at heart, for a climber's feet should not tread air. Then came a long and agonising groan, and a short silence which seemed eternity. At last came Ficker's voice, bidding me render assistance, and saying that he was firm. A short scramble brought me to Schulze, the owner of the erratic boots, lying unconscious but babbling in delirium, his blood painting crimson a little piece of snow near which he lay.[6]

Schulze had fallen some eighty feet, the full length of the rope. The ledge he landed on probably saved the lives of all three climbers, for it broke the force of the fall which otherwise would have come entirely upon the unfortunate Ficker and sent them spinning off into the void. As it was, Rickmers wrote later in admiration, 'Ficker was stout, and Ficker held.' Rickmers and Ficker somehow managed to lower the unconscious Schulze back down to the relative safety of the snowfield. It was a magnificent rescue. The ropes were frozen and the weather deteriorating. Towards the end it was Rickmers alone who was lowering Schulze – Ficker's hand was damaged and it was all he could do to abseil down to meet his sister and Muratbi.

After spending the night in their old bivouac, they reached their camp the following day. Rickmers called it a day: 'I had a wife at home and the impressions I had received within were deeper and grander than any later conquest could have roused in my soul.'[7] Cenzi and Heinz von Ficker left with him. Incredibly, though, Schulze was undaunted. Four days later he went back up the mountain with fresh companions – Helbling, Reichert, Schuster and Weber. This time he tried the wall to the left of the slab. Realising he was too high, he lowered himself down a few feet and managed to climb diagonally upwards to beneath an overhang. It was the crux of the climb. With a loose piton for protection he hauled himself over and found relatively easy ground. Two more rope-lengths and they were on the summit snowfield. The top was reached at eight, just as darkness fell and after sixteen hours of climbing. Ushba still had a sting in her tail, however. An electric storm hit them on the summit snowfield and they spent a terrified night huddled in a little hollow in the snow before the sun returned and they could descend to celebrate what was certainly one of the boldest and most technically adventurous climbs undertaken before the First World War.

It was not, however, the only German triumph on Ushba that year. Less than two weeks later a competing Bavarian party arrived in the Ushba area. Dismayed to hear that their plans for the South Peak of Ushba had been forestalled by Schulze and his companions, L. Distel, G. Leuchs and H. Pfann turned their attentions to a traverse of both peaks from north to south. The successful climb was highly innovative, the first example of the demanding multi-day traverses that were subsequently to become a trademark of Caucasian mountaineering. From a bivouac near the foot of the North Peak they completed the traverse in four days, reaching the summit of the North Peak by a new route on the North Ridge, and then finding considerable difficulty in the last 500 feet before the summit of the South Peak, before descending Schulze's route down the barrier wall. It was another extremely impressive feat, and certainly showed that the Caucasus, despite the size and relative remoteness of its mountains, was at the forefront of mountaineering development at the time.

Although 1903 was by any account the year of the great continental successes, a rather more lighthearted British expedition was active at the same time. One of what Rickmer-Rickmers described as 'two semi-attached English freebooters' was the great Himalayan climber and explorer Tom Longstaff. He was then at the beginning of a long and distinguished career, perhaps the highlight of which was the impeccably lightweight ascent of Trisul in the Indian Himalaya in 1907 – at the time it was the highest summit yet climbed and remained so until Kamet was climbed in 1931. His exploits in the Caucasus were also rather impressive, although he characteristically downplays them.

Here, as for many of his Alpine climbs, he was partnered by the New Zealand-born mountaineer, Lancelot William Rolleston. Their first ascent of the West Peak of Shkhara by its South Ridge was a particularly fine coup, and it is worth bearing in mind that it still receives a grade of 5A, the same as Schulze's route on Ushba South! We reprint here the chapter on the Caucasus from his autobiography, *This My Voyage*. It is a delightful piece of writing, full of enthusiasm for the Caucasus, its mountains and its inhabitants. Written some forty-five years after his visit, his style is noticeably lighter in tone than that of the earlier pioneers (for whom, incidentally, he has a rather touching respect) and he is sensible enough not to dwell too long on the technical details of his climbs.

1 1868: first British climbing party in the Caucasus. Seated (left) Charles Comyns Tucker, and (right) Douglas William Freshfield, leader. The central figure is presumably Arthur W Moore, third member of the team. Standing second right is their Chamonix guide, François Devouassoud

2 The Karagom Glacier, photographed by Vittorio Sella.

3 William Donkin's photograph of Ushba from Betshoi.

4 Alfred Mummery, 1855-95, most forward-thinking British mountaineer of his day. With Heinrich Zurfluh he accomplished the first ascent of Dych-Tau.

5 Clinton Dent (right), Victorian surgeon-climber and President of the Alpine Club.

6 Dych Tau South-West Face, from Shkhara. Mummery's 1888 line largely follows the left-hand of the twin buttresses facing camera. The right-hand buttress was not climbed for another seventy years – by Mike Harris and George Band.

7 William Donkin and 8 Harry Fox, who disappeared with their two Swiss guides while attempting Koshtan-Tau in 1888.

9 Koshtan-Tau and the Ullu-Auz Glacier. Donkin's party is believed to have fallen while traversing the precipitious East Ridge (left), either from this, the north side, or from the south, where their last bivouac was found.

10 Camp near the Gulba Glacier, mid-August 1888 – one of Donkin's last photographs, Dent and Fox centre.

12 Kaspar Streich

Johann Fischer

13 The Sleeping Place discovered by the 1889 Search Expedition, drawn by H. Willink from a sketch made on the spot by Captain Powell.

14 The North Face of Tetnuld, climbed by John Jenkins and Micha[el] Taylor in 1937.

15 British expedition of 1937: (left to right) Robin Hodgkin, Bob Beaumont, John Jenkins and Micha[el] Taylor.

16 Sir John Hunt (centre), leader of the 1958 British Caucasus Expedition, seen here with Misha Khergiani (left) and Josef Kachiani.

17 Vitali Abalakov survived Stalinist persecution to become Honoured Master of Sport and preeminent figure of Caucasian mountaineering.

18 The twin peaks of Ushba from the Ushba Plateau. On the left, Little Ushba.

19 Pik Schurovski from the Shkhelda Glacier (Photo: Vilem Heckel)

20 Mick Fowler radioing success from the summit bivouac on Ushba.

10
The Finest Climb

by T. G. Longstaff

In 1903, having at long last taken my medical degrees, I felt that virtue should be rewarded. I persuaded Rolleston to take two months' holiday. Now for the frosty Caucasus, the goal of the Argonauts, the last refuge of Alastor. The great days of its exploration were over: Freshfield's book and his alluring map had been published and the last great unclimbed peaks were named and known. Willy Rickmers, of the well-known Heligoland family and an old alpine acquaintance, invited us to join his large party of continental climbers; but we preferred independence. Also we meant to snatch some of the plums from our Austrian and Bavarian rivals. We read it up. We studied the detailed maps of Freshfield and Merzbacher. We learned a smattering of Russian, which should be our lingua franca in these lands of many tongues.

In our preparations Hermann Woolley proved himself a most generous mentor. He was the last of the great ones in the Caucasus, a fine exponent of mountain craft and a personality of the rarest charm. We had realized in the Alps that mobility is the essence of happy travel. Rolleston is really a sybarite, a connoisseur of good living: but he knew his stuff. It is best to burden yourself with nothing but what is essential: anything more becomes a hindrance. We took one Whymper tent and, for high bivouacs, a very light silk Mummery tent, but with the improvement of a floor sewn in to keep out wind and snow. Our sleeping-bags were of eiderdown, weighing under 3 lbs. each. Our climbing rope was silk. We were to live on the country, carrying bags of small change therefor. For the mountains we needed some tinned food and biscuits, to be bought at Odessa. Two pack-horses should be enough. There must be no waiting for the assembly of a caravan each time we had to change transport.

So off by boat and train on the 16th July. Through upstart Berlin, with its blatant self-consciousness, and frowning Thorn to Alexandrovo on the frontier. The Russians were both friendly and helpful. But the ice-axes were beyond them and suspicion is ineradicable in the Russian mind. Englishmen going to the Caucasus to climb mountains? Absurd! We were gold-seekers. Those ice-axes were miners' picks: thus! and the action was illustrated. But *nichevo*, 'what matter': the commonest and most useful word in the language. Then on to lovely tragic Warsaw, last outlier of Europe. Through 700 miles of the hot Ukraine with its unending plains of ripening corn to Odessa, in those days the leading port of Europe for the export of wheat. At Odessa shopping and money-changing took a day.

Then off again by night across the Black Sea, where Venus was reflected like a moon and even the Milky Way shone in the black mirror of the Euxine. The Chersonese; Crim Tartary; the Crimea. Along these coasts were strung, before our era, a series of Ionian Greek settlements, fringing a barbarous hinterland of Iranian tribes. Later these were occupied by the Genoese, much as our East India merchants established factories on the coasts of the Indian peninsula. Such is Feodosia. There the East came aboard: Persian traders with scarlet-dyed beards and high caps; picturesque Turkish, Bulgarian and Armenian labourers; Greeks and Karait Jews; a chained gang of sad but evil-looking Tartars with their poor families, said to be on the weary road to Siberia.

The Caucasus is usually said to divide Europe from Asia. But few realize that Asia is on the north side and Europe on the south. The mountains protected European Georgia against a succession of Asiatic invasions which swept over the steppe to the north. Only within the last century has southern Russia been added to Europe and in many districts its native population is still Asiatic. The whole tradition of Georgia is European.

The straits of Kertsch seemed a strong dividing line: once past them we began to sense the Caucasus. Forest begins. The coasts become steep and richly wooded right down to the shore. There was snow on the cloud-capped ranges inland. We passed the mouth of the Kodor rushing down from the trackless fever-stricken forests of Abkhasia, home of the great wisent, that bison so vividly depicted in the prehistoric drawings of the Spanish caves. At Soukhum Kale we discovered Georgia. The first swaggering Mingrelians came on board in pointed flapping *bashliks* and long tight-fitting coats with ornamented cartridge slots at the breast and narrow silver-studded belts with the ivory-handled *kinjal* at their slender waists. The *kinjal* is like the sword the warrior holds on a black-figured Greek vase: short, broad, two-edged blades, sharply pointed but only 15 inches long: altogether Mycenean in type. And these men are Europeans.

At Batum, anciently Georgian, later Turkish and now Russian, we sought out the British Consul. He introduced us to his American colleague who at once recommended to us one of his own camp-servants, a young Georgian, Nestor: his open face did not belie his character. He would take charge of our base camps and interpret our scanty Russian into the several Georgian dialects we should meet. We had cause to be very grateful to our American benefactor. Sound local advice is priceless at the start in any new venture.

At this time there was trouble at Baku, followed by great unrest in Batum soon after we left, and friendly Russians warned us against going to the mountains and most of all against venturing into lawless Svanetia. But the Consuls advised us that it was only along the Turkish and Persian frontiers that things were bad, though the Russian mail had just been cut up at Artvine and all the Cossack escort killed.

At Batum we took train to Kutais, the historic Cyta of the Greeks. Colchis at last, the home of Medea. And I remembered Clinton Dent – his face like Odysseus – giving a lecture at Eton on his travels in the Caucasus, and my boast that I would go there. Now the dream had come true. This river Rion was the Phasis from whose sands the Fleece was loaded with gold and which, through Greece and Rome, gave its name to our pheasant. This western Georgia has been a link between Europe and Asia for eons. Georgians have ruled and swayed policy widely: Georgian nobles had great influence at Persian courts: Georgians went with Nadir Shah to conquer India, and once garrisoned Kandahar. Prince Bagration, the hero of the Russian retreat of 1805, was from Imeretia. Marshal Stalin (Djugashvili) is a Georgian from Gori near Tiflis.

From Kutais we drove along the great Russian military road, the Ossetinsky Daroga. We were bound for Orbeli, gateway to Svanetia. I was entranced by the laurel trees, with us so suburban dull, but here decked with profusion of flowers: and we picked delicious wild figs, cranberries and raspberries, and bought a bucket of yellow peaches for fourpence. Because of a note left by Rickmers at Batum we had picked up Ernst Platz, a German painter left behind sick, and taken him along with us. Now on the road we ran straight into Makandaroff, Rickmers' dragoman: a most competent bearded desperado speaking about a dozen languages, including French. He was to convoy the invalid and assist us in crossing the barrier of the Laila. Our meeting was providential: for the road got very bad at Alpana and our driver, with flagging horses, refused to go on. Makandaroff instantly produced an *arba*, an ox-cart, into which we dumped the baggage under charge of Nestor, while we walked the last miles into Orbeli, an ancient town on the first foothills of the Caucasus. We slept on the table of the *cancelleria*, the court-house being the only available quarters for travellers in these parts. But the bugs either dropped from the ceiling or crawled up the table legs, for we were thoroughly well bitten by the morning. We now took horse and pushing ahead of the baggage rode beside the roaring Skenis Skali through luxuriant deciduous forests. There is a cowboy dash about Georgian horsemen, who make it a point of honour never to dismount for a difficulty, but rather to ride the harder the worse the track becomes: nor, however long the day, will they halt for food until the journey is done. It was pitch dark as we crossed the river and galloped into Lentekhi.

The village lies at the foot of the Laila range, at a parting of ways. Platz, with Nestor and the baggage were to cross by the easy Latpari pass, Rolleston and I to traverse the highest peak of the range away to the north-west. Makandaroff insisted on coming with us, bringing four Svans as porters, for now we had to walk. The track led through high forest beside the Kheledula torrent, past a few clearings with fields of maize. The forests are full of bears and maize they cannot resist: so in each field a platform is raised on stakes and on it is set an iron cresset to hold fire at night: all night a man must sit there, ringing a bell and uttering monotonous and doleful cries to protect the crops. We camped, that is we lit a fire, beside the hamlet of Djudari, and bought a small pig for the solace of our men.

We were off early next morning up the Skimeri glen, at first through close forest, then through thinning alpine woods and so eventually clear of the trees. At the edge of the brushwood, at about 10,000 feet, we made our bivouac directly under the peak of Laila, and slept in the open under a full moon, happy to be freed from compulsion of made trails.

The following morning we made an early start and got up to the Laila Pass of Freshfield's map. Here we left Makandaroff and the Svans to descend the easy glacier into the head of the Khudesh glen lying west of our peak. They would thence cross a secondary ridge to the north and get down to Betsho. We made a dash for our peak, Laila, 13,400 feet, and despite cloud got up easily in two hours, though cheated of the view we so much desired. In another hour we had rejoined Makandaroff's party and from the saddle of the secondary ridge, at about 9,000 feet, we got our view—a first sight of double-crowned Ushba, the Terrible: the grandest peak in the Caucasus, cliff piled on cliff soaring up ice-clad, more beautiful even than the twin-peaked Nanda Devi, its Himalayan counterpart, and putting the Matterhorn to shame by its massive symmetry of composition. We overlooked the valley of the upper Ingur and could see the village of Betsho beyond, at the very foot of Ushba. Betsho was the home of our four Svans, and they stood praying to the spirits of forest and hill and to the rivers of their homeland. These Svans are the turbulent Soanes of Strabo. The people of inner or free Svanetia were christianized so long ago, and have since lived in such isolation, that they have forgotten the tenets of their faith. The tribal elders used to keep the few churches locked except for one day in the year, when the priest was admitted to perform a service alone. I suspect that traces of Manicheanism and even of the more ancient sun-worship of Mithras might be discovered by the erudite. Virtually they were pagans, though the Russians had sent in a few Orthodox priests and a few Georgian school teachers in an attempt to reclaim them.

Still with Ushba magnificent before us we descended the flank of the Laila range to Skomari, or Tobalt as Freshfield's map has it. Here Prince Dadarkhan Dadishkiliani invited us to his house for tea, and kept us to dinner. This was a surprisingly sudden contact with western culture, for his entertainment and his family circle were completely European and we might have been in France. With all the charm and understanding of an aristocrat, the head of a clan, the prince cheerfully admitted that he had little control over his own tribesmen and none whatever in upper Svanetia, whither we were bound, where every man lived armed against his neighbour, acknowledging no master. It is tragically wasteful that such families as the Dadishkiliani should have been eliminated from Georgia by the Russian revolution.

It was difficult to withdraw from this pleasant social interlude and it was long after dark when we entered Betsho, thirteen days after we had left London. Here we met Willy Rickmers' party. After five attempts they had just climbed the forbidding south peak of Ushba. The successful ascent had been led by Schulze, of Munich, despite a severe fall at his first attempt when his life was only saved by the rope through the skill and intrepidity of Heinz von Ficker, one of the foremost young Austrian climbers of his day. The more I heard from them and the more I looked at Ushba the more relief I felt that it was not for us to attempt. We would snatch Tiktingen (15,267 feet) before Rickmers' stalwarts could recover from their ordeal. This was now the highest unclimbed peak in the Caucasus; but Tiktingen was far away on the main water-parting at the head of the great Zanner glacier: while here, from Betsho, we could make a nodding acquaintance with Elbruz and the sources of the Kuban and maybe overlook mysterious Abkhasia. With these objects in view we decided to make for Lakra, only 12,185 feet, but unclimbed: judging from the map it was the very view-point we wanted.

Leaving Betsho on the last day of July with a couple of Svan porters we walked up the wild Kuish glen to a *kosh*, as any hunter's bivouac is called. This *kosh* was just below the Kuish glacier in easy reach of our peak and a most delightful spot. Fortunately the weather was fine, for the rocks were vertical and offered no shelter. The Svans couched on the ground wrapped in their dark goat-skin *burkhas*. We were off alone next morning, going slowly up the Kuish glacier straight for the saddle between Leirag and Lakra, negotiating the upper ice fall and the final steep slope in three hours. Our climbing-irons saved time, obviating step-cutting except on the steepest ice. Then we turned southerly up the snowy north ridge of our peak. Soon Betsho horsemen.

They had no stomach for trusting themselves amongst these cut-throat hillmen, and also, it appeared, Nestor had refused them food from our scanty store. Led by Gramiton, a trouble-maker, the men struck for double pay: we refused to be blackmailed: Gramiton laid hand to his pistol: I hitched forward in my saddle exposing my holster, but did not move my hand towards the revolver, for it is a fool's trick to draw unless you are prepared to shoot at once and take the consequences. For a moment Gramiton weighed the chances, but the others gave him no support. We told him to be off instantly, using the insulting phrase a Russian would use to a dog and he seized his two horses and galloped back down the track without a word. Then one Constanti Devdarian, who knew a little French, came to our assistance, and we got off at last with two pack-horses and two Betsho men, but with no mounts for ourselves. We were now on the track to the Zanner pass, which leads over the main range to the Bezingi Tartar country. Probably our men thought we must be bound for Bezingi and feared to enter a Moslem district, for at the last village, Jabesh, where we camped that night, they announced their irrevocable decision to leave us, and cleared off. It was raining hard as we pitched our tent while Nestor stood guard over the abandoned baggage. A hunter came up, stood silent, and watched us. Without a word he started in and lent a hand. This Araman Kordiani turned out a jewel and never left us, and we had no more trouble with our men. His Russian vocabulary was as limited as ours, but it sufficed. He was a real Svan highlander: a tiny man hidden in shaggy *burkha* with *bashlik* worn turban-wise, or in bad weather with the tails draped round his shoulder, complete with sheepskin-covered rifle and the inevitable *kinjal* at his waist. Self-contained, tough, sleeping always in the open, he would carry any weight and at the end of a march or at a shout from the Mummery tent before dawn at a high bivouac, would produce tea inside ten minutes. Nestor, and how often did we bless the good American consul for lending him, was a Mingrelian and the Svans were sticky with him and he was in fear of them, but Araman could always get us a sheep or chickens if any were to be had. Best of all he knew the local men, and could secure us good porters.

Next morning we set off for our attempt on Tiktingen with a couple of hunters to carry our light mountain kit, leaving Araman to keep the nervous Nestor company at our Jabesh base camp, pitched in a thicket some distance from the village. A faint track led for two hours through exquisite woodland, broken by glades of the tallest flowers I have ever seen—great blue larkspurs six feet high and more. Then up a grassy spur studded with late alpine flowers, above the terminal ice-fall of the great Zanner glacier. We took to the ice and found it easy going until we came to the second ice-fall, which we avoided by crossing to a grassy spur on the glacier's left bank. We came across the skeleton of a fine *tur*, first cousin to the ibex: it had probably been killed by an avalanche during the previous winter, for the bones were not scattered, as by bears. Finally we selected a camp site on the edge of the moraine at about 10,500 feet. In front was the uncompromising mammoth ice of the Zanner glacier; at our back a mantle of lilac rhododendron swept up to the spurs of Lyaler. A lovely site and a gorgeous evening. But away up the glacier Tiktingen loomed most forbidding: very bare of snow for so high a peak and therefore very steep. In 1893 a strong party consisting of Woolley, Cockin, Solly and Newmarch had climbed the western ridge to within a few hundred feet of the summit. Where they had failed we thought it hopeless to try. The south face was appallingly steep and probably raked by stone falls. There was nothing for it but to try and get up to the top of the great east wall that connects Tiktingen with Salyinan Bashi, and so follow this ridge to the summit. This would mean a very long climb, for the glasses showed no possibility of getting up on to the wall anywhere near the peak.

We were up at two next morning: but the weather looked worse than doubtful and rain delayed us till three-thirty. The glacier was difficult by lantern light for its surface was very rough and crevasses numerous. Fortunately we did not encounter snow-bridges, till daylight came, murky. At six we were halted by a vicious hailstorm. Scratching a hollow in the snow we set our backs to the storm and pretended to enjoy breakfast and the lightning. The reward of good reconnoitring came when we discovered that we could reach the great east ridge by the route chosen. I was very despondent about weather prospects, but the good De'il was resolute. Another couple of hours up easy but rather rotten rock ribs, in lowering weather with more hail, landed us on the top of the east wall. This was our first close sight of the northern country: barren and inhospitable compared to the forested valleys of Svanetia, with a suggestion of approach to the naked steppe. But time pressed: we turned west along the ridge: very steep on the north and soon to be still steeper on the south. The first big tower was difficult; slabby and plastered with hail-rotted snow; we had to climb straight over it. More towers followed. It took us three and a half hours, going all out, to reach the highest tower of all, above the deep notch, so visible from afar, at the east foot of the final rocky pyramid of Tiktingen. It was Rolleston's confident resolution that had kept me going, for I hate and fear bad weather on a high peak. It was noon. If we could get down into the gap the peak was ours: but the descent from this great tower was very awkward. I tried leading straight down the rock face, but two large separate handholds gave way and I came on the rope. With Rolleston above I knew I was perfectly safe, so swung in, got holds and continued down. But it got worse, with no possibility of belaying the last man, so I gave it up and climbed back to the top of the tower. Rolleston went straight for the only alternative, a vicious curving ice ridge running very steeply down to the notch. The drop on both sides was alarming. The knife edge of ice seemed like a crouching beast hunching its shoulders to thrust us down the abyss. My companion was in his element for he is a dominating personality on steep ice; but it took him nearly an hour to cut hand- and footholds down to the notch, while I paid out only seventy feet of the rope. There he had a safe stance on good snow and I could follow. The old De'il had done the trick. We were in cold cloud but the rocks of the final peak were easier than we had dared to hope and in another one and a half hours we stood on the summit. Alas there was no inducement to stay: we built a very small cairn on an overhanging rock just west of the highest crag and turned down at two-thirty. Back through a searching cold wind and recurrent hail storms: but we had our old tracks to follow. Lower down new snow made it exhausting work: then rain fairly drenched us and to keep continuously alert was a hard strain. I think even the tough De'il was thankful to get back to camp at nine-thirty and gulp a hot drink brewed by our bearded hunter. Then the wind really got going: thunder, lightning, hail and rain all night. Tiktingen was very angry. Next morning we scurried down, still in rain, to our main camp at Jabesh, very wet and very cold. Off with our sodden clothes and into our sleeping-bags, where Nestor fed us with my own special Caucasian dish. It has great merits. A chicken is boiled in plenty of water with a cupful of rice. The diners start with as many cups of soup as they can drink. Then comes the chicken, which may literally be a *pièce de résistance*: but no matter if you are hungry. Finally, at the bottom there is the rice pudding. A complete three-course dinner in one cooking-pot.

Next day was given up to the sheer delight of idleness and the drying of clothes and gear. Still intent on the flesh-pots we bought a black, fat-tailed sheep for ten shillings, which Nestor considered a most exorbitant price—"but then Svans are swine." Araman produced a stocky, bearded hunter, Bitta Zourabiani, as a porter—a likely man who had a very old Berdan rifle which he kept permanently loaded and at full cock; the sear had gone, so the bolt was held back by a bit of stick, but if this fell out the gun went off.

The challenge of Tiktingen having been met we could now indulge ourselves in a treat. We would repeat the ascent of the great pyramid of Tetnuld (15,918 feet), one of the grandest peaks in the whole chain, whose summit view, Freshfield, its first climber, accounted the finest in all the Caucasus. As Nestor was feeling more at home and confident in our little camp in the coppice, comfortably private from the village of Jabesh, with whose people, however, he was now on friendly terms, we could take both Araman and Bitta with us, and so lighten our own sacks. On August 8th we went back to the snout of the Zanner and crossed to the right moraine of the Nageb glacier. The hunters pointed out tracks of bear and *tur*, but we were unlucky and saw neither. Near the end of the moraine we found a good *kosh* under an overhanging cliff, the back smoke-blackened by the bivouac fire of hunters. This was probably the very spot where Freshfield camped for the first ascent in 1887. That evening we prospected and marked the way on to the glacier and through the first crevasses.

In the morning we left the men in camp and got off early (2.10). Working up the Nageb glacier we made for the south ridge of our peak, while a gorgeous sunrise lit bands of cloud across the crown of Ushba behind us. Over the ridge itself the going is comparable to the Bionnas-say arête of Mont Blanc, but much steeper. Tetnuld is only a little higher than Mont Blanc, but a far finer peak, rising as an isolated cone rather than as the culminating point of a great massif. As we rose the slopes on the east side of our ridge got very steep: to the west was a sheer-looking drop of thousands of feet to the Nageb glacier. The condition of the snow was perfect for crampons and we had little step-cutting. But we both felt the altitude and went rather slowly. After seven and a half hours' actual going we reached the top (11.10) in a mild hail-storm, which drove us down to get back into the sunlight and enjoy the view Freshfield had promised us. From Elbruz to Kasbek the whole Caucasus was displayed and to the south all central Georgia backed by the mountains on the Turkish frontier and the highlands of Armenia.

We came down quickly in little over three hours to our bivouac, greeted with food ready. The men made up the loads with quick competence, refusing to let us carry anything. Bitta Zourabiani led off straight down the Negeb glacier instead of following the windings of the moraine. He was wearing oval crampons, *sheni*, made by forging together two old horse-shoes set with spikes and bound under the instep with rawhide thongs. He went at a terrific pace down the glacier, having *our* crampons inside his sack, and was immensely pleased when we had to cut a step or two where he had passed light foot. He was very intelligent and he discussed Franks of various races: yet great was his surprise to learn that Germans were Christians. Though very anti-Russian he had absorbed their profound national aversion to the 'Nemetsky'—those 'tongueless' people lacking human speech, as the Russians call the *Herrenvolk*.

On August 10th we moved down to Mujal. There we were entertained by the Russian orthodox priest, who, like all his brethren here, was glad of any break in his loneliness among unlettered pagans. Rickmers had urged us to visit the great Leksur glacier and have a shot at one of the several unclimbed peaks at its head. The Leksur is the biggest glacier system between Ushba and Tiktingen, due north of Mestia, the village of splendid towers, through which we had already ridden on our way from Betsho for Tiktingen. There is a snow pass at the head of the glacier sometimes used by travellers to Urusbieh in the Tartar country at the eastern foot of Elbruz. The upper ice basin extends about eight miles from west to east and is surrounded by a number of striking peaks, most of which had not at the time been climbed. We rode on to Mestia, pitching our tent in a clean open spot near the *cancelleria*. That night the vision of the moonrise over the gleaming white pyramid of Tetnuld with the dark stone village towers in the foreground kept me up late, and I browsed on Shelley for an hour, like a good Victorian.

In the morning we bought a sheep and a goose for eleven shillings and secured four horses and two men to carry ourselves and the gear up to the Leksur glacier. The track we now followed was the worst we had met, but we dared not dismount for our credit's sake, even when a baggage horse fell and almost rolled into the torrent. Because of the rough going we failed to reach the foot of the glacier, but camped in the last of the birch trees, where there was grazing for the horses. The following day we carried our light camp and food up the left side of the glacier and found an ideal bivouac under the steep spurs of Margyan-na with good water and a little rhododendron for our fire. From there we sent back a man to help Nestor at our base camp. From the bivouac we could now see our peaks. There was plenty of choice. Rolleston thought that the west peak of Latsga, Ullu-tau-tschana, marked 4,203 metres on Merzbacher's map, looked the most interesting, and made out a good line of attack. On the morrow we made the first ascent of this peak in glorious weather, getting up by the south-west ridge with no particular difficulty. From the top the Highlands of Armenia were clear and we thought we could make out Ararat itself: and towards the Black Sea rose the snowy peaks about the sources of the Kodor river, with the bare valley of Urusbieh and the huge dome of Elbruz to the north-west. For contrast away over beyond Bezingi to the north-east towered Dykhtau, a Rodin rock mass, and for sheer beauty of line there was Tetnuld, all steep ice and snow, standing alone. Gem-like amid the austerity of the scene a wall-creeper, crimson and plum-coloured, with half-open wings and fanned tail, clung to the final rocks of the summit. It sang a tenuous song of happy repetition as it crept mouse-like across the slabs. The wall-creeper (*Tichodroma muraria*) is my favourite bird, an old friend of the Alps and afterwards of the Himalaya, yet this was the only time I have heard the wild beauty of its song.

After a day well spent in complete idleness at our lovely bivouac we decided to try Bashil-tau (13,685 feet), an unclimbed peak we had reconnoitred from Ullu-tau-tschana. Bashil-tau lay at the extreme eastern end of the basin of the Leksur glacier, a long way from our bivouac, so we got off at midnight under a brilliant moon. We had to cross the glacier, clear of snow at this level, to the right moraine, to get round a bad ice-fall: above this we turned east, leaving the route to the Mestia pass on our left hand, and wound our way slowly through strange scenery of ice where the crevasses and schrunds were the biggest either of us had ever seen. This was the only time we felt that it was risky to be only two on the rope, and we were relieved to reach (7.20) the saddle at the foot of the north-west ridge of our peak. Looking over to the north side of the range we gazed on a new world, in complete contrast to the ice mazes we had crept through for hours. We could now see the limestone foothills edging the northern steppe and at our feet, on the Chegem side, the melting waters of the Bashil glacier sped away as the river Bashilauzu-su, bound for the distant Caspian (Su— river—is a word certainly directly imported from Central Asia). At eight o'clock we started to climb the great north-west ridge, set with gendarmes, some of which we outflanked by traverses on the forbidding west face, but the rock was so rotten that we preferred to climb several of the towers direct, sticking rigorously to the more difficult but safer crest of the ridge. Then the rocks were interrupted by an unexpectedly steep ice-slope where Rolleston took the lead again, cutting big steps. After the ice the ridge steepened, but the rocks were firm and warm in the sun, though clouds were piling up from the coasts of the Black Sea. At noon we gained the summit; our fourth virgin peak. This very good four hours' climb up the ridge, had been just difficult enough to be stimulating, but misliking the look of the sky we only remained a few minutes to nibble some food, while we admired Tiktingen which had so nearly defeated us. We retraced our morning route, going as fast as we could, for it was essential to clear those big crevasses by daylight. Just below the *bergschrund*, the big crevasse below the saddle, we were brought to a sudden stop. A huge snow-bridge, which we had safely crossed in the cold of dawn, had collapsed; forty feet of it dropped into a staggering ice-gulf with vertical sides. Our morning foot marks were cut clean at each brink. Displaying his usual ice-craft Rolleston circled the *schrund* and found a skimpy snow-bridge which would serve, if delicately handled. After many windings, but no hitch, he got us back to our morning's route through the labyrinth of big crevasses on to easier ground. We got down to our bivouac by seven o'clock. We had been out nineteen hours with few and brief halts, and now devoured all the food in camp, and as there was no breakfast to delay us, we reached our base camp in the birch grove early next morning, to gorge on Nestor's *shishlik*, gobbets of mutton alternated with chunks of fat skewered on a stick and grilled in the flames of a wood fire: a princely dish.

We now lost a few days from bad weather, with new snow on the mountains, and it was time to be off to Shkara. It would take three full days to reach its foot and by then we hoped the new snow would have settled into good order. From Mestia we rode over the Uguir pass to Ipari. Amongst some grand old fir trees we heard a grating call which was new to me: then saw, in laboured flight from tree to tree, two black, satanic-looking birds with marked crests—the great black woodpecker (*Dryocopus martius*)—a bird I had not then met in the Alps. From Ipari we rode on to Ushkul, the last village group on the Ingur river, in a barren and treeless glen. Both the Russian priest and the Georgian schoolmaster offered us entertainment, but we had to push on, and we camped an hour above the village, in a convenient thicket, with the south face of Shkara in full view.

Shkara is the second highest peak of the Caucasus. Its south face has been likened to the great Macugnaga face of Monte Rosa. The summit ridge is well over a mile long coming to a point at each end. The eastern one (17,036 feet) had already been climbed from the north by Cockin, with Ulrich Almer and Roth in 1888. The western peak (16,592 feet) which looked more impressive from our camp was unclimbed, and no one had yet set foot on the great southern wall facing us.

On August 23rd with Araman and his friend Simon, another bearded hunter, we struck up the right bank of the infant Ingur river mounting grassy slopes such as would have resounded to cowbells in the Alps. We followed the morainic ridge on the right bank of the Shkara glacier below the point marked 3,043 metres on Merzbacher's map. We pitched the Mummery tent on a natural platform at about 10,500 feet, which was not really high enough for our need, but was too tempting to pass by. Opposite was spread the whole lovely range of the Laila, its sweeping spurs forest-clad: away to the east we overlooked Imeretia and the hills of the Ossete clans, famed in war, and beyond lay the peak of Kasbek and the Dariel pass, through which goes the great road from Vladikavkaz to Tiflis, capital of Georgia. Vladikavkaz means Key of the Caucasus, just as Vladivostok means Key of the East.[7] On modern maps the name has been unromantically changed to Ordzhonikidze, but as he has been recently liquidated the name will probably be changed again.

We had examined the western peak of Shkara from the west and also in face and had seen that a well-marked ridge led directly to the summit. There was a little wall of rock just below the top which might be difficult: and again, some distance below this, were slabby, snow-covered rocks which might check us. It was a fine direct route, but we had not yet seen the way to get on to the beginning of this great ridge. It was the more unwise that we allowed doubtful weather to delay our start next morning till five-twenty. There is no risk in *starting* early in doubtful weather; but the flesh is weak. We scrambled down to the Shkara glacier and traversed snow slopes under a gloomy cliff with a blind corner ahead. This revealed a deep rock-strewn ravine with a hanging glacier above it from which stones and ice must often fall: but on the far side we could get on to our ridge. As the weather improved we bolted across the danger zone in a few minutes, and on to our ridge which began with easy snow slopes broken by rather rotten rock. Then, of a sudden, we found ourselves looking down upon a knife-edge of snow, with excessively steep slopes falling away on either hand. At our feet the narrow crest led abruptly downwards: then it ran horizontal for about 200 feet, to rise steep again to the continuing rocky crest. This passage which we had to take astride was like the well-known Brenva ice-ridge on Mont Blanc, but longer: an unpleasant place to leave behind us because the snow would be pretty rotten late in the afternoon. Beyond it we encountered easy rocks alternating with snow crests, with only an occasional step to cut in ice. As we had feared, the ledges leading up to the upper section of our ridge were particularly vile, rather steep and with ice-covered slabs dripping with melting snow. Above this warm dry rocks suggested a halt at one-forty-five. Here an eagle circled round: we could see its eyes: we remembered Prometheus. We were still fully three hours from the summit, and if we went on we would have to pass the night on the mountain. But the weather was now fine and we were both in very good form: we had only to go on and the peak was ours. So on we went, with Rolleston in the lead, along our narrowing ridge, with sheering slopes on either side, carefully noting several ledges where we could spend the night on the descent. The condition of the snow improved, but in one case steps had to be cut for a short distance into hard ice. Then we faced the final rock step below the summit. It had looked awkward through glasses, but there was a mantel-shelf on to which Rolleston boosted me, prodding my tail with his axe as I clawed at iced finger-holds. The passage seemed very exposed, but was fortunately short and we landed above it on easy snow. The actual summit (16,592 feet), which we reached at four-forty was a vast cornice and our small cairn had to be made on a rock outcrop just below it.

This was the highest climb we had made, yet we felt no effects from the altitude, unless it was the curious feeling of aloofness from the world below that we both experienced. We only had time to gaze over to the north at the great peak of Dykhtau rising so abruptly from the Bezingi glacier in the deep gulf below us. We had to hurry down, but as we moved one at a time, the heavyweight first, the last man could often spare an eye for the wonderful view over Georgia as the sun set and to Ararat, across the Turkish frontier, overlooking Persian lands. But the going was not easy for the last man, who had often to turn and come down backwards, which is hard to do quickly. Also the melting snow had now frozen on the rocks and a slip would have been very dangerous. In the very last of the light we reached the ledge at the foot of the steep final section of the ridge. We could not get down even to the highest of the sheltering rocks we had noted on the way up and had to spend the night on a narrow shelf with no hitch for the rope:

we could sit with dangling legs, but there could be no dozing. Gingerly taking off wet boots and stockings we wrapped our feet in dry socks and putties and thrust them into our rucksacks. The height was about 14,500 feet and after midnight we felt the cold. We took it in turns to hold the lantern between our knees for warmth, and later Rolleston boldly lit our little snow melter: but 'who can hold a fire in his hand by thinking on the frosty Caucasus?' His clothes were sadly scorched.

Slow and stiff we started down at five o'clock next morning. The narrow snow ridge was well frozen and we managed it quickly, reaching our bivouac without incident just before noon. Faithful Araman had seen our lantern in the night and had tea and grilled mutton ready for us. Then welcome sleep till four, and so down to camp. As we passed the tent, for we could only cross the stream below camp, we hailed Nestor to get a meal going. No answer. This was too much for Simon the Svan: 'the Georgian swine sleeps.' He unslung his rifle and loosed a shot, apparently at the tent, which brought Nestor scuttling out.

I count this as the finest climb I have ever had. The altitude is about the limit for alpine standards. There is no excessive difficulty on the great southern spur which we followed, though it is very long and demands constant attention, especially on the descent. The peak itself and every foot of the way was all new, and it was a good ending to a great season of seven peaks in twenty-nine days' climbing, five of them first ascents.

From *This My Voyage*, 1950

11
The End of an Era

The decade following the great ascents of 1903 was relatively quiet, in the Caucasus at least, if not in the world at large. There was no question of the range being played out, but it is probably true that after the successful expeditions to Ushba there were fewer obvious challenges. By now the major peaks had all been ascended. It was in many ways a situation comparable to that in the Alps at the end of the so-called Golden Age (traditionally identified with Whymper's ascent of the Matterhorn in 1865), and to that in the Himalaya after the 1950s. The time was ripe for attention to smaller, perhaps more technically difficult, peaks in outlying areas, and to new routes on the major peaks. In addition, the trend was now towards guideless climbing. Climbing with a guide, which had been the norm in the nineteenth century, now became the exception in the Caucasus.

It would be an exaggeration to say that by this stage the range had been tamed, but the central areas had certainly lost much of their mystery. Better maps were available, some sort of consensus was being reached on the names and heights of the peaks, and the rudiments of a tourist industry were beginning to be developed. In 1904 the first climbing guide to the range was published. V. A. Merkulof's *Guide to the Mountains of the Caucaus* (unfortunately available only in Russian) contained details of twenty-nine routes on or around the main peaks, including Ushba, Dych-Tau and Koshtan-Tau. It was issued by the Crimea-Caucasian Mountain Club, which was also beginning to build huts in the region. A few years later A. J. Afanasieff produced a far more comprehensive guide, with details of a hundred routes. Equally significant was the wealth of detailed information available in the journals of the British, German, Italian and Austrian Alpine Clubs. Few if any climbers in the Caucasus failed to write a detailed account of their expeditions, often with carefully drawn maps, and on the basis of these it was becoming possible to plan in advance fairly complicated itineraries. Of course, the Caucasus was (and still is) far less developed and visited than even the most out-of-the-way corners of the Alps, but no longer was it the savage and unknown quantity encountered by Freshfield and the early pioneers.

Why, then, were there no British visitors to the Caucasus between Longstaff and Rolleston's expedition in 1903 and that of Raeburn, Ling and Young ten years later? Perhaps the degree to which the Caucasus was becoming developed was responsible. Most of the Alpine Club members who went to the Caucasus in the footsteps of Freshfield during the nineteenth century were mountaineers in the traditional sense of the word. They journeyed to the Caucasus in a spirit of exploration, to cross passes that had never been crossed, to scale unclimbed peaks and to travel in a range where the majesty of the surroundings was matched by the sense of adventure that came with genuine discovery. While there was still much left to be done in the Caucasus in the first decade of the twentieth century, this primitive desire for pure mountain exploration could no longer be satisfied there. And so attention was turned to other, less travelled ranges, to the Himalaya, where Longstaff made the first ascent of Trisul in 1907, where Kellas climbed Pauhunri and Chomiomo in 1910, and where Meade made his three attempts on Kamet in 1910, 1912 and 1913; to the Rockies and the Selkirks in Canada, to the Andes and to the New Zealand Alps.

But there is another explanation for this turn to pastures new. By the twentieth century the British domination of mountaineering was well and truly over. The gentlemen of the Alpine Club and their guides no longer enjoyed a monopoly on significant ascents. The rise in technical standards that increased unabated up to and after the First World War was one to which British climbers contributed little. The great figures of the time were Austrian, German, Swiss and Italian, and their major climbs were mainly long and technically demanding rock climbs. One thinks of Paul Preuss' solo ascent of the East Face of the Campanile di Basso in 1911, or of his ascent of the South-East Ridge of the Aiguille Blanche de Peuterey; of Tita Piaz, known as the Devil of the Dolomites; of the Gugliermina brothers who made the first ascent of the Brouillard Ridge on Mont Blanc in 1901; of Hans Dülfer who invented the concept of the *directissima*; of Gustav Hasler who climbed the North Face of the Finsteraarhorn in 1904, the first of the great Alpine north faces to fall; of Guido Rey and his magnificent obsession with the Matterhorn. The only British climbers who could compare with these and other great continental climbers were Valentine Ryan and Geoffrey Winthrop Young, and it is true to say that the main body of British climbing was left far behind by the revolution in technical standards that swept through the Alps at the beginning of the twentieth century. The British went to the Rockies or to the Himalaya because there they could do what they were good at – exploratory mountaineering in a style for which there was no longer any scope nearer home.

Whatever the reason, the fact remains that when Harold Raeburn, William Norman Ling and J. R. Young went to the Caucasus in 1913 they were the first Britons to climb in the range for ten years. The intervening decade, of course, had seen a certain amount of activity. Much of it took place away from the great peaks of the Central Caucasus, in the relatively little climbed eastern and western ends of the range. The Western Caucasus was visited in 1904 by the Russian climber Alexander von Meck with the Swiss Andreas Fischer (who had already visited the range in 1889 in search of his brother who had disappeared with Donkin, Fox and Streich). They were accompanied by two guides, one of whom was Russian, and between them made first ascents of several minor peaks in the Alibek and Kistinka areas.[1] Two Italians, Vittorio Ronchetti and Ferdinando Colombo, made several expeditions to the Adai Khokh, in 1907, achieving some useful exploration and a first ascent in the Mamison group.[2] In the first decades of Caucasian exploration women had been conspicuous by their absence, with the honourable exceptions of Frau Rickmer Rickmers and the Maid of Ushba. In 1909 and 1910, however, the Austrian Helene Kuntze made a determined attempt to redress the balance, achieving first ascents of the South Peak of Nakhasbita and of Sugan-Tau in the Bogkhobashi group, as well as several other ascents. Mention should also be made of the four German climbers, Dr Walther Fischer, Viktor von Friedrichs, Dr Gustav Kuhfahl and Oscar Schuster (a veteran of the South Peak of Ushba in 1903) who climbed in the Kazbek area in 1910 and 1911, with first ascents of the South Peak of Resi-Khokh, Ziti-Khokh, and Zariut-Khokh on their first visit, and Kalasan-Tau, the Eastern Peak of Silga-Khokh, Shau-Khokh, the Central and Northern Peaks of Resi-Khokh and Tsmiakom-Khokh the following year. Fischer and Schuster returned in 1913 with Hermann Renner and added Lagau-Khokh to their list.

In the Central Caucasus five Bavarian climbers, Max Winkler, W. Gruber, Alexander Lechner, Alexander Thal and Rudolf Wandel had a particularly successful season in 1912. Their first outing was a repeat of Cockin, Holder and Woolley's 1888 route on the North Ridge of Dych-Tau, with two members of the party completing the climb and descent in a day. It was quite possibly the second ascent. Three days later they achieved a traverse of Gestola, reaching the summit by a new line on the North Face (although not climbing the face direct), bivouacking just below the summit. They then continued along the crest of the Bezingi Wall the following day to reach the summit of Lyalver, from which they then made the first descent on the north-eastern flanks to return to the Bezingi Glacier. Traverses were definitely coming into fashion in the Caucasus – two years earlier Oskar Hug and Casimir de Rham had succeeded in a traverse of the three summits of Dongusorun, describing it as an enjoyable and easy expedition. The Bavarian team rounded off their trip with first ascents of Kentchat and an unnamed peak of 4335 metres in the Adyrsu chain.

It was against this background that Raeburn and Ling made their two visits to the Caucasus in 1913 and 1914. Raeburn was already one of the great pioneers of Scottish mountaineering. In addition to the first summer ascents on Ben Nevis of Observatory Ridge, Observatory Buttress (both solo) and Raeburn's Buttress, he had been responsible for two classic gully routes which were technically far ahead of anything yet achieved either in Scotland or in the Alps. In April 1906 he made an extraordinary ascent of Green Gully on Ben Nevis, now a classic grade III/IV ice route. Three years later he led a rope of three up Crowberry Gully on the Buachaille Etive Mor in the incredible time of four hours and twenty minutes. These ascents displayed an outstanding degree of skill and courage, considering that they were undertaken on unknown ground with a single full-length ice-axe, hobnail boots and sixty feet of rope for the leader. Raeburn is less well known as an alpinist, but there too he had a fine record, including the first British guideless ascent of the Zmutt Ridge of the Matterhorn in 1906 and important exploration in Norway. Ling was a regular partner of Raeburn's in the Alps who also made many significant ascents in Britain in his own right. Amongst the routes they climbed together attention should be drawn to the first ascent in 1910 of the Spigolo Inglese on the North Face of Monte Disgrazia, a mixed route of some distinction.

Raeburn was not a prolific writer. Apart from the odd article for the *Scottish Mountaineering Club Journal* and the *Alpine Journal*, he wrote only one book, the instructional *Mountaineering Art* which was published in 1920. The articles about their expeditions that he and Ling contributed to the *Alpine Journal* are not particularly exciting, although there are occasional flashes of dry wit. Both men wrote in what had become the *Alpine Journal* house style, a form of Victorian prose which seems to level all climbers and mountains into an indistinguishable blur. Raeburn, however, kept a diary of his 1913 trip to the Caucasus which, after his death in 1926, passed on to Ling and then, after Ling's death in 1953, was bequeathed to the Scottish Mountaineering Club in whose journal a condensed extract appeared in 1955. It is this extract which we have chosen to reprint. It deals with an unsuccessful attempt to climb the North Peak of Ushba by the North-East Face, starting from the as yet unvisited Chalaat Glacier. It was an ambitious undertaking and ultimately defeated by objective dangers. As so often with mountains, however, the failures can be more interesting and produce better writing than the successes.

Raeburn and Ling made their attempt on Ushba North at the end of a long and spectacular trip. It was an expedition in the traditional style which Ling summarised rather succinctly:

> Our plan was to camp at the head of the Tsaya glen and explore the Adai Kokh group and attempt the many unclimbed peaks there for two or three weeks, and then to travel along the chain through Suanetia, over the Dongusorun Pass to Elbrus and so back to the line. As this was over three hundred miles and a good portion of it difficult travelling, in addition to the peaks we wished to assault, we had our work cut out; but, thanks to the admirable weather, we were able to carry everything through and reached London only one day later than we had intended; but we had to work pretty hard for it. We climbed seven peaks in all, five of them new. There

was a sixth which we considered we were entitled to count, but our stern leader held that it was not a separate mountain.[3]

Among the first ascents were Ullargh Khokh (which they named after the local name for the ptarmigan seen on the ascent); Tschantschachi Khokh, which they found rather hard and required forty-five hours; and Nuamkuam in the Shkhara range. As a matter of historical interest, they ended their trip by making the second ascent of the Eastern Peak of Elbrus, first climbed by Freshfield's party in 1868. Raeburn and Ling returned to the Caucasus the following year, making four further first ascents (Bubis Khokh, Vologata, Karagom East and Laboda) before the onset of the First World War turned their and everybody else's attention far from mountaineering.

12
Attempt on Ushba

by Harold Raeburn

On the 12th of August 1913 the party reached Betsho, the local centre of government. On the following day we engaged Muratbi—now somewhat old-looking ... yet a tireless walker, whose 'guide's book' went back to the early nineties, and included the names of Caucasian pioneers, personal friends of our own—to act as porter as far as a bivouac below Ushba. Young elected to remain, on photography bent, at Betsho; so the climbing party consisted of Raeburn, Ling and Rembert Martinson, an 18-year-old Russian. On the 14th we set off, accompanied by Muratbi and two horses. The walk along the main valley, and up the steep, tree-clad banks of the Gulba Glacier stream to the highest hamlet, Gul (6,370 feet), was pleasant but uneventful. We were entirely unloaded: our horses, on a good track, easily took everything. The one and, I think, the only drawback to guideless climbing is the necessity of carrying loads.

Presently we arrived at a small grassy flat where slight walls of stone and the marks of many fires made it unnecessary for Muratbi to inform us that it was the usual camping place whence two successful assaults and the other twelve or fifteen unsuccessful ones on Ushba had been delivered.

At 2 p.m. we reached a suitable site for a bivouac, the top of a little scantily grassed ridge just under the high left moraine of Gulba Glacier where a merry little trickling stream prattled down. The height was 9,200 feet. The tent was set up, our three days' provisions unloaded, and Muratbi sent down with the horses, to return two days later. He emphatically refused our chaffing offer to take him with us, although (or because?) he had once spent a night with Herr Ficker at nearly 14,000 feet on the south peak. In the afternoon I climbed to a height of about 10,200 feet on the rocks of Gulba to reconnoitre.

Ushba, from the south-east, takes the shape of a great cathedral with two towers of equal height at either end. A couloir, surely one of the greatest in the world, of very steep snow with a hanging glacier extends between the huge buttresses of the towers, which are connected some 500 to 800 feet below their tops by a narrow corniced arête, mostly ice. A more unpromising and frightfully dangerous access to a peak than this couloir I have never seen. At this hour the whole space between the peaks was almost ceaselessly alive with falling stones and ice-avalanches. Moreover, from the ominous glitter of the steep slopes, it was obvious that the greater part was composed of bare ice. It would have meant days of step-cutting to ascend it, and for most of the time the party would have been exposed to almost certain destruction. An attack at this season on the couloir route was wholly unjustifiable.

The only successful ascent of the north peak of Ushba from the south-east was made by this couloir on 28th September 1888 by J. G. Cockin with Ulrich Almer. It was after a prolonged spell of bad weather with heavy snowfall succeeded by frost. The climb to the col under these conditions was long and hard, but not difficult or dangerous. Now conditions were very different and the face of the mountain was almost black. Former snowbeds were now steep rocks and screes or sheets of glassy ice. Falling stones brought cataracts of followers with them right down to the glacier. There was, of course, another route – that by which Herr Schulze led some of Rickmers' party on the first ascent of the south peak in 1903. I had studied this from a description and now had it before me. Its lower part, at any rate, would present no serious difficulty, though long, steep and quite probably dangerous climbing.

But our expedition was not for the purpose of following in other parties' footsteps. Why not try it by an entirely novel route, from a glacier hitherto unvisited and by a face looked on as hopeless—by the north-east face, from the Chalaat Glacier?

The top part of this face, at least, is shown in one of Mr Woolley's photographs, and we had seen it two days before, though only partly on account of mist. This face is enormously large and is steeper than that of any great mountain hitherto climbed, the Meije not excepted; a much more formidable climb than the Matterhorn by the Zmutt.

There was still another way of attaining the summit of the north peak: by ascending the Ushba Glacier on the west and getting on to the north side of the peak from its head. This had already been followed by the party led by Herr H. Pfann, who traversed both peaks, also in 1903. This party were four nights out and had four days of climbing. As the mountain was now very icy, there might be quite an impossible amount of step-cutting on this route.

A point which further decided in favour of an attack upon the north-east face was that it ought to be freer from stones and avalanches owing to its aspect, and that the early morning sun would be largely kept off it by the high peak of Chatuintau or Mestia, on the other side of the great Chalaat Glacier.

15th August: To the North-east Face of Ushba.—We were up at 2.30 a.m. and away at 4.15 on a still and perfect morning. We ascended moraines and crossed a small glacier in the direction of the dip in Gulba ridge immediately south of that peak. Dawn came as we neared the col. On the rocks above, and quite within shot, a party of six tur appeared; one was quite a small kid, not yet very agile on the rocks. We gained the col (10,550 feet) at 5.30 a.m. We were rather disappointed to find that there was a big drop (1,300 feet) to the Chalaat Glacier. Down steep but easy ribs of rather crumbling rock and a good snow-couloir, we gained the glacier at 6.30. This was the West Chalaat branch, which had never been trodden by human foot before. Its upper part pours down in huge, steep icefalls below the vast wall of Ushba's north-east face and the shapely peak of Mestia.

This Chalaat Glacier is a large ice stream of a peculiar shape. Owing to its steepness and the depth of its snow reservoirs it descends lower, in spite of its southerly aspect, than any other Caucasian glacier, finishing nowadays at about 5,200 feet. We were on the western branch. The pass at the head of the Chalaat Glacier, between Ushba and Mestia peak, is interrupted by a little rock peak which may be called Little Ushba. On each side of this are passages looking very forbidding but not impossible. Starting generally southwards, the glacier, after flowing past Gulba, makes a right-angled bend and flows slightly north-east to join a larger ice stream from beyond Mestia peak, and then flows south-east to almost join the Leksur Glacier (the longest Caucasian glacier). At no distant date these glaciers did probably join.

Our aim was to reach a good sleeping-place as high up as possible on Ushba's N.E. face, and start early on the final climb. We had first to find our way through a very broken icefall which stretched right across the glacier. At first the glacier was flat and almost free from crevasses. There had evidently been a tremendous rockfall recently from the cliffs of Gulba, just above us on our left. Great blocks weighing many tons had been shot nearly half-way across the glacier, here nearly a mile wide. We kept well out till past this place. It cost us four hours of hard ice-work before we won through the icefall. The crampons proved of great service. Turning left and crossing a rather difficult bergschrund and ascending a further ice slope, we reached the rocks of the north-east face at 11.55. The climbing for the rest of the day was varied and interesting; never excessively difficult, it was continuous, and, I judge, like that met on the Brenva face of the Aiguille Blanche de Peuteret, but with everything on a bigger scale and at a steeper angle. Owing to the aspect, the icy parts were still covered with snow, rather inclined to avalanche, and requiring great care. The leader often took out 60 feet of rope before the others moved. We spent a long time over lunch, on comfortable ledges over which water ran, enjoying the pleasant sun, which we should soon lose.

Then on again at 1 p.m., and at length we came to a place which offered an ideal spot for a bivouac, as far as safety was concerned (5 p.m.). The height was just 13,000 feet. We were almost on a level with the col to the north of us, between Ushba and Little Ushba. A mass of rocks jutted out from the face; in these a cleft floored with ice and stones formed the only space level enough for three to lie down upon that we had seen for hours. The rocks overhung it in a penthouse solid enough to divert anything falling from above, and the sleeping berth had an inward tilt that would prevent anyone from rolling off in his sleep—very necessary, as a stone flung out from the edge of the bed touched nothing for 200 feet, and did not come to rest for 2,000. But it was quite a difficult climb to get into this bedstead!

The great feature of the upper regions of Ushba is a belt of real, and not in the sense often employed, *precipices*, which almost girdle both peaks, and give them their tower-like form. Their height at this point was roughly 1,000 feet, and for a long distance they seemed quite impossible, soaring almost straight up in dark-red slabs of granite or protogine, smooth, flawless, and more forbidding even than those upon the north face of the Petit Dru. Below the cliffs a sloping band slanted upwards to the north, and gradually the cliff broke down to meet it in that direction. Not far from the head of the West Chalaat Glacier a steep snow-covered edge came down to meet the band. We hoped to be able to work along till we gained this rib of snow-covered rock and ice, which obviously led up to the possible slopes of the upper peak. The crux lay in a great couloir floored with ice, which lay between us and the snow-edge beyond. There was also a minor couloir which cut across our route, nearer at hand.

A few minutes after we gained our shelter there was a loud rushing sound, and, with a thunderous roar, an avalanche swept down the channel. Though we were in no danger, the rush of air reached us in our snug letter-box, nearly carried away our hats, and covered everything with chilly snow-dust. The precipice above was some protection to us from anything falling from the steep ice slopes of the summit cap. Any snow avalanches from there were dispersed in dust before they reached us; any stones or blocks of ice flew over our heads.

We had a good supper, arranged things for the morning and then lay down at 7 p.m., watching the fading of the light. This bivouac stands out as the most romantic and impressive I have ever known; it was not for its wide views; the outlook was rather restricted. The nearest to it I recollect was on the Zmutt arête of the Matterhorn. The outlook thence is comparable in kind, though not in quality: the same trinity of elements, rock, ice and snow alone composing the landscape. Nothing else is visible. Here the scale was greater, the horizon narrower. Our sleeping-place actually projected from the face of the mountain, which was invisible for 100 feet below us owing to the overhang. One had a curious hesitation, in spite of the gigantic size of the blocks of which our residence was built, in going too near the edge lest the whole mass should be started off on its inevitable plunge to the glacier, whose wide crevasses were now reduced to almost invisible threads far below. Daylight at last faded; the planets shone and the stars sparkled in a cloudless moonlit sky. Ling and I dozed or turned uneasily on our stony beds, but young Rembert, who had carried a heavy load, and been as sure-footed and steady as a veteran, slumbered peacefully and soundly. O happy privilege of tired and healthy youth!

16th August: Defeat by the Demon Bowlers of Ushba.—A perfect morning: after a good breakfast we got away at 4.45. It was impossible to start before daylight: the climbing was too difficult, only one man being able to move at a time. We crossed the avalanche-couloir nearby and were disgusted to find that even at this height and on this aspect the snow was in bad condition: even at 13,500 feet it was already quite warm. At length (9 a.m.) at 14,000 feet we arrived at a point where it became necessary to consider very carefully the choice before us. We had come up a long slanting gully partly filled with snow and ice, which led northward up the base of the great precipice girdling the summit, now greatly reduced in height; we could see the edge of the cliffs and the ice-cap about 300 feet overhead. Unfortunately, the crack diminished and died out in an expanse of granite slabs. The immediate surroundings resembled the cliffs and slabs above the Cioch on Sgumain, in snow and ice conditions. The steep rocks were not iced, and their quality was little if at all inferior to the best of Skye or Norway gabbro. For heavily laden men without *kletterschuhe* at above 14,000 feet the slabs were impossible. We were, however, now level with the lower part of the ice-arête leading up to the summit ice-cap: this gained, our chief difficulties would be over.

Between us and this Promised Land, as we clung to the slabs of our Pisgah, stretched a couloir, a canyon rather, pitched at a very steep angle (lower down, almost vertical) and floored with polished rock and glistening ice. This was, in fact, the bowling-alley of the Jötuns of Ushba. The game had just begun, and the fun soon waxed fast and furious. Missiles of rock and ice hurtled and crashed against each other: masses of snow slid hissing down the groove, or overflowed high up on the surrounding slabs. The Marinelli Couloir on the Macugnaga face of Monte Rosa is a tame and feeble place by comparison.

The falls were not continuous. We timed the intervals, gazing with longing eyes at the short distance which separated us from the peaceful security of the steep ice-arête beyond. After an hour's debate, we were forced to the reluctant conclusion that the dice of the Ushba demons were too heavily loaded against us. It is no use playing with Jötuns if the game is skittles, and you are the skittles. Though the distance could have been run across in five minutes, the terrain was so difficult (smooth worn rock and ice at the maximum angle), that it would have taken 30 to 40 minutes to effect a passage even if nothing had been coming down.

We considered another place, where snow and rock débris was coming down. Probably the falls would stop in the early afternoon, and we might get over. This would mean spending the night on the summit. The weather was extraordinarily good, but there was the food difficulty. Enough remained for one day, but not for two. Ling and I could go on little or nothing for a day or two. We had, however, to consider young Martinson. Big, strong, active and heavy, though looking 24 he was only 18 years of age, and required more food than we did. He could hardly be expected to climb at over 15,000 feet on air, fine though it was.

We began the descent at 10 a.m. It went very well; all moved carefully. With so many places where we had to move one at a time, it was hours before the glacier seemed to get perceptibly nearer. We passed the sleeping-place at 3 p.m. Lower down, where the angle eases off a little, the route of ascent was rather hard to follow. We stopped on some warm slabs, where water was running, made tea and had a good meal, reserving merely a few fragments for later emergencies.

On the lower slabs I noticed little of the distant sunset-flushed snows; every faculty was strained to pick up the landmarks noted on the ascent, to watch every footstep of the men in front, and to look after the rope. The route on the slabs low down was difficult to follow. We had to avoid the line of least resistance. At one point it led us to a cliff, 200 feet high and overhanging. Where the route was doubtful the cairns I had erected the previous morning helped us. We hit on the exact place where the wall above the schrund had been passed. Much of the snow had gone, and it was necessary to jump the last 10 feet.

At last, at 7.45 p.m., we reached the glacier but failed to find our tracks (mere crampon traces) through the icefall. The sun had set, but a glorious full moon made the lanterns unnecessary. We failed to pick up the track and were forced by enormous crevasses to make for the lower rocks on Ushba. Here was an absolute *impasse* and, after some search, we found a long *bowsprit* of ice which came within jumping distance of a good ledge. We crossed by this and descended the rocks which, though steep, had good ledges and were still warm from the heat absorbed during the day. Our hands, chilled with handling snow-sodden rope, became dry and comfortable. Lower, we descended into a water and stone channel between rocks and ice and actually through tunnels in the ice—and so down the last great gash of the icefall, finally climbing a steep ice-arête on to the crisp surface of the lower glacier, all danger and difficulty now behind us.

We had just passed the scene of the great rockfall, moving between the outermost great boulders on the flat glacier. The scene was most impressive at this midnight hour. High overhead soared the glorious southern moon, glittering on the mighty ice-clad face of Ushba and the vast ice cataracts of the Chalaat Glacier. Still, nothing but rock, ice and snow hemmed us round. Suddenly the profound silence was broken by a low rumbling growl, gradually swelling to a prolonged and deafen-ing roar, thrown back by the steep walls of Mestia, and the icefalls of the glacier. The very glacier trembled. The solid earth itself seemed to quiver. The first thought that flashed through my mind was—an earthquake. It was, however, a rockfall on a scale appropriate to the scenery. From the cliffs of Gulba a great mass of the mountain had peeled off and was hurtling and crashing down on to the glacier. Light-nings played about in the midst of the falling mass as rock struck rock and flamed out. The dull, even, earth-shaking roar was pierced through ever and anon by louder, shriller notes from the bursting of errant blocks. From the débris a great cloud arose, canopying the glacier and blotting out the moon. Gradually the noise died away and the serene moon sailed out of the slow, drifting earth-cloud. We stopped to eat our last bite of food and take off the ropes which had been on us for 20 hours. Had we not been wet and chilly we would hardly have faced the long pull up to the Gulba Col, but lain down on the first rocks we came to. However, setting 'stout hearts to a stey brae', we climbed the 1,300 feet to the col and reached our tent again at 3 a.m., after an absence of 48 hours. Muratbi was delighted to see us safely back. There was not much to eat, but we had a cup of tea and a snack, and turned in, to sleep soundly and dreamlessly till the sun wakened us in the morning.

[Next day Muratbi and Martinson went down to Betsho, the former to recruit his strength among the fleshpots, the latter to fetch up food supplies to enable Raeburn and Ling (who remained at the bivouac, 'eating air') to try the south peak by the couloir leading up to the Ushba-Mazeri col. Next morning they set out, and made their way, by climbing which Raeburn describes as 'very severe by Lake District standards', to the col; but, though they spent a night there and made another attempt the next morning, the face of South Ushba, in the prevailing conditions, defeated them, and they had to retreat to the bivouac and to Betsho. From there they set out on the journey to Elbruz, which they successfully ascended some days later.]

From *Scottish Mountaineering Club Journal*, 1955

13

Between the Wars

In 1917 the Bolshevik Revolution erupted in Russia, plunging the country into turmoil and starting a long and bloody civil war. As they had done in the 1870s the Caucasians tried to take advantage of the general instability and free themselves from central domination. The Georgian capital of Tblisi was a prominent nationalist centre, declaring itself against the Bolsheviks almost as soon as news of the Revolution came through. Local aspirations to independence were encouraged and materially supported by the Allied Powers, with the situation further complicated by the expansionist ambitions of Turkey under Enver Pasha. For many months the Caucasus was in as chaotic a state as the rest of Russia. The Caucasus and the Transcaucasian Republics, however, were too strategically important to be allowed to determine their own fate, and as soon as the Bolshevik position was sufficiently secure in areas closer to Moscow, the Caucasus was brought back under control.

By 1923 the attempts of the Caucasians to win independence had finally been quelled, and climbing began once again. Now Russian mountaineers had the range to themselves. Traditionally, the history of Russian mountaineering is said to have begun with a mass ascent of Kazbek by twenty-five Georgian students in that very year, 1923. Two years later the summit of Elbrus was reached by nineteen climbers. It would be more accurate, though, to describe this as the beginning of post-Revolutionary or Soviet mountaineering. There was already a Russian Mountaineering Society in existence by the turn of the century, and more local clubs swiftly followed. They confined themselves, with a few notable exceptions such as the first ascent of Pik Schurovski by the South-East Ridge in 1915 by Golubev, Panutin and Frolov, to repeating the easiest routes up the easiest peaks, but this, after all, is also what the overwhelming majority of British climbers did in the Alps. One should not conclude, simply because relatively few significant first ascents were carried out by Russians until the late 1930s, that the range was penetrated only by the occasional party of intrepid Westerners. Russians had been walking, climbing, or simply taking the air in the Caucasus in ever increasing numbers since the 1890s. The 1930s, though, did see some notable Russian ascents. Particularly important was the ascent in October 1937 of the South-East Buttress of the South Ridge of Ushba South by G. Khergiani, M. Gvariani, V. Khergiani and Ch. Chartolani. The climb still receives a grade of 5B. The first Russian traverse of Ushba took place the same year, carried out by Eugene Abalakov (the younger of the two brothers) and Vassiliev. The North Ridge of Ushba North was first climbed in 1935 by V. Kiesel and B. Aleinokov, while the South-East Ridge of Shkhara had its first ascent in 1933 (A. Gvalia and V. Cheishvili, both from Georgia).

In 1928, however, Western activity in the range resumed. By this stage standards of difficulty in the Alps had increased dramatically with the growing popularity of the sport. Attention was now being turned to the great north faces whose technical difficulties and levels of objective danger had made them seem impregnable to climbers before the War. One name in particular stands out – the great Willo Welzenbach who shot to fame with the first ascent of the North-West Face of the Grosses Wiesbachhorn in 1924 and then, in the next two years before an elbow injury retired him from climbing for four years, followed this with a string of audacious climbs including the first ascent of the North Face Direct on the Dent d'Hérens, the North Face of the Eiskögele and the North Face of the Grossglockner. On rock too, great advances were made – one thinks, for example, of Emil Solleder and Gustav Lettenbauer's ascent in 1925 of the North-West Face of the Civetta in the Dolomites, using pitons only for belays.

Welzenbach, Solleder and Lettenbauer were all from Munich, members of the great school so many of whom died while changing the face of climbing in the Alps and the Himalaya. Also from Munich came Paul Bauer, leader of the Bavarian expedition which visited the Caucasus in 1928 and already responsible for several fine climbs in the Zillertal and Wetterstein Alps (although his greatest exploits were to take place in the Himalaya during the 1930s). Amongst his three companions was Heinz Tillman who was to make the first direct ascent of the Gross Fiescherhorn with Welzenbach in 1930. It will interest those who (rightly) bemoan the generally poor state of British climbing at this period that among the undertakings of this rather formidable team was the second ascent of Cockin's 1888 route on the North-East Ridge of Shkhara.

More significantly, Bauer's expedition gave a renewed impetus to the style of climbing that has become characteristic of the Caucasus – the tradition of long traverses, linking together several mountains and requiring several bivouacs in extremely committing situations. The climate of the Caucasus makes such long traverses very demanding undertakings. Even in summer the average daily temperature above the snow-line almost never rises above zero, and long stretches of uninterrupted good weather are rare. Given the remoteness of the higher peaks and the fact that it is generally far harder to retreat from a traverse than a straightforward ascent, the likelihood is that anyone undertaking a long traverse would have to climb at least some of it in bad weather. The levels of commitment are far greater than anything in the Alps, closer in fact to the challenges of climbing alpine-style in the Himalaya. It is, however, a logical style of climbing for a range in which the great peaks tend to lie on long ridges with few points of weakness.

The first of the great traverses had been, of course, Pfann and party's four-day effort on Ushba in 1903. Twenty-five years later Paul Bauer, Ernst Beigel, Hans Niesner and Heinz Tillman climbed a new route on the North Face of Katyn-Tau and then continued over Gestola and Lyalver, with several bivouacs in ice caves. 1930, however, saw one of the greatest and least known mountaineering feats of the pre-war era. Two Viennese climbers, Hugo Tomaschek and Willi Müller, made the first ascent of a technically very demanding mixed route on the North Rib of Shkhara. The route, with a height gain of nearly 3000 metres straight to the highest point of the Bezingi Wall, is still given a Russian grade of 5B (there is only one harder grade) and considered a very demanding undertaking. They descended Cockin's 1888 route on the North-East Ridge. Six bivouacs were needed to complete the traverse. This was just the beginning.

The following year Karl Poppinger, Karl Moldan and Josef Schintel-meister seized the greatest prize of all – the complete traverse of the

Bezingi Wall, which included climbing some of its peaks for the first time. Over six days (with every bivouac in a snow hole or ice cave), they reached the Main Peak of Shkhara by its North-East Ridge, continued over to the West Peak, and then traversed along the West Ridge, over the seven gendarmes of the Saw of Shkhara, to reach Pik Schota Rustaveli. From there they traversed the two summits of Jangi-Tau, and Pik Bezingi, to reach Katyn-Tau, continuing on over Gestola to Lyalver, before descending finally to the Zanner Pass. It was a sensational expedition, more than ten miles of hard climbing at altitude, extremely bold and committing. 'A monstrous big climb,' was how a later mountaineer described it. 'Cornices and again cornices . . . a path between earth and sky.'[1] In thirty-three years it was only repeated seven times, and the speed only improved upon on that seventh crossing. Even today it is *the* route to which everyone who climbs in the Caucasus aspires.

It was not just the ridges that received attention, though. Hard face routes were also being put up. In the Caucasus, as in the Alps at the time, it was the age of the great north faces. But, even though many of the climbers active in the Caucasus during the 'twenties and 'thirties were also at the cutting edge of Alpine climbing, the atmosphere was completely different. There were far too few climbers to generate the sort of competition that was seen on the North Faces of the Petit Dru, Grandes Jorasses or Eiger. In fact, there was very little competition at all. The sort of co-operation recorded by John Jenkins in the extract printed below, where detailed route information about the North Face of Tetnuld was provided by Schwarzgruber, bears little relation to the familiar story of Pierre Allain biting his nails at Montenvers and hoping that Raymond Lambert would fail on the North Face of the Dru. Perhaps unsurprisingly, as well, the accident rate was negligible in comparison. Some Viennese climbers died on Elbrus in 1930. Two Swiss, Max Mäglin and Josef Hegglin, together with two Russians, Goldowski and Levin, disappeared on the Misses-Tau the following year, while another Swiss, P. Buhler, was killed on Doppakh-Tau in 1933.

Among the face routes put up at this time attention should be drawn to the Shwarzgruber Rib on Jangi-Tau, climbed in July 1935 by Rudolf Schwarzgruber, Walter Marin, Ferdinand Peringer and H. Thaler. The route follows the North-East Pillar on the right-hand edge of the North Face, continuing on steep ice slopes to the summit. Three days were required for the first ascent.* Perhaps the outstanding effort, though, came in 1936 when Ludwig Schmaderer and Ludwig Vörg (who was to take part in the first ascent of the Eiger Nordwand in 1938) climbed an extremely bold and technically difficult route on the West Face of Ushba North. The climb started up a steep ice couloir, subsequently breaking out right onto the buttress below the col separating the two summits. The col was reached on the second day after a stretch of artificial ice-climbing. It has rarely been repeated. The same team also made the first ascent of the North Face of Shkhelda.

The first British climber to visit the range during this period was the Scot J. H. B. Bell who climbed with Russians in 1930 and 1932. His only known success was the first ascent of the South-West Arête of Bashil-Tau in 1930.

In 1937, however, a rather young and carefree group of four British climbers managed to get hold of visas and permission to climb in the range. We have selected articles from two of them to reprint here. As is clear from Robin Hodgkin's piece, written especially for the 1991 Alpine Club Symposium on the Caucasus, their approach to climbing was light-years away from that of the Munich Tigers who had dominated the range for a decade or so. With poor equipment and a shoe-string budget, they nonetheless managed an impressive series of climbs, of which the two described here (the North Face of Tetnuld and a new route on Ushba South) were the most important. The Tetnuld climb was carried out by John Jenkins and Michael Taylor, while it was Robin Hodgkin, Michael Taylor and Bob Beaumont who climbed Ushba South by the East Face and South-East Ridge.

It is sad to have to record that, like so many others of that generation of bold climbers, they paid a heavy price for their successes. Bob Beaumont was killed in 1938 on the Black Ladders in North Wales. The

---

* In 1958 John Hunt, Chris Brasher, Alan Blackshaw and Ralph Jones attempted the second ascent, but poor snow conditions forced a retreat barely 500 feet below the summit. See John Hunt and Christopher Brasher: *The Red Snows*, ch. 15.

same year Robin Hodgkin was caught in a storm high on the South-East Face of Masherbrum in the Karakoram Himalaya. He survived, but with appalling frostbite that cost him all his fingers and toes. John Jenkins died nine years later on the Brenva Face of Mont Blanc.

14

The Untrammelled Caucasus

by Robin Hodgkin

We weren't totally obtuse about Communism in the nineteen thirties; just thinking more about other things, especially mountains. John Jenkins, in his *Alpine Journal* article (*AJ* May 1938) observed that 'collectivisation in mountaineering, as in other aspects of Soviet life, seems to breed quantity rather than quality'. I was ticked off by a communist cousin for being 'negative' (in a *Times* article) when I remarked that rows of bombers on an airfield seen from the train looked 'sinister'. 'Who's side are you on, anyway?' Hard to say. Three of us were leftish, pacifist Quakers and Bob Beaumont was a splendid old-world scholar-patriot who had learnt basic Slav and had a sense of history. It was not just the prospect of new climbs that drew us but a heart-ache for high Asiatic mountains. It was now 1937 and I'd been feeling that way for four or five years.

We trundled across the Ukraine – crowded proletarian trains – till we got to Naltchik, hazy mountains to the south. Then by truck, up the Baksan Valley, to Tegenekli main base for Elbrus, where there was a spartan Intourist hotel. Even then, large parties of young Russians were on the trail for Europe's highest peak – city toilers being rewarded by the system. In their camps they were extremely kind to us; made us wash and do PE. We were slightly derisive about the few we met who climbed seriously. They were slow, under-equipped and wore funny hats. With hindsight, however, one salutes them, those few who were already breaking through the system, making it, on their own, to difficult summits – even Ushba – and also those younger mountaineers, such as Eugene Gippenreiter, friend of many British climbers. He got an 'official' breath of freedom in the Caucasus as a young conscript and then built his life around serious climbing; or Vlad Kiesel (physicist, now a silver haired professor) who made the bold repeat of Cockin's (1888) ascent of Ushba North peak in 1936. Most Soviet climbers are going to have a hard time now that official mountaineering will wither away. Let us not forget them or the possibilities of friendship and co-operation in their marvellous mountains.

By the beginning of our third week we were feeling very fit; and very hungry. We had had a wonderful ten days in the Jailik group and had done some fine new routes: the south face of Jailik (4533m) and the splendid north ridge of Adyr Su Bashi (4370m). But there were problems. We had no proper roubles with which to escape Intourist: only their meal coupons which we could rarely cash. We were determined to break away from these bonds and there appeared to be no others. So we had brought considerable quantities of dried food – porridge, pemmican, chocolate. And we bartered what we could: a rope and a sweater for some bread, mutton and strawberries. Our best map was from the back of Freshfield's book of 1869. The big climbs we had planned, for Ushba and Tetnuld, were several days' walk away, on the southern side of the range, and our two food sacks had already dwindled to one.

The Betsho pass is the most direct route over the range to the lush valleys of the south: out of Moslem Balkaria and into the margin of Christian Georgia. Into Asia. We hired a horse and driver for the solitary food sack and we all spent a wet night up near the watershed. Fifty years later, in Moscow, I met a French-Russian lady doctor who had crossed the Betsho many times during the war, smuggling Russian and Balkarian partisans, out of the range of the German army. She now lives in a remote Balkarian village and swears, on 'scientific' authority, that there are Caucasian yetis.

As we came down the moraine slopes on the southern side the pony slipped and somersaulted down the crumbling boulder clay. I have a sombre picture of the scene. John and I trying to scrape treacle from the smashed porridge box, licking our fingers and wondering what else we could salvage. However, things cheered up in the wooded valleys and turreted villages of Suanetia. There were the classic views of Ushba towering up into the clouds, getting steeper as the two peaks fell into line (Ushba South 4710m).

From Mazeri we made our way up to the meadows and moraines below the Gul Glacier and climbed the rocky peak of Gulba. John had a fall with some loose rocks which cut his leg and disabled him for several days. From the top we could gaze at Ushba's eastern wall – now called the Mirror Wall. It was very big indeed and very interesting. Why hadn't Schulze gone straight up the main south east ridge which was now our horizon? Were we being naive about that rising ledge which we could sometimes see when cloud broke? It was all foreshortened and a long way up. Even Schulze's bivouac place at the Mazeri Notch was a thousand metres above the glacier and that was where the big problems would start.

We spent four hours of darkness and dawn sweating up that immensely tedious couloir system that leads up to the notch from the Gul Glacier. Michael Taylor did most of the hard work – step kicking and occasional tricky bits. Now, at the Notch, Gulba was below us. Breakfast was a Healthy Life biscuit and water. We could look over now, to the wide expanse of snow and rock – the White Cravat – which girdled the foot of the Red Wall where, over on the left, Schulze and his party made that almost fatal first ascent of Ushba South in 1903. One or two parties had been up since but the route looked menacing and still a long way off. So it was partly laziness and partly fear that made us think it would be nice to go straight up the south east ridge and tackle the cliffs at the right hand end of the Red Wall. It was logical and direct. First came a slabby ridge which, after about 500 m steepened abruptly into the buttress where the wall turned into the eastern face. That was where we had seen The Ledge. We had better hump our bivouac gear up there and rub our noses in it.

Every afternoon in the Caucasus in summer there is a misty, monsoony storm. We had a Marco Pallis bivouac tent. All three of us – Bob Beaumont, Michael Taylor and I – just managed to pile in before the storm broke. This time it was really big stuff. The flashes lit up the fiery cliffs all round and it banged away till the early hours. Then, daybreak and snow everywhere. So down, down, down the maze of slabs and couloirs. John was at our camp in the glen but still not fit to climb. However he had made friends and had got some fresh meat. We three were keen to go back up, confident that we had spotted a promising new route. Two days later it was fine and we were grinding up those ghastly couloirs again. Technically they weren't difficult, though a modern East German guidebook warns of danger from stone fall.

A word about our level of climbing skill and technology in the late 1930s: yes, we had a Marco Pallis bivouac tent and had tried it out on the Petersgrat; we had Lawrie boots with tricounis and Everest clinkers; we had a few slings and often a chockstone in our rucksacks and the usual crampons etc. We were puritanical and romantic. I had once, rather guiltily, been on a piton climb in Norway, with Arne Naess, and I had actually handled a karabiner (*not* the done thing in the Alpine Club). Had we had the runners and nylon ropes and ice screws of the late fifties we would have been climbing with considerably less risk. Bob Beaumont would not have died on the Black Ladders (Ysgolion Du) the next year nor John Jenkins on the Brenva ten years later. Our models were light expeditions and light-hearted mountaineers – de Ségogne, Kirkus, Longland, Shipton, Tilman – all of them combining commitment to exploring with lightness of touch. Our unprotected run-outs, with that delicious, wayward hempen rope, were sometimes very long indeed; very cheap too; though at least in the Caucasus a fifty foot length of Beale would get you a couple of square meals.

So we went up close to the red-brown towers of the south east corner once again. It is rather like that section on the Meije above the Promontoire where the route steepens up with massive blocks and towers. The rock ledge that we had noticed was accessible but it steepened into a hard vertical section. Later we roped down it. So we looked further round the corner, over the spectacular precipices of the east face. And here there was a narrowing lizard ledge which led horizontally across to what might be a more broken recess. A loop round a jammed chock stone and a mini-pendule got us past the crux and we wriggled along and into the great re-entrant which kinks that eastern cliff. Large tracts of the opposing wall really were more than vertical and the icicles which occasionally fell off seemed to fall for miles. But our side was broken and more climbable. We made steady progress for about 300 metres till we found ourselves on the rocky edge of the top snow field.

We got to the summit at about 1 o'clock and looked admiringly at the North Peak and the ridge, snaking through the mist towards it. At that stage we thought that the two summits were equal in height. I think the seniority of the south peak only became established after the War. We were only faintly attracted by the idea of continuing on that long traverse. It had been first done over thirty years before: a marvellous epic in its day. But not, we felt, for us. So down we went, abseiling all the hard bits. The clouds were whisking round. From a distance Ushba often carries a fine banner in its updraft and we were soon right in it.

Next day we trekked further east, through the pretty valleys of Svanetia, past many villages prickling with defensive towers and, occasionally, a struggling little church in use. There was a Tourist House where we could cash food coupons and build up our supplies. But at the last village – Jabmush – before we turned north to cross the main range again, disaster struck. First, a wily, and doubtless needy, visitor nicked a full rucksack from inside the tent. This left us with only three pairs of good boots and only one rope for our planned, final climb on Tetnuld (4974m). Then, after having gone for two hours with a helpful packhorse its owner decided that 'the glacier' was much too far away and demanded immediate payment. He emphasised his point by drawing a nicely decorated Georgian sword, threatening, not us but our precious food sack. We paid up. When anyone talks about Sherpas and heavy loads I always think of the next few hours. But at last it was finished and we found ourselves on the far side of the Zanner Glacier in an Elysian meadow beyond the moraine.

John Jenkins and Michael Taylor were certainly our most experienced snow and ice climbers. So they set off with the bivouac tent and remaining rope for the north face of Tetnuld. 'A slender scimitar-shaped ridge curved upwards to lose itself in a steep ice wall' is how John described it and it was his finest route. It had originally been suggested to him by the Caucasian expert, Schwarzgruber. Their descent by the, to them, unknown and complex eastern face was a fine bit of mountaineering. Bob and I were happy to laze among the flowers of our glacier camp. It was the only time I've seen Venus, overhead in the midday heaven.

There followed a hard slog over the Zanner Pass and down to the endless moraines and grey mist of the Bezingi Glacier. Dych-Tau looked tremendous towering over the cloud on the far side. We thought back to Mummery and Zurfluh on their first ascent. There have been several notable British climbing parties in the Caucasus since the 1970's. I don't think, however, that any British mountaineers have repeated George Band's (1958) route on Dych-tau. nor for that matter have any done the main south peak of Ushba or the great traverse. Yet these must be a good deal less serious than, say, Fowler's and Saunders' Ushba West Face route. The traverse is rated about '5' on the European scale. Their time will come.

It was more than a month since we had escaped the Intourist net in the Baksan Valley – sixty miles from the Bezingi. But this time we much appreciated what seemed to be the positive benevolence of their safety nets. The telephone at the first village worked. The Tegenekli office got the message and within forty eight hours a Gorki-made Ford truck had arrived and it trundled us back onto the conveyor belt. Strangely, the quality of the meals at the Tegenekli Ritz had improved out of all recognition.

A paper presented at the Alpine Club's Caucasus Symposium in November 1991

Tetnuld Nordwand

by John R. Jenkins

We claim no credit for this route. It was Herr Schwarzgruber, the great
Austrian climber, who suggested it to us. His expeditions among the
great Bezingi peaks, many of which exceed 17,000 feet, were made in
the same tradition as Bauer's historic attempt on Kangchenjunga, and
his knowledge of these mountains, which approach nearer the Himalayan scale than any in Europe, is unrivalled. In 1936, from the summit
of Gestola, he worked out this magnificent route up the north face of
Tetnuld, which he cherished a great desire to climb. Much to the relief
of his wife, circumstances prevented him from carrying out this project,
and in a spirit which confounds those critics of nationalism in mountaineering, he sent us a photograph of the mountain on which his
proposed route was clearly marked.

The route appeared to us quite terrifying, and for a modest British
party to carry on where an expert Austrian party had left off (and
moreover to climb a *north face*) caused us some trepidation and no
small degree of amusement. On closer examination of the photograph,
the 'Schwarzgruberweg' appeared to be the only safe way up this steep
ice-swept face, and we entertained the hope that in actuality it would
prove less steep than it seemed.

An accident had confined me to four blissful days of idle recuperation
at the Gul Glacier Base Camp, while Hodgkin, Taylor and Beaumont
made their assaults on the south-east ridge of Ushba, the second of
which proved successful. During that time, thwarted ambition caused
the Tetnuld climb to attain exaggerated dimensions in my mind. What
I had lost on Ushba I would gain on Tetnuld; that thought alleviated
my disappointment.

Per ardua ... the Tetnuld Base Camp, in a flower garden overlooking the main Zanner glacier, was only reached through much
hardship and great suffering. The hardship was caused through the

maddening inefficiency and unreliability of Svanetian transport, and the suffering by the distorted and overloaded Everest carriers on which we strapped food-sacks and rucksacks.

During the first day we travelled the thirty odd miles to Mestia, slogging the last part of the way up the interminable dusty road of Mulkhura in the dim light of a ghostly moon. Round each bend, an eerie clump of watch-towers promised our journey's end, but it was not until 11 p.m., in the depths of despair, that we eventually staggered into the town. The Spartan luxury of the Tourist House and the cheerful conversation of Val, its Russian-Canadian commissar, restored our good spirits. Next day, in enervating heat, we pressed on up the valley and camped at its head above the village of Jabmush.

Our farewell to Svanetia concluded with a double tragedy,* and it was with considerable relief that we at last got away among rocks and snow again, far removed from the cheats and robbers of humanity. For the last four hours we had been forced to relay all the loads ourselves. Weighed down by 70-pound packs we had struggled up a steadily deteriorating track which had brought us, over dizzy slopes and by the snout of the Nageb glacier, to a rock platform above the main Zanner glacier. Descending on to the open ice, we finally reached the most perfect camp site of all; a level patch of soft turf flaming with the colours of a myriad flowers, through which ran many streams.

Early next day preparations were made for the climb, and Hodgkin and Beaumont nobly surrendered to Taylor and me the most vital items of equipment (of which we had been robbed in Jabmush). We started at 9 a.m. with a bivouac tent and three days' provisions. To reach the foot of Tetnuld's north face, we had to branch off the main Zanner glacier and follow its eastern branch to the foot of the steep wall below the Adish plateau where it has its birth. The Eastern Zanner breaks into the main Zanner glacier in an impassable barrier of séracs, and to avoid these, we had to contour over moraine débris and grassy slopes. We passed an inviting blue lake, and resting by its side, we lost ourselves in the reflection of the tumbled Zanner ice against the dark red rocks of Tiktengen. Further on, the glacier became level and, slith-

---

* A robbery and contretemps with their porters, see p. 155.

ering down a treacherous moraine, we reached the level ice. The cold wind blew the laziness out of us, and we had to exercise all our ingenuity in threading our way through a maze of crevasses reminiscent of the Mer de Glace.

At last our objective loomed round the corner, and with a sinking of the heart we searched for our line of attack. It was a perfect day, and Tetnuld presented a picture of unbelievable beauty which rivalled even the Brenva Mont Blanc or the north face of the Jungfrau in grandeur. Given a sheet of blue paper and a white pastel, an artist could have reproduced almost exactly the pattern of white snow and blue shadows of its north face. We did not get an opportunity to study the route in full detail until we sat down on an isolated boulder for lunch at mid-day.

Above us rose the north face of Tetnuld in a perfect inverted parabola of snow and ice, crowned with a hanging rim of séracs. Its upper part was hung with ice bulges, and the ice falling from them had scored out long flutings in the steep snow slopes. To the left, and clear of the bulges, a slender scimitar-shaped ridge curved upwards to lose itself in a steep white wall above. This was the line of ascent suggested by Herr Schwarzgruber; it looked steep and difficult and its feasibility turned on the question whether the wall was snow or ice—a question which could only be answered when the scimitar ridge had been climbed.

We roped up an hour later where the glacier became steeper and more crevassed. At last we began to make height and, zig-zagging back and forth, we wound our way through the crevasses, each of which some merciful Providence had provided with one bridge only. Easier névé led to a curious upper basin, the rim of which we climbed with some difficulty, kicking steps diagonally across a steep snow wall. We now saw the scimitar ridge closely above us, and made for a near-by hollow which appeared to offer a perfectly protected bivouac site. We pitched our little Marco Pallis tent at 4.15 p.m. Above us the steep white wall glinted in the evening sun, but even now we could not reach a decision whether it was snow or ice. We lay in the sun, watching the shadows lengthen among the sea of granite peaks to the west, flanked by the jagged silhouette of Ushba and the cloud-like domes of Elbruz.

It soon left us, so we began our elaborate preparations for the night.

Next morning dawned clear and fine, and by 6.0 a.m. we were climbing the steep slopes above the hollow, our crampons biting on the hard snow. We traversed in a wide sweep to the right and gained the base of an ice-swept funnel to the left of the scimitar ridge. We scampered up this nervously, and reaching its head, made an exceptionally steep diagonal traverse over a bergschrund to the crest of the ridge. The snow was in perfect condition and the slope extremely steep—exceeding 50 degrees. On the lower part of the ridge a cornice forced us on to its left flank, but later we followed its steep knife-edge, gaining height rapidly. The climbing and the situations were superb, and at 8.0 a.m. our ridge ran into a group of snow humps which hung like a balcony in the centre of the great snow face. On gaining them, we were overjoyed to find that the great wall ahead was of snow—only a thin coating on a base of ice, but enough to support the spikes of our crampons if the line of deepest snow was followed. Considerably relieved, we found a little platform and sat down for second breakfast at 8.20. Taylor took over the lead and tackled the slope direct, kicking toe steps. Striking a splendid rhythm, we mounted steadily upwards, and the surrounding rocks and glaciers sank below us, while the panorama of the great Bezingi peaks to the east rose into view. As we approached a band of rocks, the snow improved and our confidence grew. We reached their foot at 9.40, but as they were loose and ice-bound we skirted their base to the right and crossed steeper snow towards an ice gully between them and the hanging rim of séracs guarding the summit snows. A steep snow wall above a bergschrund gave some difficulty, but the foot of the gully was soon gained. This proved a tough customer and as I hacked steps in its vertical walls, Taylor, standing in the steps below, began to complain of the intense cold. Some steep and icy rocks barred the head of the gully, and I had great difficulty in climbing them. These were anxious moments, as Taylor was beginning to feel faint, and we had no belay. A short snow slope above led to a point on the north-east ridge, which we reached at 11 o'clock, to see the summit within striking distance. Straightforward climbing, firstly over ice coated with soft mush and then over névé slopes, brought us to a snow ledge under the last line of defences, a semi-circular ice-wall. Here the altitude began to tell, and putting on all our clothes as a protection against a biting wind, we broke through a breach in the ice and panted up the last slope of the summit snow cone.

The superb view was marred by the wind, and at 11.40 we ran down to shelter and made the best of a very chilly lunch. We proposed to descend the east face to the Adish plateau and from there to find a way down to the tent through the topmost ice-fall of the East Zanner glacier. At 12.15 p.m. we moved off, and keeping near the north-east ridge we found excellent snow which led us in a broad sweep to the right, over a number of crevasses, to a large snow-field at a lesser angle. Descending rapidly, we made for an obvious snow bridge across a broad crevasse below. We crossed this bridge and found ourselves on the brink of a vertical step. Retracing our steps, we crossed over to the north-east ridge and found our way blocked by an even higher ice-wall. The only alternative was to make a traverse to the east of the entire face. After negotiating a tricky sérac, easier work brought us to a corner, whence a very nasty traverse led under threatening séracs to the névés buttressing the east ridge. We found these in excellent condition and quickly ran down towards a col at the head of the East Zanner. Lower down, the snow covering had thinned out in places, and after some difficulty we reached this col on the rim of the Adish plateau and, skirting the base of a small intervening snow peak on its east, we gained the top of the Zanner ice-fall. It came as rather a shock so late in the day to find that the route of descent was not obvious. Half an hour was spent in searching for a possible weakness, and eventually at 4.30 we had to hammer an ice-piton into a crack and descend a 50-foot ice-wall on the doubled rope. The further descent of the glacier from here was very complicated and we drew several blanks. The snow kept changing in texture and we were grateful for crampons for the harder parts. After a bout of crevasse jumping, we espied our tracks of the previous day, indicating the position of the bivouac, and crossing the last slopes, we reached it at 5.10 p.m. A burden of anxiety was lifted from our shoulders, and we light-heartedly packed the tent and raced down the lower ice-fall. At 6.15 we unroped on the level ice and took off the crampons which we had worn since 6 o'clock that morning. We wearily threaded our way through the last crevasses and, on reaching the first bank of moraine, we espied one of Hodgkin's characteristic cairns, in which fluttered a piece of paper. Expecting the worst, we anxiously drew the paper from the stones and read his somewhat imperialistic message: 'Welcome to the conquerors of Tetnuld. God save the King.'

From Midland Association of Mountaineers Journal, 1938

15
The Red Snows

There were no Western mountaineering expeditions to the Caucasus between 1937 and 1958. The only non-Soviet visitors hailed from the countries behind the Iron Curtain. It was, in many ways, the period in which Soviet mountaineering came of age. Finding it hard to maintain overseas contacts, and to keep abreast of advances in technique and equipment, Soviet mountaineers developed their own climbing style. Until recently little has been known about their activities beyond their exploits in the Himalaya. When word of climbs on their home mountains did reach the West, it tended to concentrate on the Pamirs, the range north of the Hindu Kush. In many ways, however, the Caucasus has always been the forcing ground. Its peaks (somewhat lower than those in the Pamirs, many of which are over 6000 metres, and three over 7000 metres) are of a height where Alpine ethics can be relatively safely adhered to, and problems of extreme altitude are not relevant.

Now that the Iron Curtain has lifted much more information is available about the history of Soviet climbing and indeed of climbing in the Eastern Bloc countries in general. One thing that has become clear, although it was always suspected, is that for many Soviet climbers the dangers of the mountain were the least of their worries. It is ironic that mountaineering, which for so many people is a way of escape from the restrictions of politics and social conventions, should through Stalin's paranoia have become as political as any other sphere of existence. The purges which decimated so many brilliant Soviet politicians, soldiers, artists, and millions of completely ordinary people, also took their toll of the mountaineering community. Thanks to Eugene Gippenreiter, so long an invaluable link between British climbers and those in the Soviet Union, we have been able to find out about some of the more prominent mountaineers who suffered at the hands of Stalin's secret police. As he has made clear, though, the few cases we outline here were just the tip of the iceberg.

The man often credited as the first great Soviet mountaineer was

Vassily Semenowski (there is a peak named after him in the Caucasus). Born in 1884 he trained as a mountain guide in Switzerland before returning to Russia after the Revolution. In 1929 he organised the first training programme for mountain guides in the Caucasus, and in 1936 was the first climber to be declared an Honoured Master of Sport. Among his significant climbs was the first Soviet ascent (with Willi Merkl's party in 1930) of Schulze's route on Ushba South. In 1937, however, he was arrested and shot. The same fate befell Nicolai Gorbunov in 1938. An astute politician (he had been Lenin's personal secretary) and an outstanding scientist (holding the highest scientific title of Academician), Gorbunov led several expeditions to the Pamirs between 1928 and 1933. Another great pioneer in the Pamirs was Nikolai Krylenko, who led the Soviet half of a joint expedition with German climbers in 1928, as well as expeditions to the Eastern Pamirs in 1931 and to Pik Lenin in 1934. Arrested in 1938, Krylenko died in prison. His sentence was posthumously rescinded in 1954.

None of these three were just mountaineers. They had all dabbled in politics during dangerous times. The same cannot be said, though, for the Siberian Vitali Abalakov, one of the greatest and most famous Soviet mountaineers. As Victor Saunders has put it, 'Vitali Abalakov . . . dominated the scene after the Second World War to such an extent that if you take any great Caucasian face and there is an elegant rock line, that will be the Abalakov route.'[1] It is unfair, though, to consider just Abalakov's post-war career. He was one of the outstanding climbers in the Soviet Union in the 'thirties (although it is important not to confuse him with his brother Eugene who made the first Soviet traverse of Ushba in 1937, the first complete Dych-Tau to Koshtan-Tau traverse and the first Soviet traverse of the complete Bezingi Ridge, both in 1938). Vitali had shone particularly in the Pamirs, making a solo first ascent of Pik Communismus in 1933, as well as the first ascent of Pik Lenin from the north the following year and the first ascent of Pik Trapezia in 1935.

Vitali Abalakov was recovering from severe frostbite, incurred while descending from Khan Tengri in the Tien Shan in 1936, when he was arrested in 1937 on charges of counter-revolutionary activity. One of his crimes, apparently, was using foreign climbing equipment for propaganda purposes! He remained in prison for twenty months. When he tried to organise a morning exercise routine for his fellow prisoners he was placed in a special punishment cell. Fortunately for Soviet mountaineering, he was eventually acquitted and rehabilitated. His climbing career resumed after the war. Two of his climbs particularly worthy of attention are the North Face of Pik Schurovski by its North-West Rib (1947) and the North-East Face of Dych-Tau (1954). The first of these climbs is a long and intricate rock route, often compared to the Walker Spur on the North Face of the Grandes Jorasses, while the second still ranks as one of the more imposing of the classic face climbs in the range. Friedrich Bender has this to say about it: 'This is serious stuff! Anyone standing in the basin of the Mishirgi Glacier, head back, mouth wide open, and wondering whether there really can be a route up these icy cascades, should very seriously reflect whether or not to go any further. The rock-climbing is exceedingly hard, the snow sections are severely threatened by stonefall and avalanches which are the norm here.'[2]

One of Vitali Abalakov's companions on the North-East Face of Dych-Tau was the physicist Vladimir Kiesel. He had learnt to climb with Abalakov in the early 1930s and made some important ascents, including the first Soviet ascent of Ushba North in 1935 (with Aleinokov). Interestingly enough he retrieved from the summit the note which Cockin had left there in 1889! His climbing career was rudely interrupted between 1943 and 1948 when his family were designated 'enemies of the people'.

The list could be continued almost indefinitely. Boris Garf, for example, the editor of the 1952 Bezingi guidebook, spent two years in prison between 1937 and 1939. A. Poliakov was in prison camps and then in exile between 1938 and 1945. According to Eugene Gippenreiter, however, all the climbers who found themselves persecuted under Stalin were eventually acquitted, a small consolation to the many who were executed or died in prison.

Stalin's purges were, of course, not the only obstacle to mountaineering in the Caucasus during the 1940s–50s. The range was one of the battlefields in the Second World War after Hitler unwisely reneged on his agreement with Stalin and invaded the Soviet Union. At one stage half of the Caucasus was occupied by German troops and the fighting was ferocious. The Germans were anxious to cross the mountains and gain control of the oilwells to the south, but their supply lines were seriously stretched. Ironically, among the invading forces were several climbers who had been active in the Caucasus before the war, such as Wolfgang Gorter and Rudolf Schwarzgruber. The great Paul Bauer, who had led the successful Bavarian expedition of 1928, returned in 1943 in command of 2000 crack Alpine soldiers.

In August 1942 there occurred an incident that was to reverberate on through the Cold War years after the war. Members of the 1st ('Edelweiss') and 4th ('Enzian') Mountain Division, led by Captain Heinz Groth, obtained permission to attempt Elbrus. The Red Army had eleven men garrisoned in the Priut Hut, but they soon surrendered to the German troops. After three days acclimatising, an assault party set out for the summit in the early hours of the 21st. Conditions were atrocious. It was blowing a gale on the ridge, and bitingly cold. Men's eyes were caked with snow and visibility shrank to a few metres. One climber slipped and pulled off two of his companions. Luckily, the fourth man on the rope, Dr Karl von Kraus – who had climbed in the Caucasus before – managed to check and hold the fall. At 11 a.m. all the team reached the Western Summit and hoisted the Reich war flag in the snow. The message went out to the world that the swastika was flying from the highest peak in the Caucasus.[3]

The end of the war found a Caucasus devastated by fighting, its villages razed to the ground with only a few German camps left standing. Instead of helping to rebuild the area, Stalin exiled many of the Balkarian tribes for allegedly collaborating with the Germans. They were sent to the Asian republics, particularly to Kazakhstan, and allowed to return only when Kruschev came to power.

Nonetheless, it was during this period that the Soviet Union consolidated its distinctive approach to mountaineering. The trade unions set to work building the permanent camps that were to become the focal point of Soviet climbing. George Band described the highly regulated structure that he encountered on his visit to the Caucasus in 1958.

Under the direction of the All-Union Physical Culture and Sports Committee an Alpine section organised expeditions, Alpiniads and training camps which enrolled an average of 6000 climbers each year. Financial support came largely through Trade Unions who through their sports societies contributed 12–15 million roubles annually. After a few introductory climbs the novice receives a badge as a Mountaineer of the USSR. The most skilled and experienced climbers (some 200, I believe) have qualified as a Master of Sport, and come from all trades and professions. Igor Solodnev, first violin of the Bolshoi Theatre, is one, and so is the Geometer, Alex Alexandrov, the rector of Leningrad University. Competitions are held for long traverses or particularly difficult face climbs, and annual medals awarded in this so-called school for courage. Gregarious ascents are preferred, six or eight climbers often tackling a peak together, unlike our twos or fours in the Alps. Indeed, in 1935, a record was set when Elbrus was ascended by 500 collective farmers from Kabarda.[4]

However disciplined this approach may be, it is still light years away from the sort of sport-climbing that is now gaining a dangerous ascendancy in Western Europe. In many ways, as Band points out, this type of regimentation is a sensible response to the rigours of Caucasian climbing:

There seems to be a lack of easy ways off the big mountains. This means that, even in good conditions, an average party may require a couple of bivouacs on the ascent and another on the descent, in addition to a bivouac at the foot of the mountain – at the level of the non-existent hut – so that a party must be self-sufficient for at least five days away from its permanent camp. If the weather breaks – and there is no lack of storms in the Caucasus – the time out may be trebled. The Russian technique is to sit out the storm and carry on afterwards. As a result they always carry four-man tents, sleeping bags and sufficient food and fuel ... We began to understand the Russian approach. The controlled grading and group training of climbers coupled with their insistence upon safety prevents relatively inexperienced climbers being let loose on such long intimidating climbs.

George Band visited the Caucasus in 1958 as part of a nine-man expedition led by Sir John Hunt. They were the first foreign climbers in the range since the War (apart from the solitary visit of Joyce

Dunsheath is 1957). The opinion was still widely held after the 1942 Elbrus affair that all visiting alpinists were enemies and spies. It took four years of letter writing and delicate negotiations to gain permission. Once there, though, the British were largely free of the restrictions imposed on Soviet climbers and able to climb pretty much at will.

In the first of our two extracts John Hunt tells the tale of the expedition, while in the second George Band recounts its last climb, a fine new route on Dych-Tau climbed by himself and Mike Harris.

16

Welcome to the British Alpinists

by John Hunt

'*Welcome to the British Alpinists*' – this legend, prominently displayed above the entrance to the headquarters of the Spartak training camp in the Caucasus in 1958, was the 'Open Sesame' I had been seeking for four years. In 1954 my wife Joy and I had travelled to Moscow, where I was to lecture on the first ascent of Mount Everest. I gathered there had been some scepticism among Soviet mountaineers about the success of this climb, but at the end of my talk I was surrounded by a goup of eager young climbers, whose doubts had been set aside. There was spontaneous *rapport* between us. Through the interpretership of Yevgeni (Eugene) Gippenreiter, whose English was excellent and idiomatic, we discussed the possibility of British and Soviet climbers joining forces in the mountains. In all truth it was an optimistic hope, for such informal contacts between ordinary citizens of our two countries did not exist at that time.

The wheels of officialdom move slowly, but we took every opportunity to build relationships between individuals on both sides. Especially important was the friendship which developed between Eugene and myself; it was, I believe – without the usual connotation – a case of love at first sight. Everyone who knows him would agree that Eugene is an easy person to love. Tall and slim, he has one of the most unforgettable faces I know: a rather small, narrow head with a shock of unruly black hair, sallow complexion and a black moustache. The unforgettable part is less easy to define, coming from the infectiously good-humoured gleam in his dark eyes. Eugene, with his responsibilities for developing international contacts within the ambit of the Soviet Central Sports Council, has become an indispensable link with sportsmen the world over.

The opening moves were to arrange an exchange of lecturers. Charles Evans went to the Soviet Union to tell the story of the first ascent of Kangchenjunga in 1955; Master of Sport Yevgeni Beletski, accompanied by Gippenreiter, lectured before the Alpine Club in London and other mountaineering audiences about the philosophy and achievements of Soviet mountaineers. We never let an opportunity slip by to raise again the question of British climbers visiting some of the mountains in Russia. John Neill, a member of the Climbers' Club, was eager to organise a party of friends to climb in the Caucasus; and in 1957 the journalist-climber Chris Brasher asked me to join him in making a formal application to take an expedition there. I jumped at the chance. As the year drew towards its close we waited anxiously for a reply. Then, just after Christmas, a letter from Eugene Gippenreiter told that we had been given consent in principle to climb in the area of the Bezingi Glacier and Mount Ushba. It was a very exciting moment and we immediately went ahead with inviting others to join us, and with the preparations for our journey.

The party which gathered in the forecourt of the Royal Geographical Society on 25 June 1958 consisted of George Band, who had been the youngest member of the Everest expedition, and had since achieved distinction by being the first man, with Joe Brown, to climb Kangchenjunga, as well as making the first ascent of Huagaruncho in the Andes; John Neill, an industrial chemist, and Michael Harris, an engineer, both hailed from Wolverhampton; Derek Bull was a London insurance agent; Alan Blackshaw a civil servant; Dave Thomas, a geologist and Ralph Jones, a business man – both from Manchester. Chris Brasher had achieved lasting fame by winning a Gold Medal in the steeplechase event at the Melbourne Olympic Games two years beforehand. Common to all was our membership of the Climbers' Club whose main base of activity is in North Wales.

With the coincidence of three experienced rally drivers in the party we agreed to travel to Moscow by road. At this distance in time I have no regrets about that decision, although I confess I harboured considerable misgivings at the time. As it was, one of the three cars in our convoy managed to collide with a tram in Mulheim towards the end of the breakneck outward journey and, coming back, another overturned at speed on a cobbled road in Czechoslovakia, to be brought to a halt by a tree. We were obliged to leave the vehicles at the Polish border and continue our journey by train. In Moscow, where we spent two hectic days, we met Russia's leading mountaineer, the almost legendary Vitali Abalakov, Honoured Master of Sport. He was then well into his fifties; small, lean and completely bald, but reputed to be still at the peak of his stamina and skill, achieving climbs of the highest standard of difficulty. From Moscow, a plane, then bus took us on to Piatigorsk, a Caucasian resort with huge sanatoria for stomach and rheumatic troubles. The first part of our stay was to be spent at the nearby Spartak Camp.

Mountaineering in Russia is a highly organised, closely controlled, and competitive affair. Anyone who expresses an interest in climbing must attend a course, earn a certificate of competence and then, if he desires, to gain further experience, proceed through three standards towards the coveted title of Honoured Master of Sport. Only particular climbs on particular mountains within his certified competence are open to him, under the supervision of instructors, themselves Masters of Sport in mountaineering, at one of the established mountain camps. There is something to be said for this system, which is designed to limit accidents and the consequent searches and rescues. Much of the argument among our own climbing fraternity today stems not so much from a difference of principle as a difference in emphasis when it comes to developing the skills and experience necessary to cope with the risks which are an essential attraction of the sport. How far to carry the application of the principle: that is the question.

We had plenty of opportunity to observe the Soviet system in the sport of mountaineering during our stay at Spartak Camp and to discuss many climbing matters with its instructors and students. We noted the blend of discipline and freedom which governs the camp routine. It begins with a cheerful Ποβϱοθ γτϱο ('Good Morning') followed by a peremptory 'Get Up!' at 7 a.m. on the camp loudspeaker. Ten minutes later we were surprised to observe the students engaging in energetic exercises on the playground in front of the main building; others were running off in disciplined groups into the surrounding woods; some were swinging from ropes and parallel bars. One girl, evidently an aspirant speed-skating champion, was going through the movements of her skill as she slowly and repeatedly climbed a flight of steps.

Another group were preparing their skis for practice under ski champion Uri Zirianov on the slopes of Elbrus later in the day. I recall with some shame that the contribution of the decadent British climbers to all this purposeful activity was to wander round in our pyjamas taking photographs of the scene.

The morning physical training session was followed by cold showers and a gargantuan breakfast. I can almost feel the post-prandial discomfort I experienced after consuming a heavy sweet pudding. steaks with rice and vegetables, yoghurt and sour milk; *kvass* (a sweet drink made, I was told, of fermented milk and bread crusts); and tea. Then classes set off for the programme of instruction laid down, within the framework of a course lasting three weeks. It culminates in a three-day expedition, the climax of one such we were fortunate to witness. The group, consisting of twenty-five to thirty people, is returning from their excursions into the mountains, marching in step under the leadership of their instructors. They enter the exercise ground and come to a halt in front of Comrade Shevilov, commandant of the camp. The chief instructor reports that they have crossed this pass and climbed that mountain and the commandant says a few words of congratulation. The audience of camp staff, and onlookers like ourselves, applaud and the heroes, weary but delighted, break ranks. The audience moves forward and there are heart-felt handshakes and embraces; garlands and bouquets of flowers are presented. It is easy to be cynical, but I found this little ceremony rather touching, stemming as it did from the unaffected pleasure of everyone concerned. I was even more moved shortly afterwards when a teacher in electronics from a Siberian University – her name was Soya – came forward and presented me with a bunch of flowers which I had done nothing to deserve.

For our first climb in the Caucasus we chose a nearby summit, Pik Kavkaza, of approximately 12,795 feet. Being our first venture in these parts we decided that all our group of nine climbers should undertake the ascent and that we would invite some of the Russian instructors to accompany us. Commandant Shevilov deputed two swarthy Svanetians, stocky and black-moustachioed, Josef Kachiani and Misha Khergiani. We immediately warmed to these beaming, solid characters from one of the valleys on the far side of the Caucasus range. Both were highly skilled climbers, Josef being, at that time, champion rock-climber of the USSR. Later, we were to learn more of the organised competitions in mountaineering prowess which were so alien to Western European tradition. That night the whole party bivouacked on a ledge above the glacier by which we had approached and I shared a tent with Josef and Misha. Sandwiched together with Eugene Gippenreiter in the middle, acting as interpreter, we talked late into the night about mountains and mountain folk; they told me about their homes in the green pastures of Svanetia, surrounded by the dark forest; of their cattle and women folk, and the good red wine. From the voluminous depths of Josef's rucksack emerged quantities of dried, salted-fish from the Caspian Sea. So we ate, and talked.

In the dim light of 5th July we climbed up to the west ridge of our mountain and, as a beautiful day dawned, reached the summit. It made a magnificent start to the expedition, for we had clear views the length and breadth of the range. Eastwards we could see the big peaks of the central Caucasus, surrounding the Bezingi glacier which was to be our next destination. Nearby in the east rose the gentle pyramid of Elbrus, monarch of the massif, looking just like the pictures I had seen of Fujiyama in Japan. And immediately opposite, in the south, stood the double-headed Ushba with its satellite, Pik Shchurovski, Himalayan in architecture if not in altitude. I marvelled at the daring of our com-patriot Cockin who, with a Swiss guide Ulrich Almer from Grindelwald as companion, had reached its northern summit in 1888.

We were lucky to descend the mountain without mishap. The techni-cal difficulties are not great, but the rock was appallingly loose and three of our party were struck by falling boulders; I myself had a narrow escape while abseiling off a rock step when two rocks were dislodged from above, whirring down noisily within inches on either side of me. Mercifully intact, a very happy band of brothers returned to camp that evening in martial order, to be greeted by our hosts with flowers and fruit drinks. This simple but heart-warming little ceremony was so different from our experience of returning anonymously to the valley at the end of an alpine climb. At a reception later in the evening, to which Yevgeni Beletski and the inmates of neighbouring camps had been invited, we were the objects of friendly curiosity as we endeavoured to answer a battery of questions from people who had no previous contacts with the bourgeois Western world. 'What is the highest mountain in Europe?' It sounded like a question in a preliminary round for 'Mastermind', and provided an insight into the desire of our Soviet friends to be perceived as Westerners themselves, rather than to be associated in Western minds with the East. 'Elbrus,' I replied diplomatically.

The following day, staggering under loads weighing over sixty pounds, our party started up the Shkhel'da glacier for an eight-day expedition to climb Ushba. Our Russian companions this time were Anatoli Sisoyev, an artist, and a Kiev engineer, Anatoli Kustovski. This was a more serious undertaking, and our plans made it even more so, for we hoped to divide into two groups, and to make a double traverse of the mountain, one climbing from the north, the other repeating the route first climbed by the Oxford expedition in 1937. First, we had to negotiate a steep and heavily crevassed icefall to reach a snow shelf at 13,500 feet below the northern summit. The beginning of the climb was inauspicious; we set off in thick mist and drizzle, which turned to heavy snowfall as we climbed up through the crevasses. So bad were the conditions that we were forced to pitch our tents rather lower on the snow shelf (known as the 'pillow' of Ushba) than we had intended, about 1,500 feet below the summit. By next morning the tents were half buried by the new snow and bad weather persisted; but most members of the party, determined not to be defeated, succeeded in climbing the elegant pinnacle of Pik Shchurovski, which rises from the 'Pillow' opposite the north peak of Ushba, before settling down to a siege of that mountain. A Soviet group appeared through the mists and there we remained, nine Britons and eight Russians, prisoners of the elements, for the following three days and nights. Kustovski, the engineer, assisted by Band, Brasher and Blackshaw, put some of the time to good use by excavating an ice cave beneath the surface of the shelf; they whiled away the time with sing-songs and chess. The cave was designed for six, but on the third evening no less than eleven of us crowded into that confined space for the serious business of deciding, not so much whether to acknowledge defeat – for Ushba was impregnable under its cloak of heavy snow for days to come – but how to withdraw without catastrophe. Indeed, our descent of the icefall next day, with the snow still falling and avalanches thundering down on both flanks from the unseen mountainsides surrounding us, is one of my more unpleasant recollections. Once more, I experienced the misery, familiar from Himalayan expeditions in the 'thirtes, of floundering waist-deep in heavy new snow.

There was anxiety in the camp about our safety; an accident had occurred to another party and Comrade Shevilov had mustered an eighty-man rescue group to start off in case we failed to return by the time and date we had undertaken to be back. 'Control Time' as it is termed, is a matter to which the Russians attach great importance as a safeguard against accidents; any party which fails to return within their estimates gives rise to a rescue expedition and it ill behoves them to be both safe and late. Fortunately for our reputations we were just within our time schedule, but it was a wet and bedraggled group of Russians and Britishers which drew itself up, attempting a disciplined entry, marching in step into the camp precincts at 6 p.m. that night. Flowers and fond embraces, and a large hot meal, soon restored our morale.

The weather continued to be abysmally awful. 'An unremittingly terrible day' was my diary entry for the fifth continuous day of this depressing spell. But for me it has a happy memory. I had been asked to pay a call at a camp for Ukrainian schoolchildren a few miles away and, on arrival, was surrounded by a milling crowd of eager youngsters, as uninhibited as any of our own kids at home. After doing my best to answer their questions, I thought it might be worth risking a question on my part, which I have often put in similar circumstances in Britain. I asked the head-teacher if the children might have a day's holiday to mark my visit? Well, he did not need to consider the matter, for the reply was provided by the uproarious response of the assembled young people themselves.

It was now 12th July, and we were due to move further east into the central Caucasus. At a moving little ceremony, we bade farewell to our Spartak hosts, and were soon bumping in a lorry along the rough roads northwards to the plains at Nalchik, then east and, later, southward bound for the mountains again, to reach our main objective, the great mountain cirque of the upper Bezingi glacier. Eugene Gippenreiter was still with us. And to our great delight, so too was Anatoli Kustovski, the carefree humorist who could make us laugh even without understanding his many jokes. Towards evening we entered a deep gorge for a hair-raising two hours' drive, sometimes through fast-flowing torrents swollen by the recent rains; sometimes squeezing our way between huge boulders which had been dislodged from the cliffs above, wondering whether more might descend upon us. It was with a sigh of relief that we emerged in the failing light on to the uplands beyond, and came upon a sprawling half-built village.

Bezingi is the chief village of the Balkari tribe; nearby were the ruins of a former site, reputedly destroyed by order of Stalin in 1942 as an act of retribution for the encouragement given by these independently-minded people to the German armies, when they reached the Caucasus and hoisted the Swastika flag on the summit of Elbruz. The vengeful dictator banished the entire tribe to Kazakstan in Central Asia. But dramatic changes were now taking place. Nikita Kruschev had made the second of his famous speeches condemning Stalin's many brutalities, including his actions against the Balkaris and a neighbouring tribe, the Chegen-Inguzes. They were being given every assistance to return to their native valleys after an absence of fourteen years, and were beginning to rebuild their lives. It was an exciting time to be in the Soviet Union. We motored a few miles beyond the village, to the end of the road, and set up our tents in a meadow, dog-tired.

Very early next day I awoke to the sound of a querulous voice outside my tent. Peering out, I saw an elderly bearded person seated outside Eugene's tent. He had brought some donkeys to carry our loads to the snout of the Bezingi glacier, but he was clearly displeased with these intruders. Who were we? Why were we spoiling his hay? But his mood changed, his aquiline features broadened into a wide smile when he learned that we were British mountaineers. His father had told him of two other Englishmen (they were Donkin and Fox) who had disappeared on Koshtan-tau, one of the big peaks above us, in the last century. He himself remembered the German expeditions in the 'thirties. He had returned from exile the previous year, but many others, especially the younger Balkaris, had preferred to stay in Kazakstan;

some had run away after arriving in Bezingi. He invited us to his dwelling, or *kosh*, where we drank milk. We were his honoured guests.

The last lap of the journey to the glacier was unbelievably beautiful. After reading Freshfield's account of his journey in these parts, I had expected to find a barren waste; but the huge herds of goats of his day, and the human beings who owned them, had been absent for fourteen years. Nothing could have been more strikingly different from his description of 'ugliness' and 'treeless turf'. We wandered through lush meadows, knee deep in alpine flowers; And in the distance, dazzling white against a clear blue sky, was the huge rampart of the Bezingi Wall, its crest at over 16,000 feet; it was worth travelling all this way simply to see, let alone to attempt the climbs on this great barrier. That night we camped on grass-covered moraine slopes beneath Koshtan-tau at the junction of two rivers, and within a few hundred yards of a big Russian camp, occupied by an expedition of the Academy of Sciences. Further away was yet another expedition, of non-academic character: TRUD (the Union of Scientific Workers). We spent the evening with the academicians, who were most helpful in explaining the local topography and advising us on the history of climbing in the area. Boris Garf was there and with him his daughter Marina, a doughty lass who was well on her way to achieving the distinction of being a Master of Sport; as far as I am aware the masculine title includes the feminine in this case. Alex Baldin, our friend from Birmingham University was also in the group. With so much experienced advice it was not difficult to decide on the routes we would attempt on the Bezingi Wall, and to divide ourselves into three parties; it was to be my own good fortune to be with Alan Blackshaw, Ralph Jones and Chris Brasher in tackling the Schwarzgruber Rib, climbed only once previously, by the 1935 Austrian group, which traces an elegant line up the Wall and leads to the summit of Dzhangi-tau (16,564 feet). Our strongest party was bound for a point further east along the foot of the Wall, to attempt the Müller route, a buttress thrown out by Shkhara, at 17,064 feet, the second highest peak in the Caucasus; it was graded as somewhat more difficult than our climb; Anatoli Kustovski was a member of this group, with George Band, Derek Bull and Michael Harris. Eugene, John Neill and

Dave Thomas were to climb Gestola, at the right-hand end of the rampart.

The weather was now fine and looked settled. We were excited by the prospects of these challenging climbs and we lost no time in starting up the moraine of the Bezingi glacier the following morning, 15th July, leaving with the Russians a Control Time of 8 a.m. on 19th for our return. It was a long, weary plod up the valley, carrying four days' food and all our mountain gear. The glacier is T-shaped and we were walking along the stem, heading for a corner where it meets the wide basin, some three miles in length, at the foot of the Wall. Here we stopped for the night, scratching out a platform in a little ablation valley and crawling into our sleeping bags before lighting our Meta stove. In the fading light I looked across the glacier, my eye travelling slowly up the big buttress of rock and the fine ribbon of snow crest, sharply tilted, which would be the focus of all our thoughts and effort during the next three days. It looked formidable and I stayed tensed and anxious for a while before dropping off to sleep.

It was cold when we stirred ourselves at 2 a.m. Accustomed to alpine starts, we had packed everything overnight and had made a detailed examination of the lower part of the route which we would have to climb in the dark. There was a little icefall, menaced by an impending wall of séracs, but safely frozen at this hour. We swung left, climbing very steep snow slopes and a series of rock bands which led us, our limbs still numb with cold despite the strenuous nature of the climbing, on to the top of the rock buttress. It was 9 a.m. when we stepped out on to a level snow terrasse and began to thaw out in the full sunlight; we had been climbing for six hours. My tensions, sustained throughout that period and culminating in the final stretch of exceedingly steep ice, had gone; I was ready to enjoy the hard climbing ahead.

We were now following the crest of the narrow, sharply inclined snow rib; from time to time there were rock pitches, some of them difficult: a small tower, a rather holdless slab. Then I took the lead, with Ralph on my rope, as a great sweep of ice slope rose above us, about 400 feet in height and angled at 55 degrees. Thus far we had climbed without crampons and, in my concentration on the task ahead, I started up this slope without pausing, cutting steps. But with the increasing angle I stopped and, banging in the first ice peg, asked Ralph to strap my crampons on; it was no place to do the job myself. Ralph is at his best in situations like this; in a social setting he contrives to give the impression of light-hearted frivolity; he is a great yarner and a puller of other people's legs. In an awkward moment on a mountain he radiates calmness and patience; it was this latter quality which was called for as we stood in those ice steps while he fiddled with my crampon straps, refraining from the merited suggestion that I should have thought to put them on sooner.

On we went, for the next hour, up this big slope, I hammering in pegs at intervals to safeguard our progress. As we rose higher, avalanches peeled off the precipices on either hand, but we were safe on the rib and, utterly absorbed in the work, we were scarcely aware of them. As the day wore on I began to feel the altitude; we were impressed by the scale of the mountain, the Wall seemed endlessly high. It was 6 p.m. and we had been climbing for fifteen hours, yet still there was no relenting in the steepness; the rib became rather more ice than snow and more steps were needed; the light began to fail. And then, at long last, we stepped out on to easier ground. The rib was below us and the top of Dzhangi-tau appeared to be no great distance above. The technical difficulties were over. It was time to scrape a platform in the snow, crawl into our Zdarsky sack and get some food inside us, for we had been on the move for eighteen hours with very few pauses to eat.

I think we all slept reasonably well, despite the cold and the clatter of falling stones. Ralph and I snuggled close together, lying uncomfortably on our climbing rope, our feet in our rucksacks; such bivouacs are long remembered. As the light grew stronger we could appreciate the striking position of the little balcony we had chosen: jutting out over the plunging precipice we had toiled up, the glacier seemed to be vertically underneath us, 6,000 feet below, its surface creased with crevasses. Over the way was the great rock tower of Dykh-tau, first climbed by Alfred Mummery with the Swiss guide Zurfluh in 1888, on which we too, had designs. Thawing out gradually we got ourselves ready in leisurely fashion, confident that our peak was 'in the bag'.

How wrong we were! As soon as we set off it was obvious that we were in trouble. We slanted up towards the summit ridge on snow with a nasty, breakable crust into which we sank to our knees; it was back-breaking work, calling for a change in the lead every 50 yards or so. We came to a big crevasse, its far side defended by a snow wall 25 feet high; there was only one place where it could be crossed. Alan Blackshaw spent more than an hour surmounting the obstacle, ramming in two ice-axes near the top, as make-shift hand- and foot-holds; it was a fine lead. Above, we were on steeper ground which had been swept by an avalanche and the going was easier; but beyond was an area where fresh snow still lay on the hard underlying surface and it was obvious that it was only a matter of time, the effect of the sun's rays and a little human encouragement, to start it sliding down the mountain. I was with Brasher that morning and he led up this deep, treacherous stuff. We came to another big crevasse, bridged precariously by the new snow. Chris crawled across; there was an ominous creaking noise, but he was safely on the upper side of the monster and secured the rope for me to follow. Halfway over the snow collapsed and I was falling into the abyss. But only for about 25 feet, for to my relief and surprise I landed on a secondary snow bridge beneath the upper surface, frail and 'see-through', providing suggestive glimpses of the blue depths beneath, but enough to arrest my progress. This was just as well, for Brasher, placed as he was on the loose incoherent surface above, would inevitably have been dragged in too, and the others would have had a tragedy on their hands. I was hauled out, none the worse for the incident.

It was a moment for decision-making and for mountaineering judgment. There was the crest of the summit ridge, 300 feet above us; the top of Dzhangi-tau was further along the ridge to our right and perhaps we were 600 feet beneath it. But our progress in this awful stuff was terribly slow, the snow was dangerous and, if it held us while we reached the ridge, would surely peel off later, when the sun had warmed it. The unanimous conclusion was negative, we must turn back. It was, of course, disappointing, but we could comfort ourselves that we had climbed the Schwarzgruber Rib and had surmounted the difficult part of the climb, all of which would now have to be reversed; there were many hours of absorbing and taxing work before us. I have often felt sharp unhappiness about giving up a mountain, but this was a moment when I felt quite sure our decision was right.

Descending the snow wall above the lower crevasse, I was last on the rope. One of the two axes which Alan had placed as holds was dislodged by my weight and for the second time that day I was airborne, doing a neat somersault to land head downwards in the soft, deep snow 25 feet below. This time we were able to laugh – or rather, the others did—at the ridiculous spectacle. Below the bivouac site we found the ice rib a much more difficult proposition than on the way up; the ice was rotting and we took more than three hours to descend the first section, taking great precautions to avoid a slip. Again we bivouacked, less comfortably and in our weariness, slept little. The weather broke that night and the climb down to the distant glacier was something of a nightmare in falling snow and thick mist. It was quite dark when we pulled in our abseil rope for the last time at the foot of the lower rock buttress; in all, we had used this technique on ten occasions, sliding down the doubled length of rope 100 feet at a time. As it grew darker, Chris waxed vociferous, swinging wildly at the end of the rope, more or less blinded by the specially darkened snow goggles which he was still wearing and which added to his short-sightedness. I have seldom felt so weary as when we groped our way across the level surface of the glacier, arriving after 10 p.m. to spend our fourth night out beside the moraine. But for me it had been one of those great climbs and, summit or no summit, I felt deeply content with my companions and the world in general.

The only remaining anxiety was the matter of our 'Control Time'; we were several hours' fast walking away from Base Camp and must report there by 8 a.m. next morning. Chris Brasher, our Olympic hero, was the obvious man for the job. I stirred the reluctant runner at 3 a.m. and for twenty minutes, did my best to keep pace with him while the others packed up more slowly. Then he was away, and saved British honour by redeeming our pledge to be back on time.

The Gestola group were already back when we reached camp, triumphant from their climb; fortunately for them, it was much shorter than ours and they had escaped in time to avoid the bad weather. But we still waited for the return of the Shkhara party, whose 'Control Time' was set for the 20th July. Sure enough, within minutes of their dead-line, there they were on the edge of the moraine, half a mile away, in line and getting their clumsy booted feet into step for the final approach. There was no lack of flowers in the meadow all around us and we scurried about to produce the traditional bouquets for our friends. Indeed, they had earned the accolade. Like ourselves, they had been caught in the mist and snowfall which began before they arrived on their summit, after achieving a climb of considerable character and difficulty. Notwithstanding this they had made an impressive return by a different route, down the North-East Ridge, thus completing a trav-erse of Shkhara.

It was pleasant to relax after all these adventures. The rain was almost an asset to our social contacts, for we huddled into the larger tents of our friends of the Academy of Sciences and the Union of Scien-tific Workers to tell our stories and listen to their singing. For the Russians, impromptu concerts are very much part of the mountain holiday; they had a large repertoire and they sang well. In our honour they had come prepared with a song about British sailors running the gauntlet of the weather and German submarines in the Arctic convoys to Archangel, to which there was a sentimental encore about a British sailor and a Russian girl.

When I recounted our climb on Dzhangi-tau, and our decision to turn back within shouting distance of the top, our hosts were plainly incredulous. Even if this were the case, they seemed to imply, it was not customary to admit the fact. I was intrigued that our confession had unwittingly exposed a wide divergence in our approaches to moun-taineering, with deeper philosophical overtones. Not less interesting was a conversation we had at that time, when news reached us over the Russian transmitter and receiver station which is part and parcel of these major expeditions in the mountains. There was trouble in the Near East; marines from the American Sixth Fleet in the Mediterranean had landed in the Lebanon and British forces had re-entered Jordan. Soviet propaganda was making the most of the crisis. What should we do, isolated from our own people in this remote spot? Most helpfully, the Russians transmitted the question I put to our Ambassador in Mos-cow, Sir Patrick Reilly. They enjoyed the humour of the situation, too.

Sitting round a table in their mess tent for our evening gossip, someone suggested that they might help us get over the frontier into Turkey. Someone else thought this might involve our friends in considerable risk to themselves, but he said, 'Never mind. You British can enjoy some splendid climbing for the next twenty-five years or so, in Siberia.'

And we made social calls of a different kind. Two Balkari shepherds were minding a large mixed flock of sheep and goats on the meadow. They told us that wolves had become a menace to the flock, emboldened after the long absence of human beings from the valley. I was impressed by the enormous size of some wolf paw-prints I had seen in the mud beside the glacier. The younger shepherd was especially friendly; they regarded us as their personal guests in Balkaria. Every morning they placed a can of milk outside our tents, from their only cow. Askerbi took his ancient gun, dated 1850, up the hillside and shot a fine ibex, of which we had seen large herds in the valley, tame from many years without threat from human beings. The choicest meat was for us. 'But,' he begged us, 'don't say a word about this to my father in the village. He does not approve of hunting and has forbidden me to shoot.' Askerbi was a man in his late forties, his father had reached a ripe old age, common in those parts, of 107. 'And what,' he asked, 'was the hunting like in England?' We tried to conjure up the familiar scene of red-coated huntsmen, stirrup cups and the like. 'And what did a man have to pay for a wife?' We explained that expenses began after marriage, not before. 'Why (pointing to our packets of Weetabix which, with a kit inspection of our clothing, equipment and special food, we had laid out at the request of the inquisitive Soviet climbers) do you like these dried foods?' We explained the merits of lightening the climbers' burdens (the Russians like carrying heavy tins of fruit, meat, caviar and so on). We added that Vitawheat was especially popular with our women folk, as it helped them to keep slim. 'But why should they want to be slim?' We did our best to speak up for the girls, but our answer will be seen as chauvinistic today: 'Because it makes them attractive to men.' 'Nonsense,' retorted Askerbi scornfully. 'They are far more cuddly when they are fat.' Of course he was right: love in a cold climate.

There was still time for one more big climb and the choice had to be Dykh-tau. There were casualties in our ranks, but we managed to muster two strong groups: one to repeat the Mummery route on the south buttress, the other comprising our two best rock-climbers, Mike Harris and George Band, who wanted to attempt a formidable pillar supporting the east peak of the mountain, which ran parallel to the Mummery line. I was with Blackshaw, Eugene and Chris Brasher on the latter climb. Ours was a most disappointing story, for I had set my heart on climbing Dykh-tau, having stored up memories of Mummery's description from boyhood reading. Our start was unpropitious; Chris had to send a report to the *Daily Express*, which had helped us with funds. We began to climb two and a half hours later than intended, making it impossible to reach the relatively high bivouac which I considered essential to success. Then he had the great misfortune to be stricken by gastric trouble as we made height next morning. So serious was it that, within 1,500 feet of the summit, we had to settle him in a safe nook among the rocks while we made a half-hearted attempt to reach the summit and return to him within the day. But it was not possible and, about 500 feet higher, we came back and escorted our casualty down to the glacier. I shall always regret that missed opportunity, but I am glad to say that Chris recovered shortly afterwards; and the *Daily Express* had their headline: 'Hunt falls down crevasse.'

At the foot of Dykh-tau on the evening of 23rd July we found Boris Garf, with Marina and two other Russians, preparing to follow Band's and Harris's route. Another Russian party was coming across the Bezingi glacier, after giving up an attempt on the Müller route on Shkhara, recently climbed by our own group. This looked to me like an intentional policy to establish Soviet prowess. The impression was reinforced when, months later, I found that the record of the first ascent of the route, eventually forced up the east peak of Dykh-tau by its south pillar, was entered in the name of our Russian friends. Later I was told by Eugene Gippenreiter that the British achievement was recognised by Soviet mountaineers, but that the reason for its omission from the official annals was because no formal report had been submitted by our climbers. I have no reason to doubt the report, sent me by Boris himself after their climb, that his party did succeed; I applaud the many fine achievements of Soviet mountaineers in the Caucasus and elsewhere; but it is most regrettable that the prior achievement of Band

and Harris was ignored. I learned later that a second attempt to follow our party on Shkhara ended in tragedy when two Russian climbers fell to their deaths fairly low down on the Müller Rib.

Back at Base Camp, we waited anxiously for the return of Mike and George. It was 27th July and we were due to leave for home; the donkeys were waiting on the far side of the Bezingi torrent. Some of us were going to cross the range at the head of the glacier and descend through Svanetia to Sukhumi on the Black Sea, while others would escort our baggage to Moscow. But there was still no sign of our friends; their 'Control Time' was midday. A few minutes after 12 noon Boris Garf came over from his camp. 'We must organise a search party,' he said. Indeed, there was no alternative; we unpacked our mountain gear and, filled with forebodings, followed one of the Russian girls, Ulla, who volunteered to act as our guide to the northern approaches to Dykh-tau. It was raining hard and the mists were low on the mountains. As we climbed up the screes, I turned over in my mind all the sad and difficult things which might have to be done. Suddenly John Neill, just in front of me, stopped in his tracks: 'There are two figures ahead,' he said. Ralph's binoculars helped us identify them. There was a cheer, we waved our ice-axes and ran forward. They were late, but they had made a great climb; their success and their safety were the only things which mattered.

The rain continued the next day as we walked down the valley; we were dripping wet, but it mattered not at all. We had climbed in 'the frosty Caucasus'; we had been shown courtesy and kindness by everyone we met; the door was ajar for others to pass that way.

Condensed from *Life is Meeting*, 1978

17

'Sorry We Are Late':
A New Route on Dykh Tau

by George Band

Some people think caviar tastes like a dose of tapioca in cod-liver oil. But I like it. That's one of the things I discovered pretty quickly in the Soviet Union. So here I was now, seated at a long camp table, with a plateful of rusks before me and a bowlful of the delicious food at the side, just waiting to be swallowed. I set to, spreading it thickly on the rusks which I crushed noisily between my teeth. It was well-nigh impossible, except between mouthfuls, to overhear the conversation bubbling around me. Gradually I became aware that I was missing something important. I set the caviar down.

This was our first evening at the Mishirgi Camp. To make us feel at home, the climbers from the Academy of Sciences had hospitably invited us over to an alfresco meal. There was caviar, Caucasian honey, apricots, and chocolate, a pleasant change from our own camp food. My eyes shone. Only a few of the Russians joined us in eating; the rest sat around closely, smiling paternally as if we were sea-lions enjoying feeding-time at the zoo. At the head of the table John Hunt and Boris Garf conversed in fluent French, and I gathered that Garf, a Master of Sport, was anxious to help us making our climbing plans. This was kind. He probably knew the Bezingi area better than any climber, and nobody was better qualified to advise us. But can't he wait until tomorrow? I thought.

Since there were no descriptive guide-books, it was my job to make notes on suitable routes—as detailed as possible—for those we chose to climb. I could not handle maps, photographs, paper, and pencil and still stuff myself, especially as it was getting dark. On my left, Mike Harris was gathering similar information from Alex Baldin, another Master of Sport, who also knew the area, and, in addition, spoke good English. It seemed that both Garf and he were leaving early next morning on a several-day climb. In fact, they were giving up their final evening in camp—when they probably had many last-minute preparations to make—to help us. I felt I was being ungrateful. I pushed the caviar away and took out pencil and paper.

Sitting at a dinner table on the edge of two circles of conversation is to be like the donkey that stayed midway between two bales of hay. Which way to turn? Straining your ears, you try to take in both. Then, as one becomes engrossing, the thread of the other is lost.

'Mummery's route on Dykh-tau would be a splendid introduction . . .' Something more original would be better, I think.

'There are two unclimbed ribs on Mishirgi.' . . . That's more like it, but are we fit enough yet?

'What's the height of the Bezingi Wall?' A sudden question catches you napping.

Eventually I sided with Mike and Alex, who were crouched together over a map. Alex I knew to be particularly understanding and helpful. When he had been in England in the spring, studying nuclear physics, we had climbed together one week-end in Wales. Imagining himself to be completely out of training, he had said rather formally: 'Please do not regard me as a representative Soviet mountaineer.'

We had laughed about this in our party afterwards, thinking it would be a good catch-phrase to apply to ourselves in case of any short-comings. I was particularly keen that in our climbs with the Russians, whether together or in separate parties, there should not be any feeling of rivalry or invidious competition. We were extremely interested in each other's achievements and techniques, but there was no need to rush ahead and prove that one or the other was superior. Mountains are too big and men too small for that.

Although we had not discussed it out aloud, I felt that Mike and I had much the same sort of climbs in mind. It would be wonderful if we could form a climbing party together. As we picked Alex's brain, a natural 'sport-plan', to use the Russian terminology, evolved. We had two weeks more—time for two big climbs, perhaps three if we had luck, cut out the rests in between, and had perfect weather. The Bezingi Wall was a certain choice. This tremendous face of ice-slopes and hanging glacier, 7,000 feet high and five miles long, was the finest in Europe – upthrust by the same forces that forged the Himalayas.

For our first climb here it would be wise to select one where the route-finding was reasonably straightforward and the difficulties not great. The north ridge of Shkhara led directly to the highest point of the Wall. It had been climbed twice previously, first by an Austrian party in 1930, then, in 1948, by the Russians. They judged the standard of difficulty to be 5A. As there was yet one higher grade upon their scale, 5B, it could not be called impossible. In fact it seemed ideal. From Shkhara we could look across the upper basin of the Bezingi towards the southern ramparts of Dykh-tau.

Dykh-tau, like the Grépon above Chamonix, or Nanga Parbat above the Fairy Meadow, was yet another mountain made famous by Mummery's early exploits. One of my best book bargains as an impecunious undergraduate was a shilling second-hand edition of his *Climbs in the Alps and the Caucasus*. So slim seemed my chances of ever treading the same respected ground, that I had completely forgotten the chapters on the Caucasus. But re-reading them before the trip, I longed to climb this peak which, at the time, he believed to be the second highest in Europe.

Since then, surveyors have found that Shkhara wins this place by a snowy head. Dykh-tau is third. Several Russians had asked us whether we intended to tackle Elbrus, the highest of all, but we said politely, without explaining that it was an easy mountain, that our 'sport-plan' precluded us from doing it.

Although I longed to climb Dykh-tau, I felt that a repetition of Mummery's route, seventy years after he had created it, did not sparkle with originality. So when Alex showed us a photograph of the south face with its twin, tower-like summits, I looked intently. Pointing to the right of Mummery's route, to a clean, steep, rock rib which led directly from the lower slopes to the eastern peak, he said: 'It is unclimbed.'

I caught my breath. A wave of anticipation surged through me. Already I was snatched up into the clouds, clinging to the sun-drenched rock, spurred on by that half-exultant, half-dread thought: Is there a way? If a storm breaks, what then? Frozen to the marrow, hunched immobile in sodden clothes, slowly paying out the rope and wishing to shrink into a fissure of oblivion and warmth. Why does one climb? Not always for a surfeit of pleasure. New routes on high peaks call for all that is best in a man. What a magnificent route this would be – and typically English on south-facing rocks. Mummery would have leapt from his grave ... The caviar lay forgotten.

We climbed Skhara, which involved us in five bivouacs, then after a full day's rest in camp, Mike and I were back at Misses Kosh, this time bound for Dykh-tau. A picnic-party from Trud was there and the girls bashfully handed us posies of wild flowers. An unexpected kiss in return provoked much clicking of cameras and, laughing and joking, we joined them and polished off their biscuits and honey.

With a tinge of regret we tore ourselves away. I should have enjoyed a further day 'recuperating' as the Russians were so friendly, but our time was running out. If we wanted another climb it was best to allow the greatest possible time for it. Since the whole party was planning to move on Saturday, July 26th, we gave noon on Saturday as our 'control time'. Today was Tuesday, so we had no more time than on Shkhara, but on this occasion we were attempting a new route, not a proven way. Because of the need for speed, we had felt that a party of two would be best and so here I was, doing my best to keep up with Mike. Derek and Anatoli were mild casualties, with blisters and an infected thumb, so we did not feel too selfish going off upon our own.

It was good to know that we should not be alone on the mountain, for the other still-active members of the party, John, Alan, Chris, and Eugene, had teamed up to try Mummery's route. Also Boris Garf, with his daughter and two friends, revealed that they also had designs upon 'our' rib and wished to follow us a day behind. I hope they did not feel that we were stealing a march on them, but we promised not to knock down any stones.

I do not know why the Russians tend to climb in such large parties. Perhaps they are naturally more gregarious than we. Except in the event of an accident, two climbers seem the ideal number. They can romp along without waiting for or holding up the others. Life is at its simplest and most enjoyable. Climbing with Anatoli had been great fun and, in spite of our ignorance of each other's language and details of technique, we had got on extremely well together. But naturally a greater effort was required and this must have induced a corresponding strain. I am sure he must have felt it too.

Although two may be the ideal number, I was very glad to see Alan looking out for us at the German bivouac near which we had camped for Shkhara. Tea was ready and so was I. From here our routes diverged. The others struck off towards Mummery's bivouac, and Mike and I continued up a minor glacier flowing down from Mishirgi-tau. It was a gloomy, showery evening. We wondered about the weather; found a rock beneath which to sleep and passed an uneventful night.

By eight o'clock next morning we had reached the rocks at the foot of the buttress. We moved unroped at first, enjoying the unencumbered freedom this allows. Momentarily the angle steepened. I noticed a good belay, if it should be necessary, as I climbed in the lead up on to a little rib of rock. It was fairly smooth and flecked with snow but a slanting crack allowed me to jam my gloved hands comfortably. I stood up on a toe-hold. There's a handhold missing, I thought. If I put my left foot on that side-hold, what can I grasp when I've pulled up? Nothing. I moved down again.

'How about roping?' I eyed Mike.

'It gets easier just above,' he said.

'That's true.'

But to myself I thought: That doesn't make this move any easier. Then aloud: 'I'll have another shot.'

This time I had solved it: both hands jammed; left foot on the side-hold; right foot on the toe-hold. Now release the right-hand jam and reach up for that niche. Gently. . . . Wow!

I was falling. Mike's arms milled in a courageous effort to catch me. In vain. I was sliding on steep snow. I clawed desperately with my fingers and toes. And suddenly I stopped.

I was standing on a level ledge the size of a suitcase. Mike was twenty feet above. I looked down at the snow-covered slabs. If I were to drop my rucksack now, how far would it go? Two hundred—three hundred feet? Would it even stop on the snow? There was another cliff below. I felt slightly sick and breathed a prayer.

Unroped! I really had no right to be unscathed. This was the narrowest escape I had ever had on a mountain. My foot had slipped and with gloved hands on wet rocks, the jams were not enough to hold. Like a pestering fly on a horse's flank, Dykh-tau had nearly brushed me off. It was an object lesson and I deserved it. I should have insisted on roping up, not just suggested. Far better lose face than life.

We uncoiled the rope now; 250 feet of nylon medium belonging to Alan. He had very kindly lent it to us because the other long one had been cut on Shkhara. I belayed and Mike inspected the pitch. The embers of my self-esteem flickered a little as he removed his gloves and pondered the awkward bit, refusing to move prematurely and risk repeating my *faux pas*. At length he moved up neatly and belayed. I followed, thankful for the security of the rope which made it seem quite simple now. I led on, anxious to regain self-confidence. It was easier, thank goodness, and I did not stop until all the rope was out. There was no belay so I hammered a piton into the rock for safety. I felt that harmony had been restored.

There had been plenty of time while on Shkhara to look across and scrutinise the buttress we were on. The sheerest place had seemed to be about one-third of the way up, and as we looked up now we could see a great rock-tower thrusting vertically through the gathering clouds. Slightly intimidated, we stopped for lunch, and while munching sardines and crisp-bread we peered upwards searching for a route. In a corner on the left there was a crack. It seemed the best place to try so we tied up our sacks, checked our pitons, took a last swig of sweet lemonade, and launched the attack.

At much the same time the rain and sleet began. We took it in turns to lead until I began to feel that Mike could be making a much better job of the pitch I was on, particularly as it looked distinctly harder above.

Mike had probably never been fitter in his life than at present. After many years' steady and competent climbing—far more than I could claim—he had suddenly convinced himself that he was capable of leading the hardest routes. In Wales, just before the expedition, he had dashed up Cenotaph Corner to prove it. Success at severe rock-climbing is very much a matter of confidence; fitness geared to an attitude of mind. When I knew that Mike was there, it seemed silly on a route of this seriousness to potter on a problem which he could probably solve with more safety and in half the time.

With the hail peppering us, he needed a little encouragement to get started, but soon a couple of pitons were in and he had moved up into a wide, slabby groove, topped by an overhang. Although it seemed an age to me, it cannot have been long before he was dangling in rope stirrups attached to the rock with pitons and contemplating a trick move out to the left.

The friction on the doubled rope through half a dozen karabiners must have been trying for him, but eventually he swung up and over on to a ledge, and I was following. It was a fine lead, perhaps the hardest of the climb. I stood panting beside him, hardly feeling ready for the comparatively holdless cracks and grooves above. Again I let him take the lead and by giving him a shoulder enabled him to climb up where I had failed. Perhaps the unfortunate start to the day was making me overcautious, but, looking back, I do not regret it.

The angle eased. We lengthened our pitches. I pulled up over a little wall, cocked a leg over and there I was, on the knife-edge crest of the ridge. We had passed the tower! On the other side, sheltered from the wind was a small snow-ledge, ideal for a bivouac. What luck! We had not seen such a good resting-place during the whole day's climbing. We were soon laying out our bright red, nylon tent-sack on the trampled snow. Against all Russian ethics, we were doing without a tent in order to save weight. The sack was a little short and became filled with condensation which turned to snow in the night but I slept well enough.

We woke with the morning sunshine and were off to an urban start. Eight-fifteen would be a little late for most mountaineering textbooks. The mountain was kind and did not extend us unduly until it was time for lunch. Happily our route-finding was successful, and after climbing an icy chimney we perched on a little tower overlooking the great central gully. We could look across it to Mummery's Rib and wonder how the others were faring. We had seen no sign of them yet.

We were about three-quarters of the way up the rib; reaching the snow-sprinkled section visible from Shkhara. It had looked as if there would be plenty of ledges but now we could see we had been deceived.

The ledges were boiler-plate slabs tilted enough to make them awkward and covered with loose fresh snow. In a dry season they would present no difficulty but on this occasion the snow had to be laboriously scraped away to reveal sufficient holds. I was glad that I had led the previous pitch so that Mike would have this unenviable task. I sat on my perch sucking toffees and watched for an hour while he worked away. He was aiming up to the left where some bands of black rock offered steeper climbing but much better holds.

As evening came on we reached the crest again and I was daydreaming about hot soup and bivouac sites. But as I climbed over a brow, the sudden view shattered my reverie. A sheer rock-tower stood before me—smooth and unfissured like a block of hewn granite before the sculptor sets to work. Above and to the right it overhung. Were we defeated?

'Come and look at this, Mike,' I shouted. It was lit from the side by the setting sun and the rays picked out a slanting buttress just below. This offered a few holds and suggested that the only possible chance was in the square-cut corner out of sight and on the left. Mike traversed delicately on to the buttress and looked up.

'Yes, there is a crack,' he said. 'I think it will go. Can you bring my rucksack up?'

I had almost ceased to worry now as to whether we should get up or not. We had encountered so many problems. One just accepted them as they came and said 'thank you' if they were soluble. But here we might also have a race with the darkness unless the crack was climbed swiftly and we found a bivouac just above.

And so we did. Mike rushed up and, without thinking too carefully, I followed with his rucksack tied on to the rope six feet above me. It kept jamming as Mike hauled in, so I had to climb up with a slack rope and work it free from below, clinging on with the other hand. Damn the distraction! I only held on from sheer fury.

Our bed for the night was a snow-boat; scooped out of the crest of the ridge and moored to a pillar of stone. We built up the free-board to shield ourselves from the wind and snuggled down hoping for a calm voyage. It had been a grand day, and a striking sunset promised that the weather would hold for another.

We were practically level with the snow-saddle uniting the twin summits. If we could not climb the east peak at least we should be able to reach the col. A couple of rope-lengths next morning brought us to the base of the eastern tower. A few steps to the left there was a crack, and in the crack—a piton. Man had left his mark. We had joined the twin-peak traverse—the last lap of the marathon climb from Koshtan-tau to Dykh-tau.

We hitched our sacks to the piton and, stretching our backs for the first time in days, anticipated the joy of unencumbered climbing. We still had to move with care. The ascent was classed as 5A by the Russians, and some fresh snow made it no easier. Two hours for 250 feet, and we were on top. Ten o'clock on the morning of the fourth day, and it was good.

The rest was anticlimax. I was watching through tired eyes. We slid down our rope to the col and climbed the West Summit of Dykh-tau. There we had expected to find steps left by John Hunt's party but there were none. We should have to find our own way down. We did—and made an error. Turning off the north ridge a shade too early we paid a worse penalty than we had on Shkhara. Below us were unending slopes of steep ice.

We roped down, descending rotten rocks in crampons, then steep ice, more abseils. Darkness fell and we spent another uncomfortable night on a steep slope. If we had to descend much further we should be in hell itself. But there was still more ice next morning and then at last the moraine and the mist seeping up from the valley. I hesitated. By great good fortune, or even greater skill, Mike hit the route. Grass and saxifrage again, lush and living. We took off our boots and dabbled our toes in the grass.

'Hello, you fellows. Sorry we are late. How nice of you to come. Yes, thanks, we made it. A thoroughly good climb.'

Extracts from *The Red Snow*, 1960

18

Towards the Present Day

After 1958 the road to the Caucasus was well and truly open. Most people prepared to negotiate with Intourist and the Soviet Mountaineering Federation could get permission to join one of the mountaineering camps and climb in relative freedom. Not, of course, the freedom with which one climbs in the Alps, but certainly with greater freedom than was available to Soviet mountaineers. Among British climbers, however, relatively few took the opportunity to climb in 'the frosty Caucasus'. Partly, of course, the Iron Curtain was responsible. Not many were aware that it could be breached. Equally important, though, was the far higher profile of other greater ranges – the Himalaya, the Andes and the mountains of Alaska. The collective unconscious of British mountaineering, if one can speak of such a thing, was more stirred by the challenges of the great peaks to be found in the Indian sub-continent and in the Americas. Until relatively recently, there was a perceived division of labour in mountaineering. Lightweight technical climbing was confined to the Alps in summer, where hard, committing routes could be done with relatively easy approaches and a highly developed mountaineering infrastructure. Most climbers going elsewhere employed varying degrees of expeditionary tactics, and in general there was relatively little enthusiasm for applying the techniques of Alpine climbing to the greater ranges.

Of course, as with most generalisations there were striking counter-examples. The great tradition of lightweight mountaineering did not die. In the hands of a few exponents it continued, and indeed kept up with developments in the Alps. Some of these exponents were active in the Caucasus and we conclude this book by reprinting three articles which, in their own way, illustrate the tradition. The first of these is by G. J. Ritchie. It recounts an epic twelve-day traverse of Shkhelda in 1961 with the formidable Hamish MacInnes. The route was first climbed in six days in 1940 by L. Nadeshdin, A. Mazkevitsch, V. Nasarov and P. Sysojev in what was one of the last outstanding Soviet efforts before the German invasion. Hamish McInnes returned to the Caucasus in 1970, with Paul Nunn and Chris Woodall. As Paul Nunn graphically describes in 'A Dream of Ushba', they climbed an impressive new route on the North Face of Pik Schurovski. Last but not least, our final extract tells how the partnership of Mick Fowler and Victor Saunders, who have taken Alpine-style climbing in the greater ranges to outstanding extremes, straightened out the Schmaderer-Vörg route on the West Face of Ushba North to produce the West Face Direct.

Twelve Nights on Schkelda

by G. J. Ritchie

This is the story of a single climb in the Caucasus in the summer of 1961 when Hamish MacInnes, J. M. K. Vivyan and I visited the area following the invitation of the Mountaineering Federation of the U.S.S.R. to the Alpine Club and the Scottish Mountaineering Club. But as most climbing tales are novel only to the author and as the armchair mountaineer has been there before, I propose to introduce a new element by describing principally the environment into which we were fitted. I avoid controversy on the theories of Lysenko if I explain that it is an environment of the valley, and the mountaineer on the mountain remains unmodified by evolution.

Mountaineering in Russia seems unaffected by that mystique whose devotees give up work, society and civilised living. Mountaineering is a sport, benefiting health and the advancement of economic progress. It is therefore encouraged by trade unions and student bodies. The majority of the young men and women live far from mountains and mountain weather. Their climbing must be done in their 3-week summer vacation. They come to the mountains therefore not casually but as a responsibility of the Mountaineering Federation.

The Caucasus are as yet undeveloped 'touristically'. Certainly, a *téléférique* will shortly lessen the stature of proud Elbruz, but the range is very much in its pristine state without hotels, chalets, restaurants, souvenir shops, picture postcards, excursionist buses or cadres of professional guides. Starting after the war in an area razed of all habitation but an occasional German camp, the unions have established a number of permanent centres where a small directing staff and a somewhat larger summer staff of experienced instructors provide 3-week residential courses graduating through physical training, practical instruction and collective excursions to independent climbs by groups of friends. Progress is recorded and marked by the award of a classification of competency. The difficulties which could arise for inexperienced climbers in the Caucasus where distances and heights are greater, mountains wilder and weather less settled than in the Alps are mitigated by the introduction of a mountain safety organisation. The proposals of any party to carry out any climb are scrutinised both by the camp authorities and by the regional safety organisation. Instead of guide books there exist printed diagrams and descriptions of the principal climbs. The camp authorities probably make available diagrams of climbs considered suitable for the grading of the particular party. When they make their choice they write down details of the party, the proposed route, equipment, food, times of departure and return. The party may be medically examined. The camp authorities, if satisfied, pass the data to the regional safety organisation which has responsibility for rescue operations over great distances. This latter assesses the objective risks of existing conditions and weather prospects and on longer climbs may order the party to report regularly, either by signal rocket or radio telephony. Given approval the party can draw from the camp stores its food and equipment. Few have personal equipment, for the camps provide clothing, boots (tricouni for snow-covered rock with felt insoles against low temperatures and easy fitting to accommodate a succession of users), axes, crampons, karabiners, pitons, webbing harness (used instead of waist loops), ropes, stoves and very efficient mountain tents. The latter are essential, for there are no high huts, indeed no huts at all, and most serious climbs involve several days away from camp; and the complication of getting away from camp accentuates the general inclination of mountaineers to stay out on their own as long as possible. On the other hand, unreasonable failure to return at the prescribed time is seriously regarded, for then the rescue service springs automatically into action. Even so, days may elapse before the rescue party reaches the scene of an accident.

By formal agreement with the Federation our party were given freedom of choice of climbs and assurance of assistance to achieve this, as long as we observed the control time procedure. The season was late and although on our arrival at Spartak camp in the Adyl Su valley in the Central Caucasus we proposed to tackle some of the great rock faces we were quickly convinced on our practice climbs of the justice of local discouragement of these ambitions. We had visions of exploring the wilds of Suanetia and were gratified when it was proposed that with Eugen Tur from Gorky and Igor Bandarowsky from Odessa, two young Masters of Sport, we should undertake the traverse of the main ridge of Schkelda (or Shkhelda). Undismayed by the accounts of Rickmers' party which in 4 days first climbed the western summits in 1903 with a 10½-hour ascent of danger and difficulty from a distant bivouac and by those of a Russian academic party which seemed to have had six high bivouacs on a traverse of the ridge, Hamish thought we might push through in four if lightly laden. We would subsist largely over those four days on a concentrated and dietetically complete preparation, Complan, which required no other preparation than the addition of warm water. This cut down bulk and fuel requirements. Duvet jackets, boots and *pieds d'éléphant* with a spare pair of socks were our only change. Chocolate, tea, glucose and dried fruit filled the gap over the weight of rope and ironmongery in our small sacks. The Russians, with the greatest goodwill, fixed our control time at twelve days and slipped a few additional luxuries like apples, caviare and *pâté de foie gras* into the bulging sacks of our companions and we set off through the pinewoods.

I will not dwell upon the pleasures of the juniper fire at our first bivouac under a clear sky in a tiny oasis above the Schkelda glacier. My readers should toughen themselves for hard going ahead. At first light a painless descent of the moraine and traverse of the open crevasses of the main glacier took us soon on to a branch descending from the general direction of the Akhsu Pass steep enough to make progress in crampons and stiff new boots a mortification. A traverse across even steeper névé took us on to an airy ridge descending from the 1st West Schkelda, from which the distant view gradually widened to take in the mass of Dongus Arun and the snow domes of Elbruz, with the tiny tents of glaciologists under Ozengi now right at our feet. Just as MacInnes and I reached the iced rocks of the main ridge a wall of black cloud swept in from the east and great rolls of thunder told of the coming storm. Reluctant to descend the steep ice we started to cut a platform, but our companions hundreds of feet below had the tent and won the argument. Their site was certainly sheltered by a ridge, but required considerable excavation of iced-in boulders, to the great detriment of our ice hammers. Because of its general unsuitability for such work my light axe was the only one which was to survive the climb in usable state. In the midst of our effort, hailstones pelted down larger than marbles and we sought shelter in the pole-less tent. All that night and the next two days the storm continued, while we four remained in the shelter of a two-man tent pressed down with the weight of snow. MacInnes went out to bale it off with a large dixie, but his frozen fingers lost their hold and for the remainder of our sojourn we cooked for four in a pint-size tea can. Within, we were snug. Igor, a collector of playing cards, produced a Polish pack distinguished by the varied charms of the ladies upon the backs and the absence of the Royal pairs whose function was taken by numbers 2 and 3; all of which (and the local rules for all the games we played) left us somewhat at a disadvantage. Between times a discussion of real wages, housing conditions, health and social services and pensions in our respective countries spaced out the occasional drink of melted snow which marked the passing of time. On the fourth day of our trip, however, the sun broke through, blazing on a white world around and white cloud below. Hours passed as we dried out and threw snowballs at the steep slopes over the protecting rib and eventually provoked avalanches to sweep the slope clear for our ascent. Our earlier platform had already been avalanched and we counted ourselves lucky. Soon, however, we were traversing steep sloping ledges of ice covered by fresh snow and it was with relief that we attained the main ridge at the col between the two summits of West Schkelda. Hard going up steep névé and icy rocks took us to the higher summit at 14,134 feet. Supplies were now low, but the ridge had been provisioned three years before for parties which had withdrawn. We found a cache. Some tins were empty and like pepper pots with fine holes drilled by lightning. Others contained fuel, frozen sprats, meat and milk. We borrowed only sufficient for our immediate needs. Although the only level spot was on the summit we descended the far side to build a precarious tent platform on the steep slope. We were not alone long, for after 3 years' neglect the cache was soon yielding more of its riches to a party of stalwarts of the Red Army who ensconced themselves upon the summit.

From our tent door we looked along the other dozen or more summits of the tortuous ridge towards the incomparable beauties of the twin summits of Ushba. Below us was a slender ridge with occasional deep vertical brèches, the Bhàsteir face and the Thearlaich Gap on a vaster scale, and bearing the obvious name of Ridge of the Buildings. From now on the ridge, apart from two summits, was to vary in width between 6 inches and 6 feet. Teetering along in the dawn light with crampons catching and sparking and squawking like a pencil on a slate it was difficult to judge, for sheer discomfort, between the awkward clawing along the serrated ridge and the scarting, scratching, shin-barking, seat-splitting slides down doubled ropes in the tortuous chimneys of the gaps. But we did not seem to have moved more than a hundred yards as the chough flies when the buzzing of the brush discharge upon the pinnacles drove us down at express speed into the deepest gap. There, tied on to pitons, we set to and managed to hack and trundle and build enough of a platform to allow us to plaster the tent in under a sheltering overhang. Not a moment too soon. Above us the Army party lamented its fate as the heavens opened and lightning and hail descended and they lay in cracks unable to move. Eventually they joined us. Under our rock we could offer cooking facilities but no shelter, but after many hours of dangerous work they had a tent bulging with bodies hanging into space on a tiny platform. Safety ropes to which the occupants were clipped passed through the ventilators and primuses roared comfortably through the night as clouds of steam rose from wet clothes within.

Their position, as we climbed above them next morning on the loosest of ledges, was hazardous, but a few hours brought us out once more on to a snow ridge which, after a first icy descent, strung on, slender and sharp, in a series of arcs worthy of the skill of a slack wire artist. For myself, after savouring the full challenge of upright movement with slopes of inexorable steepness dropping thousands of feet on either side, I gave up my splay-footed efforts and traversed along a foot or two below the crest till the insidious sifting of fine snow all around warned us to set up the tents once more. Cutting blocks and building out with urgent haste as we saw the curtains of hail sweep towards us we soon had platforms for both parties and were snug once more with snow melting in the pot and a reward of chocolate from the Red Army for our help.

Next morning a swift dash to Scientist Peak yielded another cache and we breakfasted without formality upon hard frozen chunks of icy sprat. More tempting were the great black Bologna sausages, but at a hasty bivouac farther along the ridge when a further blizzard blew up at midday these were rejected even by the besieging choucas. The day cleared, and we pushed on by awkward traverses, hanging chimneys and uncertain snow slopes. High up on the steep flank of Aristov Peak (13,570 feet) we suddenly saw the formidable northern face and heard faint voices. Fly-sized, an Army party embarked upon a summer rock climb had found their exit in fierce winter conditions and were fighting desperately. Fortunately the party above had sufficient rope to get them off the face by nightfall that day.

Great good luck yielded yet another cache from which we 'borrowed' sparingly then climbed over the pinnacles behind the summit till a great void opened beneath us. There began a series of exposed and hazardous abseils across and down the face. We were not to go scot-free. A great rock dislodged by Hamish's rope shattered beside Eugen and Igor. The latter was struck on the knee. Retching with pain, he was lowered down further abseils until we were able to build yet another tent platform on a nick halfway down the gap and looking out on to a yet greater drop to the glacier far below. With unusual fore-thought we prepared our line of descent to give time for the compli-cated and bulging ice-runs of the great west face of Central Schkelda (14,074 feet). As we folded our tent next morning we stood politely aside to accommodate the leaders of the Army party as they abseiled on to our platform. Not till the descent of all their caravan made move-ment safe did we budge. Their leaders had found our steps and were away. A swift pursuit found them already over the abseil and we sadly retired and re-erected our tent. Despite distant ringing of axe and piton it was after midday before a figure was seen through mist and snow below us, and still fighting hard. Nightfall found them still on the face but by then we were otherwise engaged: 12 in a two-man tent drumming up for a Ukrainian party who had followed in our footsteps. Three tents soon packed the ledge; safety ropes were everywhere and MacInnes was leading a memorable ceilidh. Strung sadly on their uneasy scrapes on the face below, the military must have wished themselves transported on the wings of song as love lyrics of Burns, songs of Celtic sorrow and bawdy ballads of the Antipodes alternated with massed Russian voices rendering Kipling and songs more exotic. Next day the push was renewed. Hamish, as usual, plunged for the Direct and I—with the contents of his rucksack in mine (60 lb.)—cursed and prayed, following his convulsive writhings over ice-bulges; a point off each crampon, axe in the wrong hand, the next foot at ear level, the sack swinging, balaclava over my eyes, a wet-knotted Russian top rope caught behind in the last cleft, these were obviously going to be some of the greatest moments of my life, possibly the last. Oddly, it did not seem long till I was looking down on the Russian leader swarming hand over hand (out of all sympathy with the mountain) up the rope. No time for contemplation: on over ridge and pinnacle in gathering darkness seeking a level platform. A snow ledge below proved to lie at 50 degrees and to be largely ice; but night was on us and platforms had to be cut for the others, so we set to. Our position gave us tent-room to accept an exhausted member of the other party and we slept, five up, better than the others, seven on an exiguous ice-ledge. The morning started with a 125-foot free abseil and followed with hours of dour cutting downwards and round several great pinnacles till we came at last to the foot of East Schkelda (14,167 feet) rising even more fiercely than its neighbour. Two fine tent platforms were cut out of a cornice with a tiny casement looking to the world's evening sunshine below. The beauty of the night sky was unsurpassable. The cold was intense. Despite brilliant sunshine next morning the first very severe pitch led out on to an eyrie on the southern face, a situation which left us without feet and fingers despite 20 minutes' work undoing 10 minutes' restriction; all eventually lost toenails. We now surmounted a series of overhanging chimneys; the 10,000-foot unrestricted exposure meant only joy on warm rough rock with great incut holds. Then MacInnes again took the *direttisima*. A 50-degree ice-ribbon ran parallel with a rising rock rib which formed a constant ceiling. Every piton available went into the rock and I found the rope hanging out in space, suspended in a series of slings used by MacInnes to stay on and progress. The process of extraction was involved. I was not sad to emerge at the summit and find that with great luck another cache was available. For the last day or so a single tin of milk per day had been almost our sole ration for four. Our total food intake over the period was exactly one-quarter of the 'meagre' rations of the party then in Greenland. Brief stops for photography with the splendour of Ushba fully revealed before us and we set off along the ridge, where pinnacle alternated with steep deep snow faces. A series of long swinging rappels followed, but by now we were inured to the problems of clearing the top and were quickly at the foot of the Cock, steep fine rock presenting a problem worthy of Chamonix with a final fierce abseil to reach a cluster of rocks as night fell. First there, we found space for a tent. The others spent the night in the open before setting off down to Suanetia. We followed the south ridge till we could plunge down a couloir, one sound axe between us, to the Ushba glacier. Elation gave way to dismay as our way back over the col steepened and climbed, but then the ice-fall opened out and we descended through crevasses and under seracs at frantic speed with a final abseil on to less dangerous ground. We broke into a break-neck run through the crevasses towards tents on the glacier below. To Igor they were cigarettes; to us possibly a drink of tea. They were even better, and after firing our last 'all well' rocket at our control time, we ambled downwards in the warm afternoon sunshine with our shrunken stomachs not dissatisfied. This was the thirteenth day of our trip.

A Dream of Ushba

by Paul Nunn

The 'Jewel of the Caucasus' they called it, and Dennis Gray hooked us all. His enthusiasm was infectious. Richard and Barbara McHardy worked like mad on gear and Chris Woodhall acquired a mountain of food, but somehow no money appeared. At Easter it all reached a nadir. Dennis had to drop out to work in the Lakes. Then, when it looked a dead duck, chance played an ace. Pete Seeds, a journalist, wanted to climb, so we went to the lakes. He was enthusiastic and several long gambles paid off. By courtesy of the *Sunday Mirror* and *Fiat* we found ourselves in the Central Caucasus, complete with a specially-drafted leader, Hamish MacInnes.

The Elbrus-Ushba region is the Mont Blanc of the range, unmatched for altitude and for quality and variety of climbing. Here are the Soviet Trades Union Camps to which climbers come in the summer. Before long the area will become a major European ski resort. I was glad to be there before it all happened.

We were pushed too hard for time by a month-long visa which covered a 1,500 mile drive in each direction. The testing journey left us understandably lethargic, and negotiations with regard to objectives, together with some bad weather, strained our luck in the first couple of weeks. Frustratingly, our first objective, the North Face of Nakra Tau by the Abalakov route, never came into tolerable condition. This rather ambitious first objective (about one and a half times the length of the Matterhorn North Face and of similar seriousness and overall altitude) was subject to bad weather, soft and dangerous snow conditions, and potentially lethal serac avalanches. A near miss in bad conditions and continuing bad weather forced us to abandon the project.

Our attention shifted to the Ushba region. But new snow fell at 11,000ft. on July 20th. The inexorable scissors of time now made us give up our plans for a new climb on Ushba, which seemed unlikely to come into condition quickly enough. Instead, we grabbed at an objective which suggested itself overwhelmingly from the German or Shkhelda Bivouac – a new climb on the North Face of Pic Schurovski. With some head shaking but much sympathy, Paul Rotatiev, Vice-President of the Soviet Mountaineering Federation, agreed to our plans.

We aimed to storm it, without tents, sleeping bags, or large sacks full of food. We worked off our frustration in a brutally simple plan which placed a massive premium upon a small quantity of high quality gear, the use of Terrordactyl axes to eliminate step cutting and, above all, upon experience and speed.

On July 24th the dawn was frosty. Moving solo, Hamish, Chris and I crossed the glacier and ascended the runnelled ice above the bergschrund. In the gloom a party of friendly Russian instructors paused, lights twinkling, to observe our eccentric individualistic progress.

A steep couloir necessitated the rope. Hamish led, Chris followed and I prusiked, taking pictures. After a few rope lengths we escaped on to rock as ice particles and small stones began to bespatter the lower cliffs. Rocks (Grade 4–5) and perfect snow followed to the base of the first rock barrier. A beautiful traverse on perfect ice led out right to a granite rib and a patch of sun.

The rib was steep and a little loose, and gave way to typical Nevis mixed ground (5+ rock). The lower barrier passed with remarkably little incident, and we emerged at the foot of the Central Icefield. Luckily the sun passed away again behind the mountain, leaving the ice firm. We did not see it on the wall again that day.

At 12.00, after several rope lengths on ice, we reached a small exposed shoulder (a possible bivouac site). Probably we were nearly half way up the face. Confidence overtook us as we scrunched through our staple diet of Mapleton bar. Hamish, with his Lawrence of Arabia neck-shield flopping, led up the short and very steep ice field below the Central Rock Barrier. He had to cut a few steps in the approach to the only feasible-looking weakness, a gully-like depression between the icicle festooned walls. It became apparent that Rotatiev had been right in stressing the steepness of the face and of the Central Barrier in particular. Upon close inspection the rock went a little beyond the vertical everywhere but in our depression. Even there it was extremely steep and required devious route finding.

Hamish led the pitches in about three hours. The first was extremely difficult mixed climbing on steep insecure ice and loose rock for about 80ft., while the second was an easier groove (Scottish 3–4) to a horizontal rock traverse and a good small ledge. The climbing, typical of the harder British winter routes, was an admirable lead in any conditions. Half way up a Caucasian face it was remarkable.

To reach the upper ice field was the next pressing problem. Above were ice-decorated walls for several hundred feet. Binocular study had revealed an ice chimney and possible traverse to the lower lip of the plunging upper slopes. Chris grated round the arête in crampons, carrying the large sack which he preferred. The chimney, again far steeper than we had anticipated, involved an athletic spurt of dynamic bridging. A gloomy traverse in the gathering storm and failing light led to the edge of the ice. A small buttress of rock seemed the only feasible bivouac site.

Thunder crashed round the summit and sheets of hail swept down the ice fields as Chris and I excavated for an hour. Hamish engineered a brew in his slot. Pitons and a tiny wire sling secured our position, while my antique bivouac sheet hung down as a curtain. It seemed that we would probably be able to manage the ascent but, with four or five pitons left, we certainly would not be able to retreat.

5.00.—Hamish sets out in rapid moves across the encrusted ice to the lower outlet of the steep upper ice field. The storm has given way to a fierce frost, but white wind-torn streaks threaten its return. The upper ice field is steep but not too difficult, and the gradual fading of the sun prevents the development of avalanche danger. It is very long.

12.00.—At the base of the summit pyramid there is perhaps 700ft. to go. On my lead the clouds mass and the wind rises. The rock is much worse than we expected and the snow had seen too much of the morning sun. Chris takes the lead from a horrible stance on steep mush, just in time for the full blast of the snow to begin. As he ploughs up the deep snow, avalanches of powder drown his yellow cagoule. Seconding involves swimming up a trough of horrible, insecure snow. At one point Hamish and I inhabit a small ledge while Chris is totally lost in the maelstrom above. Eventually we follow tightening ropes up.

16.00.—The Traverse of the Screws avoids the final impossibly steep 100ft. of avalanche snow by an escape to the last few feet of the North West Ridge. A great mass of soft snow is removed; screws protect leader and second alike. On the ridge in a brief clearance Hamish swarms up the last rocks and flails up the final insecure mound to a stormy summit.

20.00.—The second bivouac is a collapsible snow cave on the Ushba plateau, after a plodding descent through deep snow which is threatened by avalanches and punctuated by apocalyptic visions of the huge ice walls of Bezingi to the east. Mist cheats us of respite at a food dump at the head of the Ushba ice-fall. The limitations of Alpine tactics in the Caucasus become apparent as we shudder through to morning in a pile of powder snow on a steep slope, with a cold wind blowing.

July 26th.—The mist clears briefly to reveal Ushba towering over us. Hamish's camera is frozen as we descend to the food dump. After twenty-four hours without drink, eating is difficult. Hycal renders one completely speechless. The Ushba ice-fall provides the sting in the tail – a nasty 80ft abseil from ice screws into a yawning green hole, followed by a run in balled-up crampons below a monster serac in the mist. Something falls, but it is too thick to see. After a moment peering up into the gloom of yet another storm, the crashing noises descend to our left. Towards mid-morning we skirt the last large crevasses and slide down soaking snow on to the upper Shkhelda Glacier. Schurovski is plastered, and streams of snow run down the lower slabs out of the mist. Ushba is hidden in mist and snow above the crumbling ice-fall. Richard waits to help us down at the German bivouac, while Tut assists in the rescue of an unfortunate Bulgar in a deep crevasse. Our toes are uncomfortable: Ushba will have to wait.

From *Mountain* 16, July 1971

Ushba:
From Russia with Love

by Mick Fowler

Work commitments prevented Victor Saunders and me involving ourselves with full scale Himalayan type expeditions in 1986 and necessitated a shorter but (hopefully) equally challenging trip.

Increasing popularity and familiarity meant that the appeal of the
traditional British playground of the Western Alps had begun to wane
and the quest for somewhere new and interesting was on. The area
needed to boast steep impressive rock and ice routes, enjoy a diverse
and interesting local culture, not be overrun with other climbers and
not be inordinately expensive.

It was Paul Nunn who first awakened interest in the Caucasus (he
had climbed there in 1970 with Hamish MacInnes) by emphasising the
fine and unfrequented climbing available. He suggested contact with
Des Rubens and Dave Broadhead who had attended the 1984 Caucasus
Camp and, apart from the late Pete Boardman, were the only
British climbers to have managed technical climbs in the area since
the International Mountaineering Camp System started in 1974.
Further information from John Town (who was active there in
1979) convinced us that the area was remote, exciting, rarely visited
by Western climbers and very much in line with what we were
looking for.

A team formed, comprising Victor, Maggie Urmston, Bert Simmonds
and myself, and we set about organising a visit. In response to a letter
of enquiry, the Sportskommittee in Moscow sent an invitation to attend
any 1986 climbing camp, and our plans began to take shape. Information on the area was very sparse and our main objective – the West
Face of Ushba North – was chosen from a Japanese book of mountain
photographs presented to Victor after his assisting in the rescue of
some Japanese climbers in the Karakoram in 1981.

Financial support was obtained from the Mount Everest Foundation and British Mountaineering Council and on 23 July the 20 or so people attending the Caucasus Summer Camp (mainly walkers) met in Moscow. A 1½ hour flight followed by a four hour coach ride saw us arriving at the Azau International Camp directly below Mount Elbrus in the Caucasus.

Several formalities were necessary before climbing could begin, although our initial apprehensions in this respect soon proved to be ill-founded. The alien bureaucracy turned quickly into an amusing charade rather than a tedious grind.

Firstly each of us had to undergo a medical examination which consisted of having our blood pressure taken before and after ten squatthrusts and then assuring the Soviet doctor that we all felt fit and healthy. Bert admitted to having a headache at this point which caused some confusion although eventually all was smoothed over and we were ready to choose our first routes.

A vast selection of mainly captionless photographs were on display ranging from shots of the Pamirs to a portrait of Reinhold Messner 'appreciating highly the camp's activity'. However some photographs were relevant and with the assistance of a guide and interpreter allocated to our team. Vic and I chose to start with the 'Islands' route on the North Face of Nakra Tau (4277m). This D Sup route was long and difficult enough to get us fit and acclimatised and would also give us a better idea of the layout of the range before we tackled our main objective.

Various forms had to be completed giving details of our next of kin and obtaining authority to attempt the route from our guide and camp chief. In practice obtaining permission was a formality as long as a sensible first objective was chosen – 'sensible' being loosely interpreted as easier than T.D.

The carrying of two-way radios is essential as is reporting to base three times per day. This is actually not as onerous as it first sounds – limited rescue services (no helicopters) and virtually no mountain mechanisation means that the seriousness of the climbing is similar to that in the West European Alps at the turn of the century. Besides, as all climbing parties are on the same wavelength it is possible to chat to other teams – which can be much more interesting than talking to base.

With our instruction on radio use complete it remained only to obtain food from the camp store and head into the mountains. The list of available foodstuffs was in Russian and naively we left it to our guide and interpreter to sort out some food for the four days we intended to be away from the valley. In fact we had brought freeze dried food for the mountains and needed only to supplement this from the store. Some time later we were a little taken aback to receive 5lbs of potatoes, 5 x 1kg jars of peas, 4 x whole salamis, 9 tins of assorted food and fruit juice and much more – all for two people spending four days in the mountains. We later discovered that the fee which we had paid ($800 each in 1986) covered each individual for 12 roubles (approximately £12.00) worth of food per day whilst away from camp. Food is cheap in the Soviet Union, hence our monstrous, virtually immovable mound of supplies. Suggestions that the food be returned prompted some confusion and eventually we left for the mountains with tins overflowing from under our beds and (relatively) light sacks.

Nakra Tau proved a fine route which presented no special difficulty but was sufficiently high and exhausting for us to feel extremely well exercised on our return to Azau. The descent also enabled us to get a distant view of Ushba which seemed to live up well to its reputation as the 'Matterhorn of the Caucasus'. At 4700 metre it could be seen to be a majestic double-headed peak with the 1800 metre West face forming one of the biggest, most impressive mixed faces in Europe.

Before arriving in the Soviet Union we had been rather apprehensive about what the Soviet authorities might think of our attempting a new line on this face, but in fact we need not have feared and enjoyed all the encouragement that we could have hoped for. Our guides first took us to the nearby Shkelda Mountaineering Camp where we were shown incredibly detailed descriptions of existing routes on the mountain. These were nothing at all like the guide-book descriptions that we are accustomed to in Western Europe and resembled expedition reports complete with pitch by pitch descriptions, details of the numbers of pegs/ice screws used on each pitch together with several photographs, all supported by a detailed Russian narrative.

Perusal of the information on Ushba revealed that the extreme left side of the West Face of Ushba North had its first ascent in 1956 and a line just left of centre was climbed over two days in 1982. Considering the paucity of information available in Britain we were hardly surprised at these discoveries and the fact that an obvious steep ice couloir leading directly to the summit remained unclimbed ensured that our enthusiasm remained undiminished.

No detailed pocket maps of the area exist but an excellent relief map at Azau Camp showed clearly that Ushba is on the other side of the range from the Baksan Valley and the effortê necessary to reach the mountain can be equated to reaching the Freney Pillar on foot from Chamonix.

Two approaches are possible: one climbs directly up the dangerous Ushba icefall to the Ushba plateau at the head of the Ushba glacier which is descended to the foot of the face – the other crosses at least two cols to make a long descent, eventually joining the Ushba glacier and so to the foot of the face. The former route was chosen primarily because the latter seemed so complicated that failure to even find the mountain seemed a distinct possibility.

Preparations were much simpler this time. Medicals were not required, food was not ordered (due to the vast quantities remaining from our initial order), petrol for the stove was siphoned from the Sports-kommittee coach and by 10 a.m. we had been dropped off at Shkelda camp and were ready to start walking.

A dreary, misty day dampened our spirits somewhat but having been assured that this was normal Caucasian weather (and being reluctant to spend any more time gorging ourselves on full board accommodation in the valley) we decided to start anyway. For the first hour natural pine forest, a rushing glacial torrent and numerous cattle with heavy sounding bell collars provided a scene reminiscent of the Western Alps, whilst the North Face of Shkelda provided a most impressive backdrop at the head of the valley.

Our approach soon led to below the snout of the glacier and after a steep, unpleasant trackless struggle an hour of monotonous walking on the boulder-strewn glacier surface took us to the point of divergence of the two possible approaches where a party of Russians were camped.

Here we enjoyed our first taste of the warmth and hospitality of these people. Cold fat and raw garlic smothered in home-made tomato sauce was forced into our hands, quickly followed by an unrecognisable substance resembling warm gelatine. Language barriers defeated attempts at conversation but arm waving and guttural noises conveyed a degree of friendship and respect for fellow mountaineers which I have never come across in Western Europe. The walk so far had been hot and exhausting and the somewhat unusual food on offer was gratefully accepted and instantly devoured – tasting nowhere near as bad as it must sound.

Our route now continued directly under the impressive North Face of Shkelda and three further hours of moraine-covered glacier brought us to a good camping place on the true right bank of the glacier. This is known as the 'Deutsch Bivouac' after the early 20th century German explorers who first camped here. It is really only a series of tent platforms cleared out of the moraine at the edge of the glacier, but there are limitless quantities of easily accessible drinking water and it provides a superb base from which many hard classic routes are approached. We had brought a tent as an insurance policy against the dubious weather and, as we were the only people in the area, this was duly pitched on the most palatial platform. The lack of other climbers and safe interim bases offered by West European mountain huts combined to give our situation a remote flavour and a sense of seriousness somewhere between the Western Alps and the Himalaya. Radio reception was very poor in the confines of the valley, thus accentuating the feeling of isolation.

A cloudy night with strong winds delayed our start but by 7am we were crossing the dry glacier to the foot of the Ushba icefall. Soviet mountaineers often speak lightly of this icefall, but there are deaths here every year and caution is necessary. The sun does not strike the slopes very early, although after our late start we were pleased to see a thin mist layer keeping the temperature below freezing. The lower two-thirds of the rise to the Ushba plateau is easy crevassed ground but the top one third is *bona fide* icefall material with occasional very large sérac falls. one of which was to completely change the terrain in the four days between our ascent and descent.

Four hours after leaving the Deutsch Bivouac a surprisingly sudden exit was made onto the Ushba plateau. This vast sloping plateau has several huge crevasses and a bad reputation in poor visibility. With this in mind we considered ourselves fortunate in being able to enjoy glimpses of the surrounding peaks as we skirted the lower edge of the plateau to reach the head of the Ushba glacier. The upper reaches of Ushba's West Face were now visible but a rock rib appeared to prevent direct access to the small glacier flowing down from its foot. Despite lengthy discussions with the guides at Azau, we had not been able to get any reliable advice on how best to get to the base of our chosen route. We knew from the detailed description at Shkelda camp that the 1982 ascensionists had reached the bergschrund by climbing directly up the glacier beneath the face, but we were also aware that a possible way existed across the retaining rock rib to join the glacier a few hundred feet below the bergschrund.

A set of old tracks on the Ushba glacier persuaded us to try and descend about 700m and skirt round the foot of the rock rib to reach the glacier leading to the foot of the face. Much delicate crevasse work resulted until, having descended 300m, it became clear that our intended route was virtually suicidal. The glacier itself could be seen to be in the form of a continuous icefall and, to make matters worse, huge serac falls regularly swept the face, triggering further falls in the icefall itself and leaving no chance of a justifiable approach route. We were both becoming increasingly tired and the prospect of returning up the Ushba glacier was not appealing – especially as no viable way of crossing the retaining rib and descending to the foot of the face could be seen.

However, the potential embarrassment of failing to reach the foot of our route persuaded us to painstakingly retrace our steps back up towards the Ushba plateau. There seemed to be only one option – not far below the plateau a prominent knoll on the rib could be easily gained and whilst the terrain on the far side was not visible it offered the only ray of hope in an otherwise rather gloomy situation. Ironically two hours previously we had carried out radio contact duties from a point level with the knoll but had decided against crossing the 150m of very crevassed glacier 'just for a look' as we were so certain that our low flanking manoeuvre would be successful. Needless to say the knoll proved to be the key to our problem and four hours after leaving the plateau we settled down on an excellent bivouac platform which we could have reached in 30 minutes down an easy snow slope!

Although the day had been generally misty and uninspiring the clouds lifted towards the evening and we were treated to a superb view of the face towering above us. It was difficult to gauge the exact angle but a 100m rock band at two-thirds height seemed likely to provide an extremely difficult crux section leading to a 400m ice couloir and the summit. The immediate vicinity was dominated by Ushba but elsewhere the traverses of Shkelda (4200m) and Mazeri (4000m) could be seen to be fine, challenging excursions while Dongus Orun (4454m) and the ethereal Elbrus (5642m) loomed in the distance.

Despite an encouraging evening the night was wet and windy: a heavy hailstorm coinciding with our 1.30am alarm convinced us to stay put and keep our fingers crossed for the day after. Naturally the weather turned out to be perfect and we were soon cursing our decision not to start.

The day was spent gazing at the face, checking the approach, drying our equipment and fashioning a 'pricker' for the stove out of a strand from Victor's head-torch wire. We were very proud of this improvisation which we hoped would solve the problem of the stove's increasing unreliability.

1.30am on 3 August proved to be as windy as the night before but the temperature was much lower, the sky clear and our minds more at ease with this apparently regular weather pattern.

An easy snow slope followed by a single abseil made a mockery of a direct approach up the glacier and placed us in a position 200m below the bergschrund, only 30 minutes after leaving our bivouac site. Nevertheless, even this far up the glacier, we were exposed to serac falls and were pleased to be across the bergschrund by 5am and making good time on 50° ice towards the first rock outcrops. The climbing was in a superb position but no great technical difficulties were encountered and, after a few sections of Scottish IV the crux section was reached at 11am. The 1982 route moves well to the left here around the left end of the steep band guarding access to the prominent couloir cleaving the upper one third of the face. From the detailed report at Shkelda Camp, it seemed that bad weather had prevented the Soviets from attempting the direct line and forced them to take a faint rib leading up to the North Ridge 100m from the summit. Our luck was holding – a superb, clear day had developed with perfect views of the entire Western part of the range.

The section above had looked to be the crux from a distance and closer acquaintance confirmed this. However, we were blessed with magnificent conditions; the thin ice smears adorning the obvious line of weakness had thawed the previous day but were now in perfect condition and offered very hard spectacular grade V mixed climbing for two pitches until we were able to gain the base of the couloir. Exhaustion and altitude were beginning to take their toll as progress slowed to a crawl. Although the difficulties of the couloir nowhere exceeded grade IV it was 8pm before we reached the summit.

Our guide had told us that a good bivouac site could be found here, so knowing the Soviets' appreciation of comfort (immaculate bivouac sites can be found in the most unlikely places) we were somewhat surprised to find a true knife edge of ice forming the highest point, with the crest of a rock ridge 30m down having been hacked away to form the only vaguely habitable spot.

With the temperature dropping rapidly to considerably below Western Alpine summer levels we struggled vainly with the stove before abandoning our efforts and succumbing to the need for sleep. We were content with the day – our main objective had materialised into a 1600m TD+/ED− mixed route which now lay behind us.

A perfect morning almost tempted us to traverse across to Ushba South but exhaustion and continuing stove problems saw us starting very late and descending the knife edge ice arête forming the North Ridge. Six hours later, after Victor had climbed 50m to free the rope on the very last abseil, we were back on the Ushba plateau.

A solitary party of four Soviets were camped here and showed us the same degree of hospitality and friendship that we had experienced on the way up to the Deutsch Bivouac. Their food lacked the ethnic value of the 'fat and gelatine' but soup and tea were gratefully accepted after our stove-enforced period of dehydration.

These climbers had never before met any British people, let alone without an attendant 'Intourist' guide (mountaineering seems to be one of the few ways to meet the Soviet people in a completely free and easy-going atmosphere) and an enlightening couple of hours was spent discussing topics ranging from mountaineering to Chernobyl.

They were setting out to do the traverse of both peaks of Ushba (TD) and their climbing equipment and sheer willpower deserve mention. Apart from the obligatory bunch of titanium ice screws and rock pegs they could have been climbing in Western Europe in the 1930s. Sailing rope, absorbent bendy leather boots, home-made flimsy gloves and ice daggers are hardly the sort of gear one would expect to see in use on a major TD route in France or Switzerland. Nevertheless, these climbers were quite happy with their equipment and in particular forcefully stressed the superiority of their sailing rope. We were full of respect for their ability and willpower and the meeting brought home to us the fact that it is all too easy to denigrate other people's efforts when using equipment designed 50 years later. We were almost embarrassed by our comparatively posh and expensive gear as we bid our farewells and headed off towards the top of the Ushba icefall.

Here we were somewhat shocked to find that the entire upper quarter of the fall had collapsed since our ascent. Our descent was accomplished by struggling as fast as possible over freshly broken ice blocks and wondering at the Soviets' apparent lack of respect for this infamous, and clearly dangerous, icefall.

In marked contrast to four days beforehand the Deutsch Bivouac was festooned with tents – all pitched on inferior sites to ours which, as the only unoccupied one, sat perched in the very best place. Again we were invited to share various interesting foods while our hosts demonstrated the effectiveness of titanium ice screws, giving their sales patter on the surface of the dry glacier. It was a surprise to see that one Russian had a series of home-made 'Friends' – his early efforts were clearly home-made with peculiarly misshapen components but his latest products were virtually indistinguishable from the real thing. Also the curious but popular 'ice fifis' were displayed and their superiority over our axes explained. This we failed to understand as the technique for their use involves making an ice axe placement first and then hooking the fifi into this exactly as a rock fifi would be hooked into a karabiner. Admittedly the fifi is normally used as an aid tool (complete with foot sling threaded through waist and chest harness) but nevertheless we failed to grasp the advantage they apparently gave and resisted any temptation to purchase these unique pieces of equipment. In fact the only really saleable items possessed by Russian climbers seem to be the ubiquitous titanium ice screws which miraculously appear in vast quantities at the slightest hint of 'exchange'. The current rate is 20 screws for a worn pair of plastic double boots, and judging by the amount of western equipment worn by leading Russian climbers, business is brisk.

The next day saw us leaving the Deutsch Bivouac, struggling down the moraine-covered Shkelda glacier, drinking our fill at superb clear springs and wandering through the lush undergrowth of the valley forests back to Shkelda camp. It was six days since we had left and just one long day had been spent on the face – we felt every minute of the six days to have been worthwhile.

From *Mountain* 14, April 1987

APPENDIX I
A History of Mountaineering in the Caucasus

Central Caucasus

1829   Killar Haschirow, a Circassian accompanying a party of Russian soldiers and scientists to **Elbrus**, highest peak in the Caucasus, was reported to have ascended its (lower) East Summit (5621m). British climbers have always been sceptical of the claim, though it is more favourably viewed in Europe.

1844   Moritz Wagner (Germany) 'explored the environs of Kazbek, and ascended that famous mountain to the lower limit of eternal snow' – he later estimated this as c.3355m (11,000ft). (Kazbek is 5047m; earlier attempts in 1807 by J. von Klaproth, and 1811 by M. von Engelhardt and F. W. Parrot are also on record.)

1852   **Silga Khokh** (near Kazbek) was climbed by General Chodzko in the course of a 16-year survey expedition, probably by its West Peak (3855m).

1865   G. Radde, naturalist from Tblisi, climbed the north-west slope of Elbrus to 4360m.

1868   The first sporting 'mountaineers' arrived in the Caucasus, and explored throughout the central section of the range. D. W. Freshfield, A. W. Moore and C. C. Tucker climbed **Elbrus East Peak** (5621m) with their guide F. Dévouassoud and two Urusbieh hunters. This they claimed as a first ascent. They had previously surmounted the virgin **Kazbek** (5047m).

1874   A. W. Moore returned as organiser of a second Caucasian climbing expedition, which included F. C. Grove, H. Walker and F. Gardiner. They took with them the guide P. Knubel. Moore was absent from the team's successful ascent of **Elbrus West Peak** (5633m). All had previously climbed Sultrankol-Bashi (3806m, Elbrus group).

1884   M. de Déchy (Hungary) with A. Burgener and P. J. Ruppen repeated Elbrus and made the first ascent of **Mamisom-Khokh** (or 'The Curtain'/ Khamkhakhi Khokh) in the Adai Khokh group above the Mamison Pass. (He revisited the Caucasus in the two following summers but made no significant ascents.)

1886   C. T. Dent, W. F. Donkin, A. Burgener, B. Andenmatten, in a season of almost constant bad weather, explored the head of the Bezingi valley, climbing **Gestola** (4860m) by its western ridge (misidentified as Tetnuld-Tau). They also partly explored the Dych-Tau group (or Koshtan-Tau, as they thought).

1887   Freshfield joined de Déchy for a 6-week tour, again accompanied by F. Dévouassoud. Peaks climbed included **Tetnuld**, 'the Jungfrau of the Caucasus' by its south-west ridge, 4974m; **Ukiu**, 4330m, by its south-east ridge; **Shoda** (3408m); **Gulba** (3790m).

R. Lerco (Italy) and his guide J. Muller climbed to the west crater of Elbrus, where they had to turn back when their Russian companion fell mountain-sick. Germans tried unsuccessfully 2 days later. (From now on there were regularly several attempts on Elbrus every year.)

1888   A. F. Mummery climbed **Dych-Tau** (his 'Koshtan-Tau', 5198m) on July 24 with H. Zurfluh of Meiringen. He also made first ascent of what is now **Pik Semenowski** (4054m).

J. G. Cockin, H. W. Holder and H. Woolley with U. Almer and C. Roth visited the Bezingi Glacier, where they vainly attempted Dych-Tau from the south-west before climbing it successfully a few days later by its northern arête. Holder, Woolley and Almer then climbed **Katyn-Tau** or Saddle Peak, North-West Summit (4970m). Holder, Cockin and the guides climbed **Salinan** (Salanchera/Saluinan Bashi), north of the Zanner Pass. **Shkhara** (north-east ridge) was climbed by Cockin, Almer and Roth, as was **Jangi-Tau East Peak** (Djanga), 5030m. Cockin and Almer climbed **Ushba North** (4696m) at their third attempt, following the great couloir which cleaves the mountain's twin summits.

Dent and Donkin, with H. Fox and the guides K. Streich and J. Fischer were also in the area, though Dent did not stay. Failing on the Ushba peaks, the others climbed **Dongusorun [South]-East Peak**, 4442m. All four failed to return from an attempt on Koshtan-Tau. Their bodies were never found, but an expedition the following year discovered the last bivouac site.

G. Merzbacher (Germany) and party climbed the west ridge of Cheget-Tau (4110m), the 'Biancograt' of the Caucasus.

1889   The Donkin/Fox search party comprised: Dent, Freshfield, Woolley and C. H. Powell, with C. Jossi, J. Kaufmann, K. Maurer and A. Fischer. From a rock cairn beyond the 'last sleeping place' it was deduced that the lost party must have fallen while traversing steep cliffs below the east ridge of Koshtan-Tau.

Woolley and Jossi made first ascents of the East Peak of **Mishirgi-East** (4918m), the south ridge of **Koshtan-Tau** (5150m), and the north-east ridge of **Ailama** (4547m, 4A). They also climbed Kazbek from the Devdorak Glacier (with Kaufmann, Fischer and Maurer) and Elbrus (with Kaufmann), but failed on Ushba South. Freshfield and Powell, with Maurer, climbed the North Peak of **Laila** (3976m), and explored in the Bezingi and Adyrsu regions.

V. Sella (Italy) with E. Sella, D. Maquignaz and three porters travelled extensively, climbing Elbrus and making first ascents of **Ullu-Auz Bashi** (4670m) to the north of Koshtan-Tau, by its south-east ridge (3A), and the Central, highest, Peak of **Laila** (4084m). They also climbed **Kogutai** (Kogotai/Chat Bashi), 3821m, by its northern ridge, **Dashi Khokh** (3730m), and Dadiash-Ushkul (3446m).

1890   Cockin and Holder, with Almer, attempted Jangi-Tau from the south without success. The party also explored the Adai Khokh group and made the first ascent its principal summit **Uilpata**, or Adai Khokh (4410m). They also climbed **Burdshula** (4358m) and **Zichwarga** (4138m). Sella climbed **Zichwarga East** (4100m); also **Bangurjan-Tau** (3840m) in the Svatgar group.

A. V. Pastuchov (Pastukhoff), a Russian military topographer, made an adventurous ascent of the West Peak of Elbrus with 3 Cossacks for a new physical map of the area. (It took them 6 days!) He also scaled **Khalatsa** (Chalaza), 3937m.

1891   G. Merzbacher and L. Purtscheller with J. Kehrer and J. Unterweger made a swift (8-hour) ascent West Summit of Elbrus. They climbed **north ridge of Dongusorun [North]-West** (4437m), and on to the Main Summit (4452m). Purtscheller soloed **Lower Dongusorun** (3760m). They also climbed all three summits of Laila, Adyrsu-Bashi and a new route on Jangi-Tau. **Sullukol-Bashi** (4259m) was another first, as well as **Gimarai Khokh** (4778m) in the Kasbek group.

1893   Cockin, F. W. Newmarch, G. Solly and Woolley – on an expedition without guides or porters – explored and crossed a number of ridges, most notably the Tikhtengen Pass (3843m). An attempt on Tikhtengen, the 'Caucasian Schreckhorn' (4610m), was halted by a rock tower on the west ridge 250 ft below the summit. Nuamkuam Pass on Shkhara-Nuamkuam ridge was ascended from the south by Cockin and Woolley. Two unsuccessful attempts were made on the South Peak of Ushba.

1894   J. Collier, Newmarch and Solly climbed **Bakh** (Great Charinda), 3578m, above Betsho. **Machkhin** (3751m) was climbed by Solly and Newmarch with a native hunter, Moratvi.

1895   **Tsiteli** (Ziteli/Tana), 4277m, climbed by Dent and Woolley, with K. Maurer and S. Moor. Woolley and Maurer later gained the Nuamkuam Pass from the north, from Dychsu Kosh.

W. Rickmer Rickmers and A. Hacker spent summer on the Karatchai group before making four unsuccessful attempts on Ushba (3 from south, one from north.)

1896   Cockin, Woolley, Holder – without guides – climbed **Adyrsu-Bashi** (4370m) by north ridge, **Gumatchi** (Cheget-Tau-Chana), 3810m, by its west ridge, and **Koia-ugo Bashi**. Attempts were made also on Jailik Bashi, Bzedukh and Ullukara.

Sella with E. Gallo and a number of 'Biellese farm servants as porters' made an extensive journey on the north side of the range, in the process climbing the second summit of **Tepli, Saudor Khokh** (a peak they called 'Skatikom Khokh'), 4050m, one of the Adai Khokh subsidiary summits, **Sugan North Peak** (4467m) and **Kom**, as well as crossing some unfamiliar passes.

Pastuchov, still surveying the Elbrus area, climbed the East Peak. He also undertook meteorological observations.

1900   W. R. Rickmers and his wife climbed Little Charinda (3316m) which he believed to be Collier's Bakh; Zalmag (Salmiag), 3992m, on the slopes of which he found a cairn; **Totan**, 'an unimportant summit' in the Ushba group, but a definite first ascent; and crossed – he believed for the first time – the Leila Pass (c.3100m), 'a glorious and magnificent route'. In the same year he was one of the founder members of the Caucasus Club formed in Vienna for self-sufficient climbers.

1902   **Maily Khokh** (4601m) climbed by N. de Poggenpohl.

1903   Rickmers brought 'a little army' into Svanetia for 7 weeks, 17 people in all –
12 in his immediate Austro-Bavarian-Anglo-Swiss party, 'two semi-
attached English freebooters' and three Georgians. 30 peaks and passes
were climbed, more than half of them for the first time. Despite a horrific
fall on his first attempt A. Schulze seized the plum **Ushba South** (Red
Corner, 5A) from the south-east (the Gul valley) with R. Helbling, F.
Reichert, O. Schuster, A. Weber. The expedition's other successes included
Dongosorun from the south, the west ridge of **Mestia-Tau**, 4130m (their
'Chatyn-Tau'); **Shkhelda,** 4320m; **Jangi-Tau** (all summits, including Main,
5051m); **Skimeri** (c.3600m); **Ledesht-Tau** (3836m); **Leirag-Tau** (3521m);
Hevai (3980m); **Dallakora** (3429m); **Shtavler** (3995m); **Chatyn-Tau**
(4363m); **'Zenzi-Tau'** (3860m); **Nashkodra (c.3950m); the west ridge of
Gestola (4860m)**; and **Lyalver** (4350m).

T. G. Longstaff and W. Rolleston – the semi-attached freebooters – climbed
Shkhara West Peak; also **Lakra, Ullu-Tau** (Latsga), 4207m, **Bashil-Tau**
(c.4200m), and **Tikhtengen** (4610m).

A major 6-bivouac traverse of both Ushba peaks (from the north) was made
by a separate party from Bavaria. H. Pfann, L. Distel and Dr G. Leuchs also
climbed **Bzedukh** (4271m) and **Osengi-Tau** (3415m).

A Miss Preobrajenska of Vladikavkas, described as the first 'amateur' to visit
the Kistinka valley, climbed to the ridge between Kuru-Tau and Schino-
Tau.

1904   **Nachar** (3789m) climbed by A. Fischer and C. Jossi, who (detouring from an
expedition with A. von Meck) also traversed Elbrus from north to south, and
went on to climb in the Eastern Caucasus.

1907   A nameless triple peak (**Ronchetti-Khokh**/Triple Peak, 3960m) in the
Mamison Group was climbed by Dr V. Ronchetti and F. Colombo.

1908   Raeburn reported a Russian climber ascending **Kurmuchi** (Kurmutshi),
4058m, in the Adyrsu district – but Egger claimed first ascent of this with
Miescher, 1914, saying he found cairns near the col, but no trace of earlier
passage on either summit.

V. Ronchetti, F. Colombo and the guide Confortola crossed the Urziwachi
Pass ('an attractive col') but failed to cross the Giulchi-Sugan group ('an
interminable row of crests' 'massive glaciers and beetling cliffs' –
Vallepiana).

1909   Mme H. Kuntze with guides J. Schaller and J. Lochmatter was active in the
'Bogkhobashi' (Laboda and Sugan group). She climbed **Nakhasbita South
and North Peaks** (4300m, 4393m); **Zichgartichon** (4136m); and **Sugantau
South Peak** (4490m).

1910   The Austrian party of Dr W. Fischer, V. v. Friedrichs, Dr G. Kuhfahl and
Schuster, with a local hunter I. Kalagoff, spent a productive season in the
Ossetian chain and Kasbek group. Peaks climbed included: **Donshenti-
Khokh; Resi-Khokh** (3820m); **Suatisi-Khokh** (4473m); **Ziti-Khokh
(3907m); Tsariat-Khokh** (Zariat Choch), 4062m and **Kaltber** (4409m).

The north-west ridge of **Nakra-Tau** (4277m), in the Kuish group, was
ascended by O. Hug and K. de Rham, who also traversed Leirag and

Ledesht-Tau, besides climbing **Dolra-Tau** (3850m). They went on to traverse all the Dongusorun summits.

1911 Fischer and Schuster returned to the Central Caucasus, this time with the painter Ernst Platz, to climb between the Terek and Ardon river valleys: a nameless rock peak between Zirkhu Bason/Sirchu Barson and Tsariat Khokh, Kazbek group (c.3900m); **Kalasan-Tau** (3839m); **Zilga-Khokh East Peak**; **Shau-Khokh**; **Resi-Khokh North** and **Central** and **Mitchin-Zup** (4371m); and **Tsmiakom-Khokh** (4136m) were all ascended.

1912 In the course of a wide-ranging expedition, M. Winkler, W. Gruber, A. Lechner, A. Thal and R. Wandel visited the Bezingi area, where they climbed the West Summit of Dych-Tau and traversed Gestola south to north-east. From the Jailik valley, they climbed **Jailik** (Dschailik-Basch), 4535m, and **Kentchat** (4170m). They returned through the uninhabited Nakra valley.

Fischer, Schuster, this time with Dr H. Renner, made the first ascent of **Lagau-Khokh** (4066m) in the Adai. They also climbed Kalper (probably previously ascended by a hunter), and a nameless point in the Tepli group.

1913 A Scottish group comprising H. Raeburn, W. G. Johns, W. N. Ling and J. R. Young with the Russian Rembert Martinson visited the Adai Khokh group. There they climbed **Tur Khokh**, **Ullargh Khokh**, Saramag (previously ascended by Russian surveyors, but their route 'almost certainly new'), Mamison Peak (traversed to include the virgin **Mamison Shoulder**), and **Tshantshakhi** (4420m). (This latter is the 'Adai Khokh' of early writings.) The three summits of **Nuamkuam** (4182m) on the main Ushguli-Ailama crest, were also climbed from the south by all except Johns. An attempt on the north-east face of Ushba by a new route was abandoned at 14,000ft because of objective dangers, as was another on the South Peak. Elbrus Eastern Summit was climbed.

1914 The Russian party of M. S. Golubev (Golubjew), Panjutin, Steinooglu and Steip claimed **Balvik** (Balik-su-bash/Baluksa, 3905m); **Mukal-Tau** (3888m); **Ksgem-Bashi** (4013m), all in Elbrus area; **Kullumkol Bashi** (4055m) in Adyrsu; and **Gidan-Tau** (4160m) Ukiu district.

Swiss climbers C. Egger and G. Miescher, in a 3-week campaign during which they also ascended Elbrus on ski, bagged several new ascents in the Adyl-su and Adyrsu areas: **Andirchi** (3913m); **Jantugan** (3991m); **Bashkara** (4241m), traversing to **Gadil** (4120m); **Tiutiu-Bashi** (4460m); and **Jailik** (4533m). Two unnamed points 4369m and 4365m (now **Yunomkara-Tau**), south and north of Freshfield's Pass, were climbed; as was Koiavgan-Bashi (Koja-ugu-asuch tschaft-Bashi), 3877m, first climbed by Cockin and co. in 1896; and **Kurmuchi**, 4058m (see also under 1908); as well as **Kurmuchi North** (c.4000m) – soloed by Miescher. (The outbreak of war just as they were about to leave Svanetia complicated their return journey and they were compelled to abandon their expedition photographs.)

Raeburn, Martinson, R. C. Richards and H. Scott Taylor climbed **Bubis Khokh** (Freshfield's 'Double Peak', 4420m); **Karagom Khokh East** (4513m), **Vologata** (4175m); and **Laboda** (4320m).

1915   Golubev, Bulygin, and J. Frolov climbed the easy south-west ridge of **Sarikol** (4160m) from the north. The same party – with Christinov – made the first ascent of the south-west ridge of Mestia-Tau (4130m). Golubev and Frolov also climbed south ridge of Kichkidar (4370m); and with Panutin made the first ascent of **Schurovski** (Shchurovsky), 4259m, by the south-east ridge.

1914–27 In the absence of foreign visitors during and after the First World War and the years of the Russian Revolution, Russian climbers gradually extended their activities, demonstrating particularly their dedication to collectivisation. 25 Georgian students climbed Kazbek in 1923, and in 1925 the newly formed Tiflis (Tblisi) Geographical Society (which also climbed Kazbek in 1924 and 1926) organised an extended tour, during which 19 of the 27-strong group climbed Elbrus East before trekking on through Svanetia and Abkhazia.

1928   Bavarian Caucasus expedition – P. Bauer, E. Beigel, H. Niesner, H. Tillman – came to the Bezingi. In the previously unexplored Kargashil-Tau chain members climbed **Tchumurtcheran-Tau** ('not a difficult climb, but a first ascent'). An attempt on Dych-Tau from the south-east had to be abandoned in a thunderstorm within a rope's-length of the summit. The high point of their trip extended the tradition of great traverses, for which the Caucasus was to become so rightly famous: Katyn-Tau was climbed by the north buttress; they continued over Adish-Tau, then Gestola and Lyalver, bivouacking twice en route. Shkhara was given its second ascent by a partly new route, but bad weather denied them Ushba.

Futnargun-Tau (4184m) in the Bezingi group was climbed by von Parijski and companions.

1929   A German team – Willy Merkl, Fritz Bechtold, Walter Raechl – arrived for the summer. Among their achievements were ascents of Naweriani-Tau (c.4130m) with Semenowski party; and Urzwachki-Tau. Ushba, unclimbed since 1903, was scaled with W. Semenowski after a 4-day attempt (South Summit – 3rd ascent). In Svatgar group they climbed Tot-Tau (c.4000m) with Semenowski; Skala Bodurku (4182m); Kulak-Tau (4062m).

Semenowski and party climbed Pik Komsomol (3690m); and H. Tomaschek's Viennese party was also active in the Svatgar chain, climbing **Asmashi** (4090m)-fore-summit at least was virgin). The last 8m of the rocky summit block of Svatgar-Tau (4109m) defeated them.

U. di Vallepiana, L. Gasparotto, both of Italy, with the American R. Herron and Bavarian R. Singer visited the Giulchi-Sugan group, making the first ascent of **Giulchi**, 4475m, by its south-east face. Vallepiana and Gasparotto climbed a rocky height 'opposite Giulchi and S of our col' (Giulchi Pass), c.4200m, calling it **Punta Ronchetti**. Three of them bagged **Little Sugan** (3900m) and two **Point of the Italians** (c.4200m). Gasparotto claimed to have made first true ski climb of Elbrus with Slezak and Tomaschek.

V. Dougan and Dr A. von Pollitzer climbed Oerelue-Bashi (Orelyi), 4066m, in the Jailik group. Dougan alone claimed Surin-Tau (4069m).

1930   J. H. B. Bell (Scotland) joined a Russian party, and with Delaunay made the first ascent of south-west arête of Bashil-Tau, 'a difficult climb'.

H. Tomaschek and W. Müller, from Vienna, climbed the difficult north rib of Shkhara (5200m), descending by the north-east ridge – a traverse demanding 6 bivouacs above 4000m. They also climbed the airy north ridge of Bashkha-Auz (4460m, 3A).

Another large Viennese group (describing themselves as '6 super-expert and 4 moderate performers') climbed Kolchaja, 3700m; made the first ascent of the very difficult **Futnargin Nameless Peak** (c.4100m) between Zurungal and Point 4054m, by Kolb and party – another summit between Nuamkuam and Shkhara, the summit being reached by a remarkable ice ridge. They traversed Nuamkuam. Heilinger and Jascynski climbed Koshtan-Tau by a gully on the south-east arête, making a new descent to the east-north-east (3 days). Two others traversed Khrumkol (4680m); Kolb and group climbed Karasu-Tau (3600m) in Laboda and Sugan group.

1931 A. Germogenov, M. Afanasjev, N. Nikoljev made the first ascent of the south ridge of Misses-Tau from the west (4320m). Four men – 2 Swiss: M. Mäglin and J. Hegglin, and the Russians Levin and Goldowski were lost on an attempt to climb Misses-Tau South-East.

Major traverses: the difficult north face of Misses-Tau was climbed by a strong Austrian group, comprising K. Poppinger, K. Frank, K. Moldan and S. Schintlmeister. They climbed Lyalver by the north-east ridge, traversed Gestola, made the first ascent of north-east ridge of Tetnuld, climbed Katyn-Tau by its north buttress, Adish-Tau, and traversed Gestola and Lyalver to the Zanner Pass and Misses-Kosh. Then followed their epic success of **the Bezingi horseshoe traverse/Bezingi Wall** (by Poppinger, Moldan, Schintlmeister): the first complete traverse of Shkhara, west to east, in which the points 5017m, 5010m, 5130m were climbed for the first time, and on to Jangi East and West Peaks, then Katyn-Tau, Gestola and Lyalver! It involved 6 bivouacs in ice caves, and for 33 years remained the swiftest crossing.

Siberian brothers V. and Y. Abalakov and Valentina Cheredova, who later became Mrs V. Abalakov, visited the Caucasus for the first time, climbing Dych-Tau with no previous Alpine experience.

Semenowski and party climbed the **Pik der Bergsteigerkurse** (c.3800m) in the Ushba group.

1932 N. Popov and B. Rukavischnibkov climbed the snowy Kukurtlu Dome (4912m) from the south.

1933 Georgians A. Gvalia and V. Cheishvili made the first ascent of south-east ridge of Shkhara.

Tiutiu-Bashi (4460m) was climbed by R. Gache, J. Lagarde, R. T. du Montcel and L. Valluet, who then traversed to **Balkar-Tau**, a first ascent, and **Gortu-Bashi**, again a first. (This is Freshfield's 'Kashtan Crest'.) A repeat climb of the north ridge of Koshtan-Tau was abandoned after a fall (happily not too serious). Kilmet-Bashi (3965m) was climbed by Gache, Valluet and the interpreter G. Marietsky.

A Swiss expedition – W. Rickenbach, O. Furrer, L. Saladin, P. Buhler and W. Weckert – got off to a disastrous start. Robbed in Moscow, beset by illness and bad weather, they were making a dispirited attempt on Doppakh-Tau, in stormy conditions, when Buhler fell to his death. Finally, Saladin and Weckert achieved the third direct ascent of Ushba South (5th ascent overall).

W. Heybrock has described a solitary 'tramp' in the south-east Elbrus region, in the course of which, after climbing Elbrus, he 'attacked a group of nameless unsurveyed peaks' and in succession climbed four points between 3400–3700m. The first bore a cairn with a note W. A. Wowa and A. Fura 1929; the others appeared virgin. He named the highest **Tusse Casteret**. Four days later, on a spur of the Bartkort range, he climbed his **'Point Byrd'** (3285m) and **'Punta Dainelli'** (3303m).

1934   N. Popov, G. Skorniakov, N. Chekmarev made the first ascent of the west ridge of **Germogenov Pik** (3993m, 2B). They also climbed Ullukara (4302m) by its south-west ridge (from the north).

B. Simagin, A. Lukin, B. Sigranski traversed Tiutiu-Bashi (4460m) from west to east.

A Swiss expedition led by Saladin, and including W. Frei, O. Furrer and H. Graf, with G. Harlampiev as interpreter, climbed first in the Adai Khokh group. They climbed Vologata by its north face, sat out a day of storm in an ice cave on the summit, and on the following morning began the traverse of the triple Vologata rock peak, continuing on to **Skatikom** after another bivouac. Then they climbed Karagom East and West Peaks. Later, two attempts on Ailama failed, but Frei and Gock traversed Bashkha-Auz-Bashi. The party made the first ascent of **Mishirgi-Tau Main (West) Summit** (4926m) from the south, before going on to climb Misses-Tau. Saladin and Gock climbed Pik Schurovski by its steep west face (a first ascent), and with Furrer climbed Elbrus East in record time.

First winter ascent of Elbrus East Peak by A. Gusev and W. Korsun.

1935   The Russian N. Gusak, with German companions, made first winter ascent of Elbrus West Peak.

Russians V. Kiesel and B. Aleinokov climbed the north ridge of Ushba North (4696m, 4A).

Kogutai was traversed north to south by P. Rototajev and B. Fried.

The climb and traverse West Peak 1 to 2, Shkhelda West (4310m) was achieved by O. Aristov, A. Anfilov, A. Isorgina, V. Meierovitsch. Aristov with G. Deberl, L. Nadeshin and W. Zeidler climbed the east ridge of Jantugan (3991m).

Pik Woolley (3960m) was climbed from the south-west by L. Nadeshdin, A. Sheltikov, E. Rubbach, B. Schirjajev.

The first ascent of **Bzedukh** (4271m) by its south-east ridge from the north was made by S. Metreveli and A. Beljajev.

Eleven Austrian mountaineers visited various Caucasian ranges with considerable success: R. Fraisl, F. Krobath, H. Peterka, E. Schlager and L. Spannraft were busy in the Sugan and Dychsu groups where they made first ascents of: Sugan-Tau south arête (4490m); **Sugan-Bashi** (4447m); Ailama north-east face and east arête; **Zurungal** (4222m) by its north-west arête; and made a horseshoe-traverse of Shkhara North-East Peak, climbing by the so-called 'Trapeze' or east ridge and descending the north-east ridge to the Dykhniaus Pass. They also climbed the South Peak of Tujala-Tau by its west arête and made the first ascent of the south-west flank of Koshtan-Tau.

Meanwhile in the Bezingi area the difficult north-east pillar of the main peak of Jangi-Tau (5051m) was climbed by R. Schwarzgruber (leader of the expedition), W. Marin, F. Peringer, H. Thaler. This is the celebrated 'Schwarzgruber Rib'.

Peringer and H. Bocek traversed Bzedukh-Tau, descending its north face.

A German expedition active at the same time in the Tepli group – A. Goettner, G. Rosenschon, L. Schmäderer and L. Vörg – bagged **Kolota-Tau** (4167m); **Tepli-Tau** (4423m); and **Arkhon-Tau** (c.4150m) which they traversed. In the Adai, they climbed the south ridge of Tur Khokh; Ullargh Khokh; Tvilisis (c.4300m); Bubis Khokh South by its rocky and dangerous south-west face, traversing to **Bubis Khokh North** (believed to be first ascent). They climbed Songuti North Peak. On Ushba, they put up an extremely difficult route on the South Peak of Ushba then traversed to the North Peak where they were caught in bad weather. This second traverse of the peak (the first in this direction) required four bivouacs. Finally, Gottner and Vörg climbed Dych-Tau by its north-west arête, another first ascent.

W. Heybrock undertook a 'Second Caucasian Tramp' through the Adai Khokh and Tepli massif, making glacier observations and checking place names.

1936   Austrians returned to the Bezingi area. This time the party comprised W. Frauenberger, F. Krobath, F. Peringer, H. Raditschnig, F. Wolfgang, with Schwarzgruber again as leader. Various long traverses were made, some sections of which were first ascents: Tiktengen; Shkhara – Janga; Gestola – Lyalver; Dych-Tau – Mishirgi-Tau; Khrumkol-Bashi – Koshtan-Tau; and Katyn-Tau (Bezingi 'face') – Adish-Tau. For this latter Krobath and Wolfgang teamed up with Schaeffer and Schweizer.

Other Austrian and German teams were also active. Vörg and Thurstein traversed the entire Bzedukh-Tau ridge; L Schmäderer and H. Paidar climbed Sheklikh-Tau (4320m) in the Ushba range; Vörg and Schmäderer made the first ascent of Ushba west face, attaining the North Summit and descending via the north arête.

Russian ascents included: Oru-Bashi south-west ridge by A. Sjusin, V. Birman, A. Gertschik, F. Juschnarev; Jailik south-east route by B. Simagin, A. Lapin, E. Litvinova, A. Olschanski; and Mishirgi W Peak W Ridge (from the south) by G. Prokudaev, I. Korzun, V. Naumenko. V. Abalakov led ten of his pupils up Dych-Tau.

1937   Four-man British expedition (B. Beaumont, R. Hodgkin, J. Jenkins, M. Taylor) got into training by notching up most of the peaks around the Junom Glacier, including Urubashi, Junomkara, Kichkidar and some previously unclimbed and unnamed; as well as Jailik by its south face (a new route). Next, Jenkins and Hodgkin climbed the jagged north-east ridge of Adyrsu-Bashi, while Beaumont soloed Oru-Bashi. The team traversed

Gulba by a new route, and made a significant variation to the Schulze line on Ushba South (avoiding the Red Corner). Jenkins and Taylor put up a new route on the formidable north face of Tetnuld.

South-east buttress of Ushba South south ridge (5B) went to G. Khergiani, H. Gvariani, V. Khergiani, Ch. Chartolani. A. Siderenko and A. Slobadakoi put up the western route on Little Ushba (4320m) from a bivouac on the Ushba plateau. Siderenko also established an easy new route on Gumatchi north ridge with G. Odnoblijudov. On Shkhara South (4316m) the south-east buttress of south ridge (3A) was climbed by Georgian climbers: A. Gvalia, G. Zurebiani, A. Kvitsiani, L. Meshishvili.

North-east ridge of Bashkara (4241m, 3B) climbed by E. Ivanov, A. Sidorov, V. Orliankin, Y. Smirnov.

1938   North-east ridge of Dongusorun West Peak (4437m) was climbed by V. Markov, A. Glatenko and A. Gusav. Dongusorun East (4442m) by its north pillar and east ridge fell to A. Gvalija, V. Belezkaja, and M. Gvarliani. A simple route on the east ridge of Lower Dongusorun (3760m) was made by V. Gretscheninova and E. Gret.

A long and difficult traverse of Ullu-Tau (4207m) from east to west was achieved by A. Solotarev, F. Kropf, W. Mauer and V. Nesterov.

1940   The long and sustained rock and ice traverse, west to east, of Shkhelda (4320m, Grade 5B), still one of the most demanding in the range with complicated route-finding and some tricky sections, was successfully accomplished over 8 days by L. Nadeshdin, A. Mazkevitsch, V. Nasarov and P. Sysojev.

1946   An important new route on the north face of Nakra-Tau (4277m) was put up by V. Abalakov, A. Borovikov, N. Gusak, and I. Leonov of the Spartak sport society (Left Pillar, 4B).

D. Gudkov, M. Svesdkin, G. Odnoblijudov and M. Tschertkov climbed the steep Shield route on north face of Ullu-Tau West Peak (4203m).

1947   An uncomplicated traverse, east to west, was made over the crests of Irikchat (4050m) by P. and L. Kovalev, and A. Eighorn. On Pik Schurovski (4259m) a long and difficult rock route was put up on the north-west rib (5B) by V. Abalakov, A. Borovikov, I. Leonov and V. Tscheredova (Mrs V. Abalakov), all of the Spartak sport society; the mountain's north-east ridge (4B) was climbed by V. Pelevin, Y. Arkin, K. Faddeeva, L. Filimonov, M. Chemodakov.

1949   Abalakov with Y. Arkin, N. Gusak, I. Leonov, V. Martynov, J. Moskalzov, V. Pelevin and V. Tscheredova climbed Khrumkol (4680m) east ridge from the north, a hard, mixed route. The same party climbed east ridge of Mishirgi East (4918m, 4B).

B. Garf climbed east ridge of Germogenov (3993m, 3B) with B. Boldin, V. Mikhailov, N. Nekrasov, P. Povarnin, I. Rozovskaja. Jantugan (3991m) was ascended by its south-west ridge (3A) by V. Nefedjev, B. Gorunov, D. Librovski, V. Proshina; and its north-west ridge by B. Baldin, B. Garf, K. Karavaev, V. Mikhailov, P. Povarnin, N. Nekrasova, I. Rozovskaja, A. Sharunin.

1951   The north ridge of Misses-Tau (4320m) was climbed by A. Ivanishvili, I. Bakradse, A. Kavtaradse, D. Kandesili, W. Kvatshandadse, G. Kiniani, R. Natadse.

North face of Nakra-Tau (4277m) climbed by the right-hand buttress (4B) by E. Zamora, A. Kaspin, J. Kachiani, A. Kuzin, B. Lundin, V. Nekrasov.

North-west ridge of Germogenov (3A) climbed by A. Starostin, I. Burov, Y. Pafunina, F. Pustometinko.

Mazeri north face (4A) climbed by V. Staritski, V. Annenkov, I. Borushko, V. Kozhin, S. Skovoroda.

1952   The long and very steep north rib of Mishirgi East (4918m, 5B) was climbed by V. Pelevin, A. Borovikov, V. Kiesel, I. Leonov and V. Rubanov of the Spartak sport society, Moscow.

B. Garf with A. Baldin, S. Repin, A. Romanovich, K. Tumanov, Y. Shirokov climbed the right rib of the 'triangle' on north face of Chatyn-Tau (4368m, 5B).

On Shkhara B. Khergiani established new 5B route on the buttress of south face of Main Peak (5200m) with fellow Georgian climbers I. Gabliani, M. Gvarliani, V. Khergiani, C. Chartolani.

North face of Ispanii Pik (Free Spain Peak, 4200m, 5B) climbed by V. Kiesel, N. Gusak, L. Filimonov of Moscow.

1953   Abalakov climbed the north-east face of Schurovski Pik (5B) with M. Anufrikov, V. Buslaev, V. Kiesel, I. Lapshenkov, I. Leonov, L. Filimonov.

1954   Abalakov led a serious new route on Dych-Tau north-east face (5198m), the Central Pillar (5B); with him were M. Anufrikov, J. Arkin, V. Buslajev, V. Kiesel, I. Lapschenkov, L. Filimonov and his wife, V. Tscheredova. The north buttress of north-east ridge Chatyn-Tau was climbed by I. Leonov, P. Budanov, K. Tolstov, V. Martynov, V. Rubanbov, S. Tenishev and F. Lulumbekov (5B).

O. Abalakov, R. Likucheva, V. Solovjev, B. Utkin climbed the right spur of south-west ridge of Dych-Tau (5198m, 4B).

An elegant and difficult ice route on the north-west face of Bzedukh (4271m) was made by J. Naumov, J. Sbukov, I. Kavlaschvili, and V. Tur.

Ullukara north buttress (4302m, 4A) climbed by east ridge by V. Zaitsev, Y. Zubkov, M. Rozhkov, Y. Tur.

Mazeri north rib, 4B, climbed by S. Savvon, G. Dulnev, A. Kaspin, V. Ziskindovich, V. Potapov.

1956   On Shkhelda, a north face route was established on 3rd Western Pik (Pik Aristov, 4229m, 5B) by L. Eliseev, V. Galkin, A. Ivanov, A. Manukhin.

North-west buttress of Ullukara (4302m, 4B) climbed by V. Ivanov, A. Crachev, B. Zakharjev, A. Lysov, A. Osintsev, V. Smoliakov, Y. Snetkov.

Ushba North north-west face (left side, 5B) climbed by I. Erokhin, A. Belopukhov, V. Ivanov and A. Osintsev; and the south-east face (5B) by V. Staritski, V. Bekehin, D. Ivanov, L. Kaluzhski, R. Stroganov.

1957 Globe-trotting British woman Joyce Dunsheath made a private visit to the Caucasus where she climbed Elbrus with Eugene Gippenreiter and other Soviet mountaineers. The visit was an important ice-breaker in the Cold War. That year Masters of Sport M. Khergiani and J. Kakhiani made a new north wall ascent on Dongusorun (4452m, 5B).

1958 New route on Dych-Tau East Summit via south couloir (5180m, 4B) established by B. Garf, M. Garf, A. Gurjev and E. Kudriavtsev.

Nine British climbers, led by Sir John Hunt, climbed with Soviet mountaineers in the Central Caucasus during July, the first group from any country in the 'free world' to be allowed in since the Oxford/Birmingham party of 1937. Others in the party: Alan Blackshaw, George Band, Derek Bull, David Thomas, Chris Brasher, John Neill, Michael Harris, Ralph Jones.

For part of their stay they were based in the Bezingi region and between them climbed Shkhara north buttress (Muller route); the Schwarzgruber Rib on Jangi-Tau (but not to the summit); and Gestola. Band and Harris made first ascent of south buttress on the East Summit of Dych-Tau.

Georgian climbers climbed the south-west face of Shkhara West (5057m, 5B) – D. Oboladze, D. Dangadze, A. Dzidziguri, O. Kapanadze.

V. Ivanov and A. Osintsev climbed the north face of Ailama (4547m, 5B).

North-west rib of Ushba North (4696m, 5A) climbed by K. Barov, G. Akstinas, V. Livshits.

1959 An easy route on Ortokara (4250m, 2A) via its north-east ridge was climbed by D. Suchodolski, I. Anangev, V. Iwanova and P. Kabanov.

A hard and important north face route in the classic style was made up the steep ice of Gestola (4860m, 5B) by M. Khergiani, S. Margiani and I. Polevoi. Two north face routes, both 6A, were put up on Chatyn-Tau (4368m) by A. Snesarev, V. Barzykin, B. Korablin and V. Stepanov of the Trud sport society; and L. Myshliaev, O. Kosmachev, A. Simonik.

East rib of Ushba South (4710m, 5B) went to V. Nekrasov, A. Bitnyi, A. Demchenko, G. Zhivljuk, Y. Zarichnjak, K. Rototaev.

On Dych-Tau the south spur left-hand route was climbed by L. Alexashin, V. Koptev, Y. Minin.

German mountaineers R. Kuhar, O. Kopah, C. Zerman climbed the ice slopes of Dongusorun north-west face (5A).

East face of Ispanii Pik (Free Spain Peak, 4200m, 5B) climbed by I. Myshliaev and O. Kosmachev.

French mountaineers under B. Pierre made a number of fine climbs, mostly early repeats.

1960 R. Andreev, A. Assorov, N. Isaev and A. Shrkrabkin climbed north-west face of north rib of Khrumkol (4680m, 5B).

North-east face of Ushba North (4696m, 5B) went to A. Snesarev, V. Barzykin, B. Kashevnik, B. Korablin, V. Savin, G. Stepanov of the Trud sport society; while the north-east ridge (also 5B) was claimed by M. Suponitski, R. Ivanov, A. Manukhin, N. Kusel-Moroz, S. Nikanorov.

North-east rib of Mishirgi East (4918m, 5B) climbed by St Petersburg group: A. Timofeev, V. Zhyrnov, V. Ivanov, L. Kadykov, A. Pepin, G. Chunovkin.

1961 An extremely hard climb up the enormous right-hand pillar of the north face of Koshtan-Tau (5B) was made by A. Simonik, I. Kudinov, E. Sokolovski, and V. Schutin.

Another hard north face climb was put up on Ullu-Auz-Bashi (4670m, 5B) by A. Naumov, N. Andrejev, B. Dauter, and G. Naumova.

Jantugan (3991m, 3B) north face climbed by Y. Chervinka, I. Baltar, V. Schmida and M. Jaschkovski. North face of west shoulder of Bashkara (4241m, 6A) achieved by V. Livshits, B. Britanov, I. Lusik, G. Polevoi from the Ukraine.

H. MacInnes with G. Ritchie from Scotland with Russians E. Tur and I. Bandarowsky were caught by storm traversing Shkhelda's summits west to east in what proved a 12-day epic.

1962 The long north-west rib on the north-west face of Ushba South (4710m, 5B) was climbed over 7 days of July/August by G. Zhivljuk, A. Bitnyi, J. Gavrikov, P. Goncharov, A. Demchenko and W. Logvinov.

Kunjum-Mishirgi (4500m) was climbed by its long, moderate north ridge by A. Beda, V. Daruga, A. Svesdkin, V. Platejorov-Severski, A. Tkatschenko, R. Tscheremisinov.

M. Khergiani climbed the north face buttress of Schurovski Pik (4259m, 5B) with A. Amshokov, M. Zalikhanov, J. Kakhiani, D. Kakhiani, G. Stepanov. Another north face route, also 5B, was made a few days later by L. Kensitski, I. Kashin, V. Monogarov, N. Maschenko, B. Subartovich, B Shaposhnikov.

North-west buttress of north-east ridge of Dongusorun climbed by K. Rototaev, S. Artukhin, I. Goriachev, E. Zhizhin, V. Ruzhevski, G. Solodovnikov, A. Tkachenko, S. Shatski.

1963 V. Jegerov, E. Antipenko, V. Solonnikov completed the scenic and obvious traverse at the eastern end of the Bezingi Glacier, taking in Piks Warsaw, Sella and the highest, Bashka-Auz (4460m).

The north ridge of Little Ailama (4010m, 4A) went to I. Bandurovski, V. Goncharov, O. Grippa, V. Eletski, V. Koziavkin, D. Lavrinenko from the Ukraine.

Mishirgi East south face (4918m, 5B) climbed by M. Finogenov, A. Pugachev, L. Puchkov, V. Solonnikov, A. Tkachenko, Y. Shevchenko, I. Shestipalov.

North-east rib of Ispanii Pik (4200m, 5B) climbed by B. Subartovich, E. Vaisberg, P. Tepliakov, L. Tibeikin.

1964 First ascent of south pillar route on Pik Freshfield (4050m, 3A) by A. Paunknis, G. Shirnova, K. Kalakuzkaja, P. Povarnin and M. Tshernych.

Another route on north-west face of north rib of Khrumkol (4680m, 5B) climbed by G. Chunovkin, Y. Komarov, A. Pugachev, V. Solonnikov, V. Stankevich, M. Finogenov, Y. Shevchenko, I. Shestopalov.

East Germans and Czechoslovaks (6-man group) were first non-Soviets to repeat Bezingi Wall traverse since its inauguration and the first to improve on the time of the Austrian pioneers (7th traverse overall).

North face of Mishirgi East (4918m, 5B) climbed by a Polish team: E. Mikhailski, E. Varmeresevich, T. Laukaitis, E. Hrobak.

East face of Ushba North (4696m, 5B) went to V. Monogarov, M. Aleksjuk, L. Kensitski, V. Kovtun, E. Kondakov, N. Maschenko, all from the Ukraine.

1965   Slovak party led by I. Kluvanek met with bad weather and uncertain conditions but succeeded in making first ascent of north-west face Shkhara in 3 days. (An objectively difficult route that had cost the lives of P. Cernik and Z. Studnicka in an attempt the previous year.) Further success was the first ascent of north-west ridge of Koshtan-Tau in two days. The east rib of Shkhara South (4350m, 5A) went to A. Naumov, V. Benkin, N. Grishkov, I. Kudinov; and the east face of Shkhara Main (5200m, 5B) to M. Khergiani, A. Akhvlediani, V. Gabelashvili, D. Gugava, D. Kakhiani, T. Narchemashvili, G. Zerediani of Georgia.

Austrians E. Vanis, P. Lavicka and P. Kernthaler made 9th Bezingi Wall traverse. This 17km route, which hugs the 5000-metre level, remains one of the most important undertakings in the range. About 80 per cent of the ridge is snow and ice climbing, the rest rock.

The first winter ascent of Ushba was made by Vladimir Shataev, and Volodya Kavunenko, with Boris Studaenin and Vladimir Bezlyndny. Starting from the Ushba Plateau, the north-east ridge was followed to the North Summit; the intention had been to repeat the Pfann traverse, but in that, they failed.

South face of Pik Pushkin (5100m, 4B) climbed by N. Garevski and others.

Bashkara north face (4241m, 6A) first ascent by Ukrainian climbers: Y. Grigorenko-Prigoda, Y. Bakhtigozin, Y. Sizyi, V. Shumikhin.

North face climb on Nuamkuam (4182m, left rib 5B) by A. Naumov, Y. Kozlov, I. Kudinov, M. Trofimov.

1966   Another new route went up on Pik Pushkin south face (left spur, 4B), this time by A. Pugachev and companions. On Nuamkuam, the right-hand rib of north face (5B) fell to I. Kudinov, B. Golubkov, V. Daruga, Y. Saratov.

1967   A fine new route was put up on the Monarch (or Monk) ridge of Jailik (4533m, 5A): V. Ruschevski, L. Belov, K. Saizev, K. Kaspaov, I. Nugmanov, J. Porochnja climbed this south ridge from the upper plateau of the West Yunom Glacier. On Pik Schurovski, the 'Surok' (Marmot) route on the west face, 5B, went to Ukrainians L. Kensitski, R. Badygin, A. Blankovski, P. Goncharov, V. Gromko, O. Markovski. And the west ridge buttress of Kukurtlu (4623m, 5B) was claimed by E. Zhizhin, D. Makauskas, L. Matushin, I. Hatskevich, A. Chmykhov.

New 6A-line established on north rib of Khrumkol by A. Tomofeev and others.

1969   South face of Shkhara Main Summit (5200m, 5B) went to Georgian climbers S. Mirianashvili, G. Abashidze, D. Dangadze, O. Hazaradze.

1970   Friedrich Bender (subsequently author of many Caucasian guidebooks) put up a beautiful long route of moderate difficulty on the East Peak of Pik Kavkaz (4160m, 3A). He climbed the north-west route with H. Brumlich and G. Kretschmer.

H. MacInnes headed another British expedition, which also included: A. McHardy, P. Nunn, P. Braithwaite, C. Woodall, P. Seeds. MacInnes, Nunn and Woodall made first ascent of 'Centenary Climb' on north face Pik Schurovski over 3 days in July (3000ft of mainly steep mixed climbing).

Climbers from Mirianaschvili climbing school in Georgia (S. Mirianashvili, G. Bavasheli, L. Glonti, D. Dangadze, O. Hazaradze) opened a difficult new route on the near-vertical south face of Shkhara West (5057m). 180 pegs were used on the 5-bivouac 1500m climb.

Chatyn-Tau (4368m) north face climbed by K. Klezko with 5 companions, making a variant to the Mischljaew route. On Ushba South, west rib climb (6A) went to Y. Artsischevski, P. Volkov, V. Kuznetsov, Y. Manshin.

1972 North face of Nuamkuam (4182m, 5B) climbed by A. Levin, A. Babinin, A. Blankovski, I. Dudchenko, E. Kalashnikov.

South-west rib of Ushba South (4710m, 6A) went to Ukrainian climbers Y. Grigirenko-Prigoda, V. Bakhtigozin, A. Vselubski, Y. Grushko, V. Tkachenko, V. Shumikhin.

1973 Direct east face route on Ushba South (4710m, 6A) fell to I. Hatskevich, V. Volkov, A. Kuznetsov, M. Nikulin, M. Ovchinnikov, V. Popov, S. Sobolev.

1974 In the Elbrus massif west face of Kukurtlu (4623m, 6A) went to R. Giutashvili, A. Borovski, G. Vardanjan, G. Zumbadze, G. Starchik.

North-east rib of Jantugan (3991m, 3B) climbed by V. Verbenski and others.

Bezingi camp climbers V. Daruga, N. Efremov, I. Korkin and E. Porokhov climbed north-west face Salinan (4510m, 5B).

A variant to south-west rib of Ushba South was claimed by G. Shalaev, V. Bolizhevski, S. Labzhinski, S. Senchina, O. Nikolaichuk, Y. Gresko.

1975 East face climb on Ushba South (5B) made by I. Hatskevich, Y. Boldyrev, G. Poliakov, G. Pshakin, G. Shumikhin. Ushba North north-east rib (5B) went to L. Kensitski, V. Gromko, V. Zasypkin, H. Kornysj, V. Ledeneev, E. Umanets of the Elbrus camp.

1976 Czechoslovak climbers climbed south-west face of Shkhara West (5057m).

1977 Czechoslovak climbers made first ascent south-west face of Shkhara (left-hand side).

The west face of Ushba South (4710m, 5B) was climbed by I. Slesov, G. Dzhinoev, V. Mikhalev, N. Shevandrin.

An exciting route up the 'Cascades' of the north face of Mishirgi East (4918m, 6A) claimed by Y. Shevchenko, V. Parfenenko, V. Cherepov, V. Jarslavtsev of the Bezingi camp.

1978 Georgian climbers established new route up centre of south-west face of Shkhara West (5057m, 5B): O. Hazaradze, G. Abashidze, S. Barliani, S. Gabisiani, S. Mirianashvili.

Ispanii Pik (Free Spain Peak, 4200m) was climbed by the east face (left-hand side, 5B) by V. Kolomytsev, V. Elagin, Ne Kurkin, S. Penzov of Moscow.

1979   John Town made a private visit to climb Kogutai, Elbrus and two minor peaks in the Adyrsu, and reported there were no longer significant barriers to a small party from the West wishing to climb in the Caucasus.

Three Bavarians were killed attempting the north-east ridge of Shkhara.

1980   Direct route on Shkhara West north face (5057m, 6A) climbed during Bezingi summer camp by A. Blankovski, I. Krainov, A. Levin, V. Melentjev.

1981   Czechoslovak climbers spent a productive three weeks in Adyrsu valley. On the north face of Tiutiu they put up a new steep ice route to the right of the existing Khergiani line; M. Smid soloed a new route on north face of the very steep Ullu-Tau (80 degrees in places), followed by a traverse of the ridge. Two women – Z. Charvatova and A. Stehlikova – repeated hard routes on Ullu-Tau north face and north buttress of Tiutiu (Khergiani line).

Another new route on north face of Shkhara West (6A) went to Y. Razumov, V. Alimov, A. Kolchin, B. Silin.

North-east face of Ullukara (4302m, 5A) climbed on its left-hand side by A. Simakov and others.

1982   B. Danihelkova, Z. Herman and M. Hurtik climbed a steep ice route on north face of Pik Shchurovski.

Czechs T. Bradac, I. Ullsperger and J. Kapoun, made first ascent of route on north face of Aristov.

A new route up the centre of Tetnuld north face was claimed by S. Tjulpanov, V. Andrienko, N. Ivanov, V. Lazarev, M. Mukhortov. On Khrumkol (4680m) V. Melentjev, E. Belousov, E. Gasilov, V. Ivlev, M. Trofimov put up a 6A-route on Khrumkol north face.

A direct north face route on Mishirgi East (5B) went to Ukrainians V. Grischenko, S. Belinski, V. Zasypkin, V. Kuliamin, A. Moldovanov, A. Tolstousov.

The icefalls of the north-west face of Ushba South (5B) were climbed by the Spartak group: V. Forostjan, A. Kulichenko, G. Lebedev, V. Likhachev, K. Rybalka; and the north-west face of Ushba North (6A) went to Moscow climbers: V. Kolomytsev, I. Grebenschikov, V. Elagin, S. Pensov. On Ushba North, a route following the left side of north-east face (4696m, 6A) went to V. Grischenko, A. Barsukov, S. Belinski, G. Vasilenko, V. Kuliamin, V. Pilipenko, S. Sentsov, A. Tolstousov.

1983   North face of Shkhara Main (5200m, 5B) climbed by I. Krainov, V. Akifjev, E. Belousov, E. Gailov, V. Ivlev, V. Makarov, V. Melentjev, M. Trofimov of the Bezingi camp. Their companions claimed a new north face route on Shkhara West (5057m, 5B): A. Laletin, V. Gurevich, S. Zhukov, A. Neplokhov, Y. Razumov, Y. Stroganov, N. Shustrov.

Direct north face route on Ailama (4547m, 5A) went to St Petersburg mountaineers: M. Mukhortov, V. Bolonin, A. Gershtein, V. Andrienko, N. Ivanov, N. Sobolev.

1984   Reported winter ascents 1983–4 included new Polish route on north face of Shkhelda Central (4295m) by M. Nanowski and Z. Skierski. R. Kolakowski, T. Kopys and J. Wolf made first winter ascent of Kensicky Route on north face of Schurovski.

In July East Germans R. Mittag and R. Treppte put up new line on the left side of north face of Adyrsu-Bashi. W. Schonelebe and M. Urbczat climbed new predominantly ice route on west face of Ullu-Tau.

G. Steimann and G. Knobloch climbed a new steep, direct ice route up north face of Pik Germogenov (3993m).

Dych-Tau (5198m) was climbed by its south-west side by E. Gasilov, S. Zhukov, V. Zanjkovski, G. Rudenko.

Desmond Rubens and David Broadhead were Scottish representatives on the International Caucasus mountaineering summer camp. They traversed Dongusorun and Nakra which, in fog and blizzard conditions, had 'a real Scottish flavour'; made a swift lightweight ascent of Ushba North ridge; an ice climb on the north face of Ullukara-Tau, and the obligatory ascent of Elbrus.

(It was reported that 659 climbers from 18 countries had taken part in Soviet climbing camps during the year – but these included those in Pamir, Tien Shan and Altai as well as the Caucasus.)

1985   Polish climbers made winter ascents of the north face Abalakov route on Pik Schurovski (Z. Czyzewski and M. Nanowski) and a new route on north face of Bashkara (4241m) by R. Kolakowski and T. Kopys.

In the summer a west face route was established on Jantugan (3991m, 4B) by M. Gorbenko, P. Serenkov, M. Sitnik and B. Shamrakov of Odessa.

Repeats of two impressive big wall climbs on Ushbas North and South were done by a 4-member Polish team (2 of whom were women). 40 climbers attended the International Caucasus Meeting.

A new route up the ice 'board' of Shkhara Main north face (5B) went to St Petersburg climbers Y. Bushmanov, B. Maleev, A. Nekrasov, V. Panasjuk.

North face route (up right side of face) on Nuamkuam (4182m, 5B) by Y. Ovsjannikov, V. Zhuravlev, D. Krivko, V. Makarov, G. Hasanov – from Bezingi camp.

1986   First winter ascent of Khergiani route on Dongusorun north face by J. Barszczewski and Z. Winiarski, of ice couloir route on north face of Schurovski by J. Wolf and K. Smieszko. L. MaKay, J. Cernik and F. Piacek made first winter ascent of Kolomyjcev route on north-west face of Ushba North.

Mick Fowler and Victor Saunders (members of a 4-person British team) climbed Nakra Peak and a new west face direct route on Ushba North (4696m – 5B).

Ullukara north-east face (4302m) climbed by its right-hand side by A. Simakov, I. Danilina and A. Shalaev of Moscow.

During the Bezingi camp, direct north face route was put up on Khrumkol (4680m, 5B): A. Kolchin, E. Gasilov, V. Makarov, V. Nikonova.

Semenowski Pik (4054m) was climbed from the west, up glacier by V. Makarov, A. Kolchin and others.

1990 New 6A route on left side of Ushba South, south-west face by M. Zholobov, A. Antonov, Y. Perevoscchikov, S. Tatiankin, P. Shabalin (from Kirov).

1991 Avon Mountaineering Club were guests of Georgian Alpine Club (Bristol is twinned with Tblisi) and climbed Vakhushti (4000m) and Tetri Utsnobi (4114m), both in Svanetia, and Kazbek (5047m).

Eastern Caucasus

This for years has remained a little-visited area, although its isolated massifs are beginning to come in for attention now. When Leonid Zaniatnin from St Petersburg visited remote villages here soon after the war, he was stared at wherever he went. 'We have not seen any Russians since the Revolution,' an old peasant woman told him.

1884 The south-west ridge (2B) of **Uilpata** was climbed by M. de Déchy of Hungary with A. Burgener and P. J. Ruppen.

1890 G. Yeld and G. P. Baker (with G. Realini, of Tblisi, as interpreter) visited Daghestan where they climbed **Bazarjuzi** (4466m) and **Kishin-Dag** (c.3800m).

1892 G. Merzbacher (Germany) on his second Caucasian visit climbed peaks in the Tushinish-Tchetchen and Dagestan groups: **Diklos-Mta** (4189m), **Donos** (4135m), **Komito-Tawi** (4272m), **Tebulos** (4507m), **Tugo** (4206m), **Addala-shyugko** (4140m), **Antshowala** (4098m), **Botshoch-meer** (4120m), **Kosaraku** (4091m).

1897 De Déchy climbed **Machkos** (3809m).

1903 **Little Kuru** (3620m) climbed by M. Preobraschenskaja.

1904 A. Fischer and C. Jossi climbed the three south-west summits of **Kuru-Tau** and **Schino-Tau** in the Kistinka/Chewsurish group.

1951 Chanchakhi (4420m): north face climbed by V. Ablakov with M. Anufrikov, V. Kiesel, B. Nagaev.

1954 The north buttress of Mamison (4358m, 5A) was climbed by K. Barov, R. Abduramanov, M. Greshnev, B. Koshevnik, V. Livshits, S. Semenov, E. Tur.

1964 Mamison (4358m) on the main Caucasian ridge in the upper reaches of the Ardon river was climbed by the north rib of east shoulder (5A) by Y. Bolizhhevski, A. Malyi, Y. Rabinovitch, V. Shumikhin. Another route was put up on the mountain's north face (5B – left rib of the Triangle) by G. Polevoi, V. Bubenov, A. Klokova, V. Khromov.

On Uilpata, the 4th buttress of the south ridge (4B) went to G. Polevoi, A. Karatsuba, V. Kolesnik and V. Polevoi.

1967 The right rib of Mamison's north face Triangle (5B) was climbed by Y. Grigorenko-Prigoda, V. Bakhtigozin, A. Zavgorodnyi, V. Neborak.

1968 Chanchakhi (4420m): central bastion of north face (6A) climbed by L. Popov, V. Bolizhevski, V. Kovtun, Y. Paramud, A. Fomin, V. Khitrinski. Three years previously the right bastion (5B) had fallen to V. Neborak, Y. Bolizhevski, Y. Grigorenko-Prigoda and L. Oleinik.

On Uilpata, the third buttress of the south ridge (5A) went to P. Nelipovich, N. Korolenko, S. Kulev, V. Ovcharenko and E. Smichkus.

1970   Central bastion of north-east face of Chanchakhi climbed by Y. Grigorenko-Prigoda, V. Bakhtigozen, Y. Bolizhevski, V. Shumikhin.

1971   The left bastion of Chanchakhi's north face (6A) climbed by B. Korablin, R. Andreev, V. Velikanov, V. Gerasimov, P. Panjukov, I. Shestopalov. On Uilpata, the south ridge (5B) went to I. Shestipalov, D. Korshunov, L. Korshunova, while the second buttress of the south ridge (5A) was claimed by M. Konjkov, A. Choikashvili, B. Lunev, R. Porskuriakov.

1972   An east face route (right-hand side) was established on Sugan-Bashi (4447m) in the Digory gorge by A. Zadorozhnyi, V. Lankin, E. Meretski, E. Khokhlov.

1976   The right part of north-east face of Sugan-Bashi (6A) climbed by E. Khokhlov, G. Dzhioev, A. Ishakhov, I. Slesov.

1977   The west face of Javakhishvili (3780m, 5B) went to Georgian climbers: S. Mirianashvili, T. Abashidze, S. Barliani, I. Gabisiani, D. Dangadze, O. Hazaradze.

1980   A route following the right side of the north face of Mamison (5B) was climbed by the Kiev group of V. Bodnik, V. Barsukov, A. Derkach. I. Kharinjak. G. Artemenko and others climbed up the centre of the north-west face of Chaukhi North (3842m, 5B).

1981   The left bastion of Chanchakhi's north-east face (5B) fell to A. Martynov, V. Goloschapov, B. Gorishnya, V. Sychev from Kharkov city; Goloschapov had led another (5B) route on the face the previous year with G. Artemenko, A. Babitski, P. Goncharov, V. Ovcharenko, V. Tarasenko.

The right side of north-west face of Erydag (3887m), a 5B route, went to E. Radoshkevich, L. Bezrukov, S. Belousov, V. Grischenko, A. Ivenkov, M. Poliakov – all from Donetsk city.

1982   On Javakhishvili the north-west rib (4B) went to T. Lukashvili, T. Tarkhnishvili, I. Chichinadze, T. Sharashenidze, and the north-east rib (4A) to G. Chelidze, I. Geldiashvili, T. Lukashvili, T. Sharashenidze – all of Georgia. Georgians also climbed the north-west face of Abudalauris Chaukhi (3845m, 5B): T. Lukashvili, I. Geldiashvili, D. Kelekhsashvili, D. Tarkhnischvili, M. Chichinadze, T. Sharashenidze. A new route up the right side of the north face of Abudalauris Chaukhi was established by V. Goloschapov, A. Gordienko, V. Gorishny, V. Tarasenko, from the Tsei camp.

1983   A 6A north-west face climb on Erydag was achieved by Kharkov climbers V. Goloschapov, S. Bonarenko, V. Gorishnyi, V. Pecheritsa and A. Tanets.

Ukrainians climbed up the centre of the north face of Abudalauris Chaukhi (5B): V. Kuzjmuk, V. Barsukov, P. Serenkov, O. Zakanjan.

On Gai-Komd, Main (3192m) on the rocky Skalisty ridge in Checheno-Ingushetia, a new south face route (5B) was found by A. Kurochkin, M. Govorov, G. Evsjukov, A. Lukonenko, V. Smirnov, N. Sitnikov.

On Mamison, the north face Triangle direct (5B) was climbed by A. Rusjaev, V. Glushko, A. Kotelnikov, G. Kachan, A. Odintsov, and P. Chaika; another north face route (up the icefalls, also 5B) went to V. Shopin, I. Denisov, V. Kozyrev, E. Maiorov, V. Oshe. Both groups were from St Petersburg.

1984   Mamison's left north face icefall (5B, again) was claimed by L. Volkov, P. Evteev, B. Poliakovski and P. Sizonov.

1986   A. Kharitonov led a 6A route up the centre of Gai-Komd south-east face, with K. Andrjushkevich, S. Bernatski, V. Panasjuk, V. Polianski, V. Smirnov.

1990   The south rib of south-west ridge of Uilpata (4B) went to V. Remenjuk, I. Krjuchkov, A. Kuchumov, R. Kuchumova, E. Smirnova, A. Chalei – all from the Torpedo camp.

1992   British climbers M. Doyle, E. French, P. Knott and A. White joined Ukrainians M. Bogmapov and Y. Cherebko for an informal expedition. Diklos was climbed by a new route, finishing on the south ridge, and the mountain traversed. A new snow and ice route on the north-west face of Addala East was climbed from an impressive cirque north of Addala-shukgelmeer.

Western Caucasus

1901   A. von Meck crossed Klukhor Pass with A. Fischer and Ch. Jossi, and the guide Jani Bezurtanoff, of Gwilety.

1904   A. Fischer and Jossi climbed **West Bjelakaja** (3851m) and **Semenov-Bashi** (3608m); von Meck seized **Dschalowtschat** (3824m) and **Sunachet** (3600m).

1912   **Kluchkara-Tau** (3578m) was climbed by its northern snow pass ('Karatau Pass') and west ridge by A. Keller and S. Erismann of a Swiss expedition. Then with S. Manuel and F. Crinsoz de Cottens they attempted Dombai-Ulgen from the east. A long, difficult ice couloir brought them to the same notch in the north ridge that Fischer had reached from the other side in 1904. The attempt was abandoned when Manuel was injured by a falling rock.

1914   **Dombai** (4040m) was finally climbed by W. Fischer and Dr O. Schuster on their fifth visit to this Western region. Essentially, they followed the A. Fischer line and north ridge. Earlier they had claimed first ascents of **Sofridschu** (3785m) and three unnamed points – **P 3896, P 3710, P 3427** – to the south-east of it.

1929   Bäcker, Beuge, Hildebrandt and Timm had a successful expedition, climbing **Dokutai** (3750m), **'Excursia-kara-Tau'** (3600m), and **'Prekrasnui Vid'** (3600m – Bäcker solo).

1936   The east ridge of Ptysh (3250m), on the Akbenkski Ridge, Dombai area, was climbed by V. Miklashevski, V. Ivanov, Lunin.

1937   Dombai-Ulgen West was climbed from the west (4B) by V. Sasorov, M. Korshunov, K. Sobolev, A. Askinasi. P. Minin, N. Sviatogorski and others gained Kirpich (3800m) from the Mordy Pass.

1946   The north buttress of Amanauz in the Dombai area (3760m) was climbed by V. Ivanov, G. Velikson, G. Kvatter.

1951   Dombai-Ulgen West was climbed, this time from the Dombai Pass (5A) by V. Nesterov, V. Barkov, A. Volzhin, I. Galustov, Y. Chubanov.

1961   The south face of Kirpich (3800m, 5B) went to Y. Chernoslivin, Y. Nikolaev, A. Potapov, and G. Senachev.

1962   The Kichkinekol and Mordy gorges became the target of the Trud sport society. The north face of Dalar (3979m, 6A) was climbed by A. Snesarev, A. Artanov, B. Korablin, V. Naugolnyi, V. Stepanov, V. Cheryshev; and the north-east rib (5B) by V. Stepanov, A. Artanov, O. Dracheva, V. Chekryzhev. Ukraine climbers claimed the north-west face of Dombai-Ulgen West (5A): G. Polevi, A. Klokova, A. Lutsjuk, V. Lutsjuk, Neborachek, V. Ovcharov.

Trapetsia (The Trapeze), Main Summit 3743m, was climbed by the face of the east rib (4A) by Moscow climbers K. Rototaev, S. Artjukhin, A. Tkachenko and S. Shatski.

1964   The Spartak sports group climbed the east face of Dalar (5B): V. Kavunenko, H. Magomedov, L. Poliakov, V. Shataev. Kavunenko, A. Balashov, B. Utkin and Shataev – all from Moscow – put up a 6A east face route on Amanauz (Dvuzubka), 3600m.

1968   Dalar's west face (5A) went to B. Korablin and others.

Trud climbers Y. Manoilov, E. Antipenko, I. Antonovski, B. Vasiljev and V. Solonnikov put up the difficult 'Romb' climb on the west face of Kirpich (6A). Others took the south face (5B): V. Ruzhevski, A. Zadorozhyi, V. Lankin, A. Nepomiaschiy, S. Raspopov, E. Khohlov.

1969   The north-west face of Kirpich (5A) went to S. Sogrin, Y. Baichenko, V. Zemerov and V. Malutin.

1973   The west rib of Dombai-Ulgen (West) went to V. Sukharev, L. Volkov, V. Neborak of the Alibek camp. Lajub (2998m) in the Krasnodar region was climbed by its north-east face (5B) by O. Mazurov, G. Abarbarchuk, V. Saltykov, A. Sorokin.

1975   More new routes yielded on Dalar: the north-east face buttress (6A) to B. Korablin, B. Gladkih, V. Krjukov, E. Snetkov, M. Surzhik (all of Uzunkol camp), and the right-hand side of the north face (5B) to many of the same: V. Shopin, B. Gladkih, V. Krjukov, E. Snetkov, M. Surzhik. The Triangle of the west face (4B) went to Y. Zhemchuzhnikov and O. Leonovich. Pik Shokoladnyi (Chocolate Peak), 3650m, was climbed by its south-west face by French climbers, P. Despie and others.

1976   Dalar north face buttress (5B) went to V. Grakovich of Moscow, climbing with M. Warburton of the USA. The south-east face of Trapetzia (5B) went to V. Kavunenko, V. Bashkirov, A. Zybin, V. Kaprov and O. Korovkin (all from Moscow).

1977   On Dolbai-Ulgen, the centre of the west face (5B) was climbed by S. Senchina, V. Bolizhevski, O. Nikolaichuck. Amanauz north-east face (6A) was climbed by V. Bodnik, A. Bychek, A. Verba and L. Volkov of Kiev. In the Krasnodar region the east rib of Lajub went to V. Krivov, V. Azhinov, E. Avakumiants and V. Chumak.

1978   Dalar north-east face (5B) fell to Mikhailov, G. Evsjukov, V. Ponomarev, V. Sedelnikov, V. Smirnov. On Kirpich, a variant south face route (5B) went to

B. Vasiljev, E. Oshe, V. Popov, G. Shedrin of St Petersburg. Zamok's south face (3930m, 5B) was climbed by B. Korablin, B. Vasiljev, A. Grachev, E. Oshe, G. Schedrin of St Petersburg.

1981   A. Hafizov and others climbed the south-south-east face of the west ridge of Zamok.

1990   A variant (also 5B) of the French route on the south-west face of Pik Shokoladnyi was put up by A. Kostromitinov, A. Moskalev of the Uzunkol camp.

APPENDIX II

Who got there first? Was Killar the Circassian the first man to climb Elbrus?

KASBEK AND ELBROUZ
TO THE EDITOR OF THE TIMES

Sir,—On our return to England we find that the notice which appeared in your columns of our journey in the Caucasus has induced a writer in a German paper to set up claims for his countrymen to the first ascents of Kasbek and Elbrouz. These claims, which the writer has the assurance to support by reference to well-known works (in fact directly contradicting his assertions), have obtained a wide circulation at home and abroad, and, unless contradicted, will yield to foreigners that which in truth belongs to Englishmen. The German writer says:—'It is a mistake to suppose that Kasbek and Elbrouz were ascended for the first time by the three Englishmen. As for Kasbek, it was ascended by Moritz Wagner about 1844.'

Now, Herr Wagner, in his book, *Der Kaukasus in die Jahren*, 1843 *bis* 1846, says:—'I explored the environs of Kasbek, and ascended that famous mountain to the lower limit of eternal snow.' He fixes, in another passage, the point reached at about 11,000ft.

'Elbrouz,' it is further stated, 'was ascended in 1829 by Kuppfer the mineralogist, Meyer the botanist, and other philosophers, with some Circassian guides;' and Kuppfer's *Voyage dans les Environs du Mont Elbrouz; rapport fait à l'Académie Impériale de St. Petersbourg*, 1830, is quoted as an authority for this statement.

On reference to Kuppfer's work I find that none of the scientific members of the expedition make any claim to have gained the actual summit of Elbrouz. M. Lenz, who advanced beyond the rest, stopped at a point estimated at 600 French feet below it. So much for the German claims.

I am well aware that a Tcherkess named Killar is said by Kuppfer to have reached the summit, but his success is supported by such weak evidence, and is so inconsistent with the rest of the narrative, that we may, I think, in common with the best-informed Russians whom we met in the country, reasonably reject his story, and regard our own as the first authentic ascent of the highest mountain in the Caucasus.

I am, Sir, your obedient servant,
DOUGLAS W. FRESHFIELD.

Tunbridge-Wells, Oct. 21, 1868

Douglas Freshfield's round dismissal of Killar's success echoes the views of an earlier academic, the Reverend Hereford Brooke George, first editor of *The Alpine Journal*. With a waspish lack of charity George remarked in 1865 that 'obviously it was not in Killar's interest to deny having reached the summit when he could obtain 400 roubles by holding his tongue.'[1] He was referring to the bounty offered to the first man up by the Russian general sent to make a military promenade in the Caucasus. Though he rejected the narrative as 'meagre, vague and entirely unsatisfactory', George did supply, in the second volume of *The Alpine Journal*, a translated extract from Kupffer's account of the 1829 expedition.

Kupffer was a mineralogist and chief of the savants attached to General Emmanuel's suite. He was one of the party to attempt the mountain, blackening his face with gunpowder for protection against the effects of high-altitude sun and snow blindness. But he could do nothing against fatigue, giddiness and 'an undefinable sinking' and, along with a number of other Cossacks and Circassians, abandoned the climb at what he estimated was a height of 14,000 French feet (14,921 English feet). Monsieur Lenz, accompanied by two Circassians and a Cossack, climbed on up a ridge of rocks to some 600 feet below the summit before also turning back in the face of knee-deep, sun-softened snow. Kupffer wrote:

> During this eventful day the general, seated before his tent, had watched our progress with an excellent telescope I had left at his disposal. As soon as the morning mists disappeared he saw us ascend the snow cone, and reach the foot of the rocks towards the summit, while the others halted. But suddenly he observed a single man far in advance of the rest, who had already almost crossed the track of snow between the summit and the head of the rocky staircase. This man was seen to approach the scarped rock which forms the actual summit, walk round it, disappear for a moment against the dark-coloured rock, and then vanish behind the mists which again filled the valley, cutting off the view of Elbrouz. This took place at 11 a.m.: the general could no longer doubt that one of us had reached the summit; he could see by the colour of the dress that it was a Circassian, but the distance was too great for his features to be distinguished.
>
> Killar, as the Circassian was named who had attained the summit of Elbrouz, had known how to profit by the morning's frost better than we had. He had crossed the limit of eternal snow long before us, and when Monsieur Lenz reached his highest point, Killar was already on his return from the summit. As the snow did not begin to soften till eleven, he found it firm to the very top, and only in the descent encountered the same difficulties with us. A bold hunter, and well acquainted with the country, he had before ascended to considerable heights, though he had never tried actually to reach the summit. He returned to camp a good hour before us, to receive from the general the reward due to his courage: but the general waited for the arrival of the whole party, in order to render the ceremony more solemn. Having spread out on a table the reward which he had promised to the man who should first reach the summit, he handed it to him in sight of all the camp, adding a piece of cloth for a caftan; and we all drank to his health in certain bottles of champagne, which our Mussulmen, not to infringe the law of the prophet, consumed with great satisfaction under the name of sherbet.'

The reader must decide whether he finds Kupffer's narrative as meagre and unsatisfactory as George suggests—from a scientific point of view; it is certainly a charming and vivid piece of writing. From the Reverend George's further aside that 'at any rate none of the *herrschaft* made the ascent', he seems to be implying that even if one were to accept Killar's claim, as a native ascent, it could have little validity. Certainly that was the view of Francis Fox Tuckett, writing in 1868:

> Whether Killar really did or did not attain the highest point, and whether the latter was not, indeed, hidden by the 'mists', which are a weak feature in the evidence, he, at any rate, received the promised reward of 400 roubles, and appears to have enjoyed locally the reputation of having succeeded. In any case, however, the recent ascent by our countrymen and F. Devouassoud is the *first that has been effected by any but a native mountaineer.*[2] [Editorial emphasis]

Periodically, mountain historians have re-examined the Killar question, but almost always from a standpoint of disbelief. In *The Alpine Journal* in 1966, T. S. Blakeney was dismissive: 'So nebulous and unconfirmed a claim as that of Killar cannot seriously be entertained unless some further evidence is produced and made available to support it.'[3]

In 1970 a Polish mountaineer, Boleslaw Chwascinski, pointed out that Kupffer's was by no means the only account of the 1829 climb. The Polish and Russian press of the day had covered the matter in some detail. He himself had tracked down a letter from Lenz to the Polish Academician, Parrot, another from an officer in General Emmanuel's detachment and one from Kupffer to the Vice-president of the Russian Imperial Academy of Sciences. All were unanimous that Killar had reached the summit.[4]

Chwascinski made the point that Killar would not have known General Emmanuel was watching him through his telescope, nor when he passed Lenz's group going up, that they would not get to the top. But it would have been clear to him that if followers found no footprints in the snow up there, everything would be lost from his point of view, the money and the effort. 'I think,' Chwascinski said, 'the Reverend H. B. George underestimated the physical possibilities of the uplanders. Two uplanders were with the Fresh-field party and C. C. Tucker marvelled at their physical condition . . . One can even add . . . that the porters were carrying the burden and the alpinists went without any load, or with a small load only.'

The slope was an easy one, and only the soft snow compelled the scientists to return. Killar's tactic of setting off at night was a lesson not lost on Lenz, who in his letter to Parrot wrote, 'we didn't reach the summit but I don't see any reason why we couldn't do so next time. We just have to spend the night on the highest point reached, and then we should be able to get to the top before the snow thaws.'

Chwascinski allowed he may have been a little harsh on Freshfield; it was the attitude of the Reverend George that really raised his hackles, making Killar out to be a fraud who tried to fool money out of General Emmanuel. But then, he added, it was a Russian affair: they should stand up for Killar. And in a sense, they have. Their academics seem never to have questioned the climb and surveyors named at least two peaks in the Baksan Basin in honour of Killar. Is this the time for us in Western Europe to be less grudging over Killar's achievement?

Perhaps, too, we should spare a regret for Freshfield. One way or another, he was destined to have to relinquish his place in history as the 'conqueror' of Elbrus. By the time F. Gardiner, F. C. Grove and Horace Walker climbed the West Summit of the mountain in 1874, it was already known to be higher than its twin, the eastern peak scaled by Freshfield and Devouassoud with A. W. Moore, C. C. Tucker and the two Urusbieh hunters.

Source Notes

Chapter 2: Snows Without Name pp. 8–13

1 'Praeterita Caucasica' (*AJ* 30, 1916) pp. 189–90.
2 'Reminiscences of François Joseph Dévouassoud' (*AJ* 31, 1917) p. 198.
3 Quoted by Arnold Lunn in *A Century of British Mountaineering* (Allen and Unwin, 1957), p. 120.
4 *Travels in the Central Caucasus and Bashan* p. 161.
5 ibid. pp. 218–19.
6 ibid. p. 238.
7 ibid. pp. 300–1.
8 ibid. p. 330.
9 ibid. p. 361.
10 ibid. p. 362.
11 ibid. p. 417.
12 *AJ* 46, 1935 p. 175.

Chapter 3: pp. 14–15

Crossing The Karagom Pass. Freshfield: *The Exploration of the Caucasus* (Arnold, 1896) pp. 128–34.
A Skeleton Diary of Six Weeks' Travel in the Central Caucasus in 1887. Freshfield: (*AJ* 13, 1887).

Chapter 4: A Peak in the Bag pp. 46–9

1 Moore: 'The Caucasus in 1874' (*AJ* 61, 1956) pp. 158–9.
2 ibid. p. 126.
3 Longstaff (*AJ* 62, 1957) p. 134.
4 Donkin: *Mountaineering in the Caucasus* (*AJ* 13, 1887) p. 251.

Chapter 5: pp. 50–66

The Ascent of Gestola. Dent: *AJ* 13, 1887.

Chapter 6: Annus Mirabilis pp. 67–72

1 Freshfield: *The Exploration of the Caucasus* Vol. II p. 22.
2 Bender: *Classic Climbs in the Caucasus* (Diadem, 1992).
3 Holder: 'An Expedition to the Caucasus' (*AJ* 14, 1889) p. 182.
4 ibid. p. 184.
5 ibid. p. 197.
6 ibid. p. 200.

Chapter 7: pp. 73–87

Dych Tau. Mummery: *My Climbs in the Alps and Caucasus* (Fisher Unwin, 1895) pp. 258–84.

Chapter 8: 'Herr Gott! Der Schlafplatz' pp. 88–104

1 Quoted by F. F. Tuckett in Fox's obituary, *AJ* 14, 1888, pp. 132–4.
2 Dent: 'Notes of an Expedition to the Caucasus' *AJ* 14, 1888, p. 94.
3 This and future extracts are taken from the letter reprinted in *AJ* 14, 1888, pp. 311–14.
4 From Dent's obituary of Donkin in *AJ* 14, 1888, p. 131.
5 Quoted in Holder: 'An Expedition to the Caucasus' in *AJ* 14, 1888, p. 190.
6 Quoted in Freshfield: *The Exploration of the Caucasus* Vol. 2 p. 65.
7 Quoted by Dent: 'The History of the Search Expedition to the Caucasus' in *AJ* 15, 1890, p. 26.
8 Both passages quoted in Freshfield, op. cit.
9 Translated and quoted in a letter from Dent and Freshfield published in *The Times* on October 15, 1888. The letter is reprinted in full in Dent: 'Notes of an Expedition to the Caucasus'.
10 *The Times*, October 6, 1888 and quoted in Dent: 'Notes of an Expedition to the Caucasus'.
11 Dent: 'The History of the Search Expedition to the Caucasus', p. 28.
12 ibid. pp. 34–5.
13 Freshfield: *The Exploration of the Caucasus*, Vol. II, pp. 83–4.
14 Dent: op. cit. p. 434.
15 Dent: ibid. p. 436.
16 Dent: ibid. pp. 38–9.

Chapter 9: The Second Invasion pp. 105–12

1 Holder: 'A Month among the Southern Valleys and Mountains of the Central Caucasus' (*AJ* 15, 1891) p. 521.
2 *AJ* 15, 1891, p. 558.
3 W. Rickmer-Rickmers: 'Ushba: Suanetia in 1903' (*AJ* 22, 1904) p. 342.
4 ibid. p. 345.
5 ibid. p. 345.
6 ibid. p. 346.
7 ibid. p. 347.

Chapter 10: The Finest Climb pp. 113–29

Longstaff: *This My Voyage* (John Murray, 1950) pp. 41–61.

Chapter 11: The End of an Era pp. 130–5

1 See A. von Meck: 'In the Western Caucasus' (*AJ* 22, 1905) and A. Fischer: 'Climbs in the Caucasus' (*AJ* 22, 1905).
2 See Vittorio Rochetti: 'A Climb in the Mamison Group' (*AJ* 24, 1908–9) pp. 218–28.
3 Ling: 'Some New Climbs in the Caucasus' (*AJ* 204, 1914) pp. 132–3.

Chapter 12 pp. 136–44

Raeburn: 'Attempt on Ushba' *SMJ*, 1955 pp. 3–327.

Chapter 13: Between the Wars pp. 145–50

1 Erich Vanis in 'The Bezingi Wall' *AJ* 72, 1967, pp. 57–64.

Chapter 14

The Untrammelled Caucasus pp. 151–6. Hodgkin: Text of a paper delivered at the Alpine Club Caucasus Symposium, 23 November 1991, and previously unpublished.
Tetnuld Nordwand pp. 157–62. Jenkins: *Chronicles of John Jenkins* (privately published, 1987).

Chapter 15: The Red Snows pp. 163–8

1 In *The Mountains of Europe*, edited by Kev Reynolds (Oxford Illustrated Press, 1990).
2 Friedrich Bender: *Classic Climbs in the Caucasus* p. 276.
3 Richard Gilbert: 'Svanetia: The Legendary Kingdom of the Caucasus' in *AJ* 1992–3, pp. 142–3. Gilbert refers to P. Carrell: *Hitler's War on Russia* (London, Harrap, 1964). And authors' correspondence with E. Gippenreiter.
4 'The British Caucasus Expedition, 1958' in *Mountaincraft*, summer 1959, p. 2.

Chapter 16: Welcome to the British Alpinists pp. 169–85

Hunt: *Life Is Meeting* (Hodder & Stoughton, 1978), chapter 10.

Chapter 17: 'Sorry We Are Late' pp. 186–94

Band: in *The Red Snows* by John Hunt and Chris Brasher (Hodder & Stoughton, 1959), pp. 107–10, 131–8.

Chapter 18: Towards the Present Day pp. 195–218

Ritchie: 'Twelve Nights on Schkelda', *SMCJ* 1962 (pp. 220–7).
Nunn: 'A Dream of Ushba', *Mountain* 16, July 1971 (pp. 25–7).
Fowler: 'Ushba: From Russia With Love', *Mountain* 114, April 1987 (pp. 20–5).

Appendix II

1 *AJ* 2, 1865, p. 175.
2 *AJ* 4, 1868, p. 168.
3 *AJ* 71, 1966, pp. 312–13.
4 Correspondence between B. Chwascinski and D. F. O. Dangar of the Alpine Club, and incorporated into Dangar's note in *AJ* 78, 1973, pp. 265–6.

A Caucasus Bibliography

1   A Selection of books about the Caucasus Mountains
Mainly on climbing, but including some early travel as well as general
background items

Afanasieff, R., *100 Kaukasus Gipfel*, 1913 (With Appendix c.1914).

Bender, Friedrich, *Classic Climbs in the Caucasus, a guide for mountaineers*, London: Diadem, 1992

(Bender is author of a series of Caucasus guides published in German.)

Bryce, Viscount James, *Transcaucasia and Ararat, being notes of a vacation tour in the autumn of 1876*, London: Macmillan, 1877.

Collomb, R. and Wielochowski, A., *Mount Elbruz Region: Baksan Basin – Ingur Valley*, (Guide and maps 180 000 & 1:210 000) Reading: West Col, 1992.

Cunynghame, Sir Arthur Thurlow, *Travels in the Eastern Caucasus, on the Caspian and Black Seas, especially in Daghestan and on the frontiers of Persia and Turkey, during the summer of 1871*, London: John Murray, 1872.

Dechy, Moriz von, *Kaukasus: Reisen und Forschungen im Kaukasischen Hochgebirge*, 1905–07, 3 vols.

Demidoff, E. (Prince San Donato), *Hunting trips in the Caucasus*, London: Rowland Ward, 1898.

Dumas, Alexandre, *Impressions de voyage: le Caucase*, 1865, 3 vols.

Dunsheath, Joyce, *Guest of the Soviets: Moscow and the Caucasus 1957*, London: Constable, 1959.

Egger, Carl, *Im Kaukasus: Bergbesteigungen und Reiseerlebnisse im Sommer 1914*, 1915.

— *Die Eroberung des Kaukasus*, Basel: Benno Schwabe, 1932.

Ellis, George, *Memoir of the Caucasus States*, 1788.

Fischer, Andreas, *Zwei Kaukasus-Expeditionen*, Berne: Schmid, Francke, 1891.

Freshfield, D. W., *Travels in the Central Caucasus and Bashan including visits to Ararat and Tabreez and ascents of Kazbek and Elbruz*, London: Longman, 1869.

— *The Exploration of the Caucasus*, London: Arnold, 1896 – 2 vols (with photographs by V. Sella).

Grove, F. C., *The Frosty Caucasus: an account of a walk through part of the range and of an ascent of Elbruz in the summer of 1874*, London: Longmans, 1875.

Heckel, Vilem, *Climbing in the Caucasus*, London: Spring Books [1959]. (Photo album, with text by Josef Styrsa.)

Hunt, Sir John and Brasher, Chris, *The Red Snows: an account of the British expedition 1958*, London: Hutchinson, 1960.

Maclean, Fitzroy, *To Caucasus the End of all the Earth: an illustrated companion to the Caucasus and Transcaucasia* London: Cape, 1976.

Merkulof, V. A., *Guide to the Mountains of the Caucasus, with a special Excursion Map of the Black Sea Litoral and the Central Caucasus* (in Russian, but extract translated in *AJ* 26, 1912), St Petersburg: M. D. Lomkovski/Crimea-Caucasian Mountain Club, 1904.

Merzbacher, Gottfried, *Aus den Hochregionen des Kaukasus: Wanderungen Erlebnisse, Beobachtungen*, 1901. 2 vols.

Mounsey, A. H., *A Journey through the Caucasus and the interior of Persia*, London: Smith, Elder, 1872.

Mourier, J., *Guide au Caucase*, 1894.

Mummery, A. F., *My Climbs in the Alps and Caucasus*, London: Fisher Unwin, 1895 (Many reprints).

Pereira, M., *East of Trebizond*, London: Bles, 1971.

— *Across the Caucasus* London: Bles, 1973.

Phillipps-Wolley, Clive, *Savage Svanetia*, London: Bentley [1884?].

(Other books with relevant Caucasus chapters will be found in the chronological section of this bibliography)

2 Bibliographies

Useful Caucasus bibliographies are to be found in: *Alpine Club Library Catalogue, 1982*; *Guest of the Soviets* by Joyce Dunsheath and *Across the Caucasus* by M. Pereira, 1973.

Jill (W. R.) Neate's *Mountaineering and its Literature*, 1978, incorporates historical and bibliographical Caucasus references (p. 72); she enlarged the bibliography in her revised edition, *Mountaineering Literature*, 1986.

3 General Caucasian Source Articles and Extracts

The following represent the principal sources for a general review of mountaineering activity (over and above those books already listed).

Abbreviations: AJ   *Alpine Journal*
GJ   *Geographical Journal*
SMCJ   *Scottish Mountaineering Club Journal*
ZDÖAV   *Journal of the German and Austrian Alpine Clubs*

H. Woolley, *List of Principal Peaks Ascended in the Central Caucasus Prior to 1912*, AJ 25, 1912.

H. Raeburn, *A Further List of Peaks Ascended in the Central Caucasus in 1912, 1913, 1914 and 1915* AJ 30, 1916.

R. L. G. Irving, *The Extension of the Playground*, Caucasus forms part of this chapter in *The Romance of Mountaineering* 1935.

— *Ushba*, in *Ten Great Mountains*, 1940.

John Neill, *The Mountaineering History of the Caucasus*, in *The Red Snows* by Sir J. Hunt and C. Brasher, 1960.

— *The Caucasus*, chapter in *World Atlas of Mountaineering* by W. Noyce and I. McMorrin, 1969.

John Cleare, *Caucasus*, in *Collins guide to Mountains and Mountaineering*, 1979.

Edward Pyatt, *Western Asia – The Caucasus*, in *Guinness Book of Mountains and Mountaineering*, 1980.

A. V. (Victor) Saunders, *The Caucasus*, in *The Mountains of Europe*, edited by Kev Reynolds, 1990.

Ken Wilson, *Caucasus, An Alpinist's Briefing* in *High*, October 1992, with an appendix of 'Useful Information' compiled by Jill Neate.

4   **Exploration of the Caucasus**
Here articles and extracts are listed in chronological order of the
activity described.

H. B. George, 'Mount Elbrouz, and the attempted ascent of it by a Russian Expedition',
AJ 2, 1865–6.

D. W. Freshfield, Kasbek and Elbrouz, letter to the Editor of *The Times*, dated
21.10.1868.

F. F. Tuckett, Claims of early ascents of Elbrus and Kazbek refuted by *AJ* Editor, *AJ* 4,
1868.

T. S. Blakeney, 'The First Ascent of Elbruz' (note refuting Killar claim), *AJ* 59, Nov
1954.

[*AJ* ed], 'Elbruz' (Russian first ascent still doubted), *AJ* 76, Nov 1966.

D. F. O. Dangar, 'Elbruz – observations on the supposed first ascent in 1829 . . .'
(Chwascinski turned up some evidence to support claim), *AJ* 88, 1973.

D. W. Freshfield, 'Praeterita Caucasica' (the first expeditions to the Caucasus), *AJ*
30.

— Itinerary of a Tour in the Caucasus made by Messrs D. W. Freshfield, A. W. Moore,
and A. A. Tucker, with François Devouassoud, of Chamouni, and Baqua
Pipia, a Mingrelian servant *AJ* 4, No. 23.

F. Gardiner and others, 'Itinerary of expedition to the Caucasus in 1874', *AJ* 7.

F. Gardiner, 'The Second Expedition to the Caucasus', *AJ* 30.

A. W. Moore, 'The Caucasus in 1874' (Transcript of Moore's diary, in 2 parts, issues
Nos 291, 292), *AJ* 60, 1955 and *AJ* 61, 1956.

Anon, 'Caucasian Literature' (reviews of Cunynghame's *Travels in the Eastern Caucasus*, and Mounsey's *A Journey through the Caucasus and the interior of
Persia*, *AJ* 6, 1874.

D. W. Freshfield, 'Caucasian Literature' (notices of German-language Caucasus
books by H. Abich and Dr G. Radde), *AJ* 9, 1880.

Maurice de Dechy, 'Itinerary of a Tour in the Central Caucasus', *AJ* 12, No. 86, 1884.

— 'The First Ascent of Adai Choch', *AJ* 12, 1885.

C. Comyns Tucker, Review of *Savage Svanetia*, by Clive Phillipps-Wolley, FRGS, 2 vols
(London: Bentley), *AJ* 11, 1884.

[Ed], 'New Expeditions in 1886 – Central Caucasus', *AJ* 13, No. 93, Aug 1886.

Clinton Dent, 'The Ascent of Tetnuld Tau' (ie Gestola), *AJ* 13, No. 96, 1887.

W. F. Donkin, 'Mountaineering in the Caucasus' (Bezingi glacier region, 1886), *AJ* 13,
No. 96, 1887.

D. W. Freshfield, 'A skeleton diary of six weeks' travel in the Central Caucasus in
1887', *AJ* 13.

— 'Climbs in the Caucasus, Part I', *AJ* 13.

— 'Climbs in the Caucasus, Part II', *AJ* 14.

[Ed], 'New maps of the Caucasus', *AJ* 14, No. 101, Aug. 1888.

[Re: A. F. Mummery], 'Mountaineering in the Caucasus' (23.8.1888, newspaper item in
St James's Gazette)

[Ed], 'Exploration of the Caucasus in 1888', *AJ* 14.

A. F. Mummery, 'Dych Tau', Chapter in *My Climbs in the Alps and Caucasus*, 1895.

C. A. Russell, 'One Hundred Years Ago' (ie 1888), *AJ*, 93, No. 337, 1988–9.

Clinton Dent, 'Notes of an expedition to the Caucasus', (With remarks on the recent
accident) *AJ* 14.

Henry W. Holder, 'An Expedition to the Caucasus' (1888), *AJ* 14, No. 103, Feb. 1889.

Clinton Dent, 'The History of the Search Expedition to the Caucasus' (loss of Donkin and Fox), *AJ* 15, No 107, Feb 1890.

D. W. Freshfield, His lecture on the Search Expedition, delivered to the RGS, 10.11.1890, reported in *The Standard, The Times* etc., 11.2.1890.

C. A. Russell 'One Hundred Years Ago' (ie 1889), *AJ* 94, No 338, 1989–90.

Jeffery Parrette 'The Sleeping Place' (The loss of Donkin and Fox in the Caucasus), *Appalachia*, 15.6.1988.

[Ed], Memorial service being held for Harry Fox, 1-page feature in *Wellington Weekly News*, 31.8.1988.

M v Dechy, 'Neuere Forschungen und Bergreisen im kaukasischen Hochgebirge'. 1889–90 activity. A cutting, not clear in what and when published.

Vittorio Sella, 'Nel Caucaso Centrale. Note di Escursioni colla Camera oscura', *Bollettino del Club Alpino Italiano*, Vol xxiii, 1890.

D. R. Peacock, 'Travel in the Caucasus' (short note on temporary difficulties), *AJ* 15.

[Ed], 'Alpine Notes – Caucasus' (short note of Purtscheller/Merzbacher tour), *AJ* 15, 1891.

[Anon], Book review: *Zwei Kaukasus-Expeditionen*, Von Andreas Fischer (Bern: Schmid, Francke, 1891), *AJ* 15.

D. W. Freshfield, 'The Solitude of Abkhasia, concluding with a note on the High-Level Routes of the Caucasus', *AJ* 15, 1890.

H. W. Holder, 'A Month among the Southern Valleys and Mountains of the Central Caucasus, with Ascents of Tsforga, Boordooil (Bordjula) and Adai Choch', *AJ* 15, 1891.

G. P. Baker, 'Signor Sella's 1890 Caucasian Photographs' (note), *AJ* 15, 1891.

— (Short section on 1890 expedition in his) *Mountaineering Memories of the Past* (Privately printed, 1951).

George Yeld, 'Daghestan and the Ascent of Basardjusi', *AJ* 16, 1892.

D. W. Freshfield, 'A Note on the Map of the Adai Khokh Group', *AJ* 16, 1892.

J. G. Cockin, 'Shkara, Janga, and Ushba', *AJ* 16, 1893.

[Ed], 'Alpine Notes and New Routes – Central Caucasus', *AJ* 16, 1893.

Godfrey A. Solly, 'Suanetia in 1893', *AJ* 17, 1895.

[Ed], 'New Expeditions in 1894 – Central Caucasus' *AJ* 17, No. 128.

[Ed], 'New Expeditions in 1895 – Central Caucasus' *AJ* 17, No. 130, 1895.

[Ed], 'New Expeditions in 1896 – Central Caucasus', *AJ* 18, Nos 133, 134, 1896.

[Ed], 'Exhibition – Mr A. D. McCormick's Caucasian Sketches', *AJ* 18, 1896.

Sundry papers July 1986 etc, Reviews of *The Exploration of the Caucasus* by D. W. Freshfield.

C. T. Dent, 'Fine Art and Mountaineering', *Art Journal*, 1896.

Hermann Woolley, 'Mirshirgi-Tau and Ailam', *AJ* 18, 1897.

Vittorio Sella, 'The Caucasus in 1896', *AJ* 18, 1897.

H. W. Holder, 'Climbs among the Peaks of the Adyrsu, Central Caucasus', *AJ* 18, 1897.

[JWG], 'The Caucasus', *Nature* 11.3.1897.

[Anon], 'The Caucasus' – Review of *Hunting Trips in the Caucasus* by E. Demidoff, Prince San Donato (London: Rowland Ward) *Pall Mall Gazette*, 6.9.1898.

[Ed], 'Western and Eastern Caucasus' (note), *AJ* 19, 1898.

C. T. Dent, 'The First Ascent of Tsiteli' (Central Caucasus), *AJ* 19, 1899.

W. Rickmer Rickmers, 'Ushba', *AJ* 19, 1899.

[Ed], 'New Expeditions in 1900 – continued – Central Caucasus', *AJ* 20, 1900–1.

[Ed], 'New Expeditions in 1903 – Caucasus' (various), *AJ* 21.

J. H. Wigner, 'In Western Suanetia in 1903', *AJ* 23, 1904.

L. W. Rolleston, 'Climbing in Suanetia' (1903), *AJ* 23, 1904.

T. G. Longstaff, 'Caucasus' (chapter 3 of his book *This My Voyage*, 1950, relates to 1903 journey).

John F. Baddeley, 'Some Remarks on the Nomenclature of Ossetia and Adjacent Countries, with Special Reference to Dr Merzbacher's Map', *AJ* 22, 1904.

W. Rickmer Rickmers, 'Personally Conducted: Suanetia in 1903, Parts I & II' *AJ* 22, Nos 166, 167, 1904. (Part II of this article subsequently repeated in *Mountain Craft* magazine in 1964).

R. L. G. Irving, Describes the 1903 climbs in his *Ten Great Mountains*, 1940.

Heinz v Ficker, Adolf Schulze & Dr G. Leuchs, 'Uschbafahrten 1903', *ZDÖAV* 1904, Vol. xxxv, Innsbruck, 1904. (Some photos and illus. by Ernst Platz).

[Ed, *Alpinismus*], 'Klassische Fahrten' (Short retrospective article with pictures of 1903 climbs), *Alpinismus*, November 1981.

M. Kurz (ed), 'Robert Helbling und Albert Weber als Teilnehmer der Rickmers-Expedition 1903', *Berge der Welt*, 1948.

Alexander von Meck, 'In the Western Caucasus', *AJ* 22, 1905.

Dr Andreas Fischer, 'Climbs in the Caucasus, Part II' *AJ* 22, No. 170, 1905.

M. Kurz (ed), 'Andreas Fischers zwei Expeditionen 1889 und 1904', *Berge der Welt*, 1948.

Dr Vittorio Ronchetti, 'A Climb in the Mamison Group' (Caucasus), *AJ* 24, 1908–9.

[Ed], 'Caucasus – Bogkhobashi Group' (notes on Mme Kuntze's climbs), 'Caucasus – Kasbek Group' (notes on Fischer party climbs), *AJ* 25, Feb 1911.

Dr Walther Fischer, Dr Gustav Kuhfahl & Oscar Schuster, 'Aus dem Zentralen Kaukasus', *DÖAV* 1911, Vol xlii, Munich 1911.

Dr Walther Fischer, Ernst Platz & Oscar Schuster, 'Zwischen Terek und Ardon – Kaukasusfahrten im Sommer 1911' *DÖAV* 1912, Vol xliii, Vienna 1912.

[Ed], 'The Kazbek Group in the Caucasus' (note on Oscar Schuster) *AJ* 26, 1912.

[J. P. F. (Farrer)], 'Central Caucasus' (notes on Schuster & Winkler expeditions, 1911 and 1912), *AJ* 27, 1913.

M. Kurz (ed), 'Keller, Erismann und Seelig bei der Rikli-Reise', 1912, *Berge der Welt*, 1948.

A. Keller, 'Hochtouren und Erstbesteigungen im Westlichen Kaukasus' in the book *Natur-und Kulturbilder aus den Kaukasuslaendern und Hocharmenien* by M. Rikli.

[Ed], 'Central Caucasus' (further notes – 2 separate references – on Schuster expedition), *AJ* 27, 1913.

D. W. Freshfield, 'Caucasica' (Merkulof's Guide reviewed), *AJ* 26, 1912.

— 'The First Ascent of Adai Khokh', *AJ* 27, 1912.

[Ed], 'Caucasus' (notes on Adai Khokh, Mamison Khokh, Saramag, Tshantishachi Khokh, Shkhara and Ushba Groups), *AJ* 28, 1914.

W. N. Ling, 'Some New Climbs in the Caucasus (1913: With Raeburn etc, Adai Khokh and elsewhere, 5 first ascents), *AJ* 28, No. 204, with notes in 203, 1914.

[Ed], 'Excursions and Notes – SMC Abroad in 1913' (Caucasus trip of Ling, Raeburn, Young and Jones noted), *SMCJ* 13, 1914.

Harold Raeburn (ed by J. H. B. Bell), 'Attempt on Ushba' 1913, *SMCJ* 1955.

[Ed], 'Excursions and Notes – SMC Abroad in 1914' (Caucasus trip of Raeburn, Scott Tucker and Richards noted) *SMCJ* 13, 1915.

George Kennan, 'An Island in the Sea of History: The Highlands of Daghestan', *National Geographic* 24, pp. 1087–1140, Oct 1913.

[Ed], 'Notes on the Caucasus' (Afanasieff's Climbing Guide, Schuster's Travelling Tips), *AJ* 28, No. 204, May 1914.

D. W. Freshfield, Correspondence: 'The Twin Summits of Elbruz', *AJ* 28, No. 204, May 1914.

O. Schuster, 'Notes on the Caucasus' (Kuish Group, Central Caucasus, with bibliography), *AJ* 28, No. 205, Aug 1914.

Harold Raeburn, 'Central Caucasus – Adai (Uilpata) Group' (1914 expedition), *AJ* 28, No. 206, Nov. 1914.

D. W. Freshfield, 'Notes on the Caucasus' (Caucasian Place-Names, mention of Egger/ Miescher expedition, 1914), *AJ* 28, No. 206, Nov. 1914.

Harold Raeburn, 'In the Caucasus' (1914), *AJ* 29, No. 208, May 1915.

— 'The Highest Peak of the Adai Khokh Group, Central Caucasus', *AJ* 29, No. 208, May 1915.

D. W. Freshfield, 'Caucasian Notes: travel in the Caucasus', note in *AJ* 39.

H. Niesner, 'A Bavarian (1928) Expedition to the Caucasus' (with notes on nomenclature by D. W. Freshfield), *AJ* 41, No. 238, 1929.

Paul Bauer, 'In dem Swanetisch-Tatarischen Alpen' (Munich expedition, 1928), *ZDÖAV* 1930, Vol. lxi, Innsbruck 1930.

Hugo Tomaschek, 'Die Erschliessung der Swjekgarkette' (Viennese expedition, 1929), *ZDÖAV* 1930, Vol. lxi, Innsbruck 1930.

Paul Bauer, 'Bavaria and the Caucasus' (opening chapter of his book *Kanchenjunga Challenge*, 1955, describes 1928 expedition).

Willy Merkl, Walter Rachl, Fritz Bechtold, 'Deutsche Kaukasus-Kundfahrt 1929', *ZDÖAV* 1931, Vol. lxii, Innsbruck 1931.

Ugo di Vallepiana, 'Mountaineering in the Caucasus, 1929', *AJ* 42, No. 241, Nov. 1930.

— 'Kaukasus-Fahrt 1929', *Berge der Welt*, 1946.

J. H. B. Bell, 'Across the Caucasus in July 1930', Note in *SMCJ* 19, No. 110, Nov. 1930.

Hugo Tomaschek, 'Bergfahrten im Kaukasus 1930', *ZDÖAV* 1932, Vol. lxiii, Innsbruck • 1932.

[Ed], 'Caucasus Notes' (mainly 1930 activity, including Shkhara traverse of Muller/ Tomaschek), *AJ* 42, No. 241, Nov. 1930.

J. Schintlmeister, (Reports, in German, on 1931 activity – including ascents Lyalver, Gestola and Tetnuld, and Jangi-Tau/Shkhara traverse – in *Salzburger Chronik* for 29 August and 10 October, 1931. Further brief accounts in Mitteilungen des DÖAV, Jan. 1932 and *Der Bergsteiger* 1930/31.)

— 'Kaukasus, 1931/1963', *Oesterr. Alpenzeitung*, Jan/Feb 1965.

[Ed], 'Caucasus Notes' (1931 activity, including Shkhara traverse of Poppinger etc) *AJ* 43, No. 243, Nov 1931.

M. Kurz (ed), 'Maeglin und Hegglin verschollen 1931', *Berge der Welt*, 1948.

J. Lagarde, 'Caucasus Notes' (the French expedition, 1933), *AJ* 46, No. 248, May 1934.

W. Weckert, 'The Swiss Caucasus Expedition, 1933', *AJ* 46, No. 249, 1934.

E. H. Stevens, 'Caucasus Notes' (remarks on French expedition, 1933), *AJ* 47.

Two Caucasian Journeys: W. Heybrock, 'A Solitary Tramp', L. Saladin, 'The Swiss Expedition, 1934', *AJ* 47, No. 250, 1935.

M. Kurz (ed), 'Expedition Saladin und Gefaehrten 1934', *Berge der Welt*, 1948.

W. Heybrock, 'A Second Caucasian Tramp', *AJ* 48, No. 252, 1936.

J. Schintlmeister, 'Die bergsteigerische Taetigkeit der wissenschaftlichen Kaukasusexpedition 1935', Mitteilungen des DOAV 12/1935.

R. Schwarzgruber, 'The DÖAV in the Caucasus, 1935', *AJ* 48, 1936.

— 'The DÖAV in the Caucasus, 1936', *AJ* 49, No. 254, 1937.

John Jenkins, *Chronicles of John Jenkins, 1913–1947* (Caucasus diary, 1937, edited by Dulcibel Jenkins), 1987.

— 'Climbing in the Caucasus', *Geographical Magazine*, May 1938.

— 'A light expedition to the Central Caucasus, 1937', *AJ* 50, 1938.

— 'Tetnuld Nordwand', Midland Association of Mountaineers, June 1938.

— 'Towards Ushba', *Rucksack Club Journal*, 1938.

M. S. Taylor, 'Caucasus Commissariat' *Rucksack Club Journal*, 1938.

Robin Hodgkin and R. L. Beaumont, 'Two Caucasus Climbs', (Adyrsu Bashi, and Ushba), *Climbers' Club Journal*, 1938.

Robin Hodgkin, 'The Untrammelled Caucasus in 1937', address to AC Caucasus Symposium, November 1991.

[Anon], 'Highest Peak in Europe Scaled by British Woman', *Moscow News*, 20 November 1957 (One of several Russian newspaper features).

Joyce Dunsheath, 'Adventure in the Caucasus', *Mountain Craft* Summer 1958.

John Hunt, 'British Expedition to the Caucasus' (basic summary of 1958 expedition), *AJ* 63, No. 297, Nov. 1958.

M. J. Harris, 'The East Summit of Dych Tau', *AJ* 64, No. 298, May 1959.

A. Blackshaw, 'Jangi Tau', *AJ* 64, No. 298, May 1959.

John Neill, 'Notes on Pik Shchurovsky and Gestola' *AJ* 64, No. 298, May 1959.

John Hunt, 'Welcome to British Alpinists 1958', in his *Life is Meeting*, 1978.

George Band, 'The British Caucasus Expedition, 1958', *Mountain Craft* Summer 1959.

Chris Brasher, 'Climbing in the Caucasus, with the British Expedition', *The Observer*, 20 July 1958.

Ralph Jones, 'Climbing with the Russians', *Geographical Magazine* June 1959.

Bernard Pierre, 'Central Caucasus' (brief report on French expedition, 1959), *AJ* 69, No. 299, Nov. 1959.

Hamish MacInnes, 'The Traverse of Shkhelda', *AJ* 67, No. 304, 1962, and *Soviet Weekly*, November 1, 1962.

— 'The Frosty Caucasus', chapter in his book *Look Behind the Ranges*, 1979.

G. J. Ritchie, 'Twelve Nights on Schkelda', *SMCJ*, 1962.

Erich Vanis, 'The Bezingi Wall' (1966 traverse, translated by Hugh Merrick), *AJ* 72.

Paul Nunn, 'A Dream of Ushba', *Mountain* 16, July 1971, and reprinted in his *At the Sharp End*, 1988.

John Town, 'Back in the USSR', *AJ* 86, No. 330, 1981.

David J. Broadhead, 'The International Mountaineering Camp 1984', *AJ* 92, No. 336, 1987.

A. V. Saunders, 'The British Caucasus Expedition 1986', *AJ* 92, No. 336, 1987.

Mick Fowler, 'Ushba – From Russia with Love' (1986 trip), *Mountain* 114, April 1987.

Richard Gilbert, 'Svanetia: The Legendary Kingdom of the Caucasus, *AJ* 97, No. 341, 1992/3.

Roger Alton and Dick Bradbury, 'On the Roof of Europe' (climbing Elbrus), *Guardian*, 2.11.91.

[Ed], 'Mountain Info' (rarely visited area of the Caucasus opening up to climbers), *High* 124, March 1993.

Index